Women's and Girls' Pathways
Through the Criminal Legal System

Women's and Girls' Pathways Through the Criminal Legal System

Addressing Trauma, Mental Health, and Marginalization

Dana DeHart and Shannon Lynch

Cognella Series on Family and Gender-Based Violence

Series edited by Claire Renzetti

SAN DIEGO

Bassim Hamadeh, CEO and Publisher
Amy Smith, Senior Project Editor
Abbey Hastings, Associate Production Editor
Jess Estrella, Senior Graphic Designer
Stephanie Kohl, Licensing Coordinator
Natalie Piccotti, Director of Marketing
Kassie Graves, Vice President of Editorial
Jamie Giganti, Director of Academic Publishing

cognella® | ACADEMIC PUBLISHING
3970 Sorrento Valley Blvd., Ste. 500, San Diego, CA 92121

Brief Contents

Detailed Contents

Introduction

GETTING REAL 0.1

Sharon is a 26-year-old African American woman. The following narrative is taken from Sharon's own words and description of her experiences during a research interview. Sharon is incarcerated for a violation of probation. She had done crimes to get money for drugs. She was reporting to a probation officer and was getting dirty urine tests because she was still on crack. Her sentence is 3 years. She was doing drugs because she found out she was HIV-positive. She was pregnant at the time. She thought that the world was going to end, so she might as well have fun while she had time. The crack led her to doing the other things—forgery, theft. Growing up, Sharon lived with her mom, who smoked crack. There were hardly ever lights, water, or food in the house, but her grandmom provided for her. When she was 8, Sharon was molested by a neighbor. She told her grandmom, and he went to jail. They put Sharon through counseling, but she didn't stay for long. She kind of outgrew it. She started having sex just to be having sex. The guys were older, and her boyfriend was 24. When she was 11, she was raped by a bunch of men. She was sitting on her boyfriend's porch, and they just picked her up and took her off to an abandoned house. One of them took her to her grandmom's house, and her grandmom called the police. Half of them got locked up for it. "They should have got me more counseling or something—someone to talk to—because when you're that young and something like that happens, a person's mind goes through a lot. You feel you're not worthy. I started messing with any man willing to give it to me." Then she started drinking hard liquor. Sometimes her and one of her homegirls would go, and they'd drink it out of the store. Sometimes they'd steal her mom's liquor out of the cabinet. When she got older, she was drinking every day. That's when she was about 14, and her mother's boyfriends started messing with her, trying to pay her to have sex with them. Her mother didn't believe her. Sharon's momma was good but messed with the wrong people, smoked crack. Sharon wouldn't be alive if it weren't for her grandmom. Sharon was wild, but her grandmom put her foot down. Sharon started staying with her, and it was a good environment. Sharon moved out when she was 17, with her oldest two children. Her boyfriend would come stay with her. They fought all the time. He'd call her "bitch" and "whore," but she wasn't doing nothing. He gave her black eyes, swollen lips. He'd fight and she'd fight back harder. Sharon's brother told him he better not put his hands on her. She got tired of it and left him. After that, she met a drug dealer. She was wanting to tote pistols, wanting to hang out and sell drugs. She got a drug charge at 18 but it was dropped. She married her husband when she was 19 and is still married to him. They fought sometimes. She had her own place and started to get in more trouble with the law—acting out, fighting the police. She was selling drugs and stealing check cards because she was trying to make money for drugs without prostituting herself—which she did do, and she's not ashamed to say. She almost shot a woman who was messing with her husband. She did 2 years for pointing and possessing a firearm. When Sharon got locked up, she had just started messing with the checks a little, but she didn't know it well. She got out of prison and started thinking about it—what she could do better. The day she was out, she was using again. Sharon's getting older, and she knows drugs ain't for her. She wants her children back, wants to get out of prison and get a job. She wants it to be like it used to be when she was 17—she didn't do drugs, and she had a job.

Think about Sharon's experiences. What are some things that contributed to her crimes? What things could have led her on a different path? What could help her now?

Women's pathways through the criminal legal system are shaped by a variety of factors, ranging from their demographic backgrounds and life experiences to laws and policies within the jurisdiction in which they enter the system. This book describes these pathways as framed through the lens of two key theoretical perspectives—the feminist pathways perspective and intersectional criminology—as well as two applied approaches to prevention, risk reduction, and intervention—trauma-informed approaches and the sequential intercept model. The theoretical models help us to understand how women became system involved and how they may be differentially impacted by that involvement. The applied approaches provide us with the knowledge and resources to do something to keep girls and women from slipping further into the system. In this introduction, we provide a brief overview of each theoretical and applied model. As you read this book, stop periodically to think about how each of these models relates to what you are reading.

Feminist Pathways Perspective

Feminist pathways theorists consider the unique or gendered experiences of women and girls that increase the risk of engaging in behaviors labeled as criminal. This theory reflects the idea that women and girls are differentially exposed to risks, perhaps via the nature, severity, or intensity of these risks, as compared to boys and men (Salisbury & Van Voorhis, 2009). Thus, while there are risks described as gender-neutral (e.g., education, criminal history, criminal peer networks) and associated with both men's and women's criminal behaviors, there are also specific factors (e.g., victimization, mental health problems) that differentially increase risk for women entering the system (Brennan et al., 2012). The pathways approach recognizes not only that men and women may have different risk factors, but also that there are differences within groups—for men and boys and for women and girls (Wattanporn & Holtfreter, 2014). In particular, the pathways approach recognizes increased risk for women and girls with marginalized social identities (Belknap, 2014)—people of color, with disabilities, lower socioeconomic statuses, sexual minorities, and others. The pathways approach adds to existing theories by addressing the etiology and progression of crimes committed by women and girls, as these groups have not been well addressed in traditional theories of criminology. In addition, the pathways approach offers guidance for addressing risks for offending, addressing women and girls' treatment needs, assessing gender-responsive risks and needs, and responsivity of justice and service interventions (Andrews & Bonta, 1994).

Intersectional Criminology

An important thread throughout the book will be intersectional criminology. Potter (2015) defines intersectionality as placing the "lived experience" of individuals at the center of analyses and considering individuals' identities including race, ethnicity, gender, sexuality, disability, nationality and socioeconomic class. *Intersectionality* is a theoretical approach that recognizes that all people have multiple identities (e.g., race/ethnicity, gender, class) that contribute to their lived experience (Potter, 2015). In addition, proponents of this theory recognize that identities like gender, class, or race/ethnicity are socially constructed. In other words, gender, race/ethnicity, and class shape our experiences because they are "structuring influences that affect how people behave, how others react to and define that behavior, [and] who has the power to label behaviors" (Lynch, 1999, pp. 4–5). Further, this model of identities emphasizes that our identities intersect in ways that enhance or limit our power. When a social identity or combination of identities is most likely to decrease one's power, we often use the term *marginalization* or *marginalized* to describe these disadvantages. One example of how we can examine intersections of identities and disadvantage is to look more closely at who is most at risk of living at or below poverty level. We often hear that women earn lower wages then men and also that average income varies by ethnic group in the United States. If we take a moment to examine the intersections of income, gender, and ethnicity when we look at who is living at or below the poverty level in the United States, we see that while about 9.3% of men and 12.8% of women lived at or beneath the poverty level in 2016, 22.8% of Indigenous women and 21.4% of Black women lived at or below the poverty level (Patrick, 2017).

By applying an intersectional lens throughout our writing, we will address ways that women and girls' identities within multiple social categories places them in positions of power and/or inequality, impacting vulnerability at each stage of the criminal legal system. We will illustrate that intersectionality is associated with differential risk of women and girls becoming system-involved, differential experiences within the system, and differential success in reintegrating into communities. This has particular practical importance in implementation of assessment, intervention, and systemic advocacy pertaining to criminal legal issues. We underscore that addressing complex needs (i.e., "poly-problems" if viewed solely at the individual level) necessitates a systemic lens that recognizes marginalization and requires integrated, multi-system approaches to eradicate systemic barriers, gaps, and redundancies (i.e., structural problems that marginalize those at the intersections).

Trauma-Informed Approaches

This book will address impact of trauma, adversity, and mental health on women's and girls' pathways through the criminal legal system, including girls' and women's experiences of entry into the system, incarcerative experiences, and reentry into communities. Specifically, we will highlight ways in which women's and girls' exposure to interpersonal violence and other adversity increases risk of entering the system, represents unmet treatment needs and risks while in the system, and increases the risk of recidivism post-release. At each stage, we will discuss assessment of trauma, mental health, and individual/family needs in conjunction with recommendations based on the trauma-informed approach (Substance Abuse and Mental

Health Services Administration (SAMHSA), 2014). In its simplest form, a trauma-informed approach consists of four basic principles. First, individuals working from this perspective *realize* victimization or trauma is a common experience and that traumatic experiences impact how we behave. Next, a trauma-informed approach includes *recognition* of signs and symptoms of traumatic distress. This recognition informs the third principle, which asserts that policies and procedures are *responsive* to trauma survivors, in particular not utilizing methods that increase risk of *retraumatizing* individuals. Of particular importance for this book, a trauma-informed approach would include providing training to key personnel who interact with trauma-exposed women and girls at risk of entering the criminal legal system. Such an approach would also involve closely examining practices and procedures used by police, actors within the legal system, and corrections officers to reduce retraumatization. One example of this type of approach would be using trauma-informed risk and needs assessments when making pre-trial detention or probation recommendations. Another would be considering trauma that may occur during booking procedures and limiting practices that retraumatize women and girls. As you will see, by combining a trauma-informed approach with the intercept model, we can consider ways to decrease risk of entry into the criminal legal system and offer alternative paths to address social issues labeled as criminal (e.g., substance use, sex work, truancy, running away).

Stages of Legal Processing and the Sequential Intercept Model

Girls and women come into contact with the legal system in a number of different ways. Youth are sometimes referred to the juvenile legal system through schools, while both children and adults are subject to calls or patrols in the broader community. Figure 0.1 demonstrates the sequence of events in the criminal justice system.

In the most general terms, the process of legal involvement often occurs as follows. When crimes or delinquency are observed by an officer or reported by members of the public, officers may make an arrest and/or take the person into custody based on a valid warrant or reasonable belief that an offense has been committed. Arrests are followed by booking and detention, and within a number of hours, the defendant will appear in court, at which time a determination will be made whether she may be released and if bail is required. Likelihood of bail is based on the court's interpretation of the severity of the offense, likelihood that the defendant

What is the sequence of events in the criminal justice system?

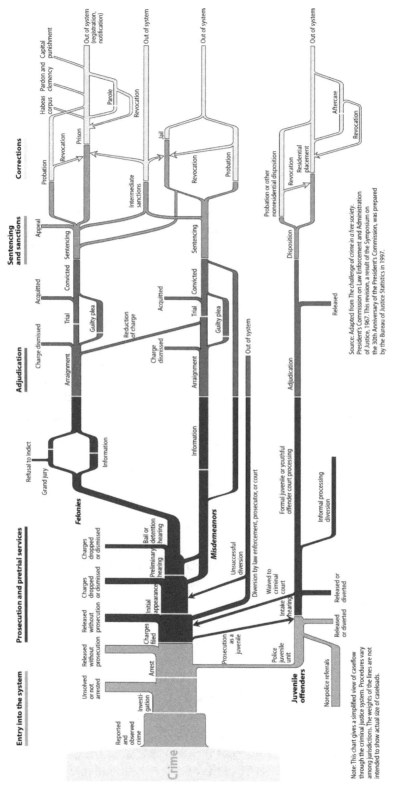

Note: This chart gives a simplified view of caseflow through the criminal justice system. Procedures vary among jurisdictions. The weights of the lines are not intended to show actual size of caseloads.

Source: Adapted from *The challenge of crime in a free society*: President's Commission on Law Enforcement and Administration of Justice, 1967. This revision, a result of the Symposium on the 30th Anniversary of the President's Commission, was prepared by the Bureau of Justice Statistics in 1997.

FIGURE 0.1 Criminal justice flowchart.

will flee, and the defendant's prior record. A court-appointed attorney may represent the defendant if she does not already have a lawyer. During subsequent hearings, a judge and/or grand jury will examine evidence presented by the prosecution to determine whether there is sufficient evidence to indicate the defendant committed an offense. The case may move forward to trial, during which the courts determine whether guilt of the defendant can be determined beyond a reasonable doubt. A "not guilty" verdict results in the defendant's release, whereas a "guilty" verdict is followed by penalties imposed by the judge. These penalties may include involvement in the correctional system, including community corrections or incarceration. Good behavior during incarceration may be identified as the basis of conditional release, under which the individual may be subject to supervised parole. Upon completion of the correctional sentence, the individual returns to the community through the process of reentry (GetLegal.com, 2016).

Throughout this process, there are numerous points at which the individuals involved (e.g., community members, law enforcement officers, youth intake officers, defendants, prosecutors, judges, correctional officers, probation/parole officers) have a degree of discretion in determining whether and how the event proceeds. There are also jurisdiction-specific and institution-specific protocols that may shape the way that the event unfolds. Finally, community norms and resources dictate whether an event is perceived and reported as a crime, as well as how an individual is received back into the community upon reentry. All of these factors impact the human toll and economic impacts of the event on individuals, families, and communities.

The sequential intercept model (Figure 0.2) was developed by Munetz and Griffin (2006) as a conceptual framework that could be applied during different stages of processing through the criminal legal system. The model was developed with a specific focus on identifying and addressing mental illness among persons who commit crimes, but it has potential for broad applicability around other issues requiring screening and connecting persons to resources and services in communities. The model centers around the idea that persons with mental illness who commit crimes should be diverted to appropriate services rather than becoming deeply enmeshed in the criminal legal system.

Each stage of criminal legal contact—from law enforcement and emergency services through detention, courts, jails and prisons, and community corrections—offers an opportunity to identify persons with mental illness and intervene. These opportunities are referred to as "intercepts," and they occur in a predictable sequence based on the criminal legal process.

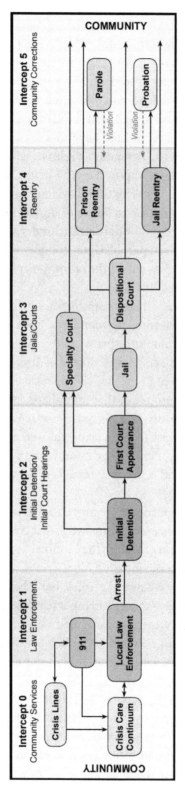

FIGURE 0.2 Sequential intercept model.

Munetz and Griffin (2006) describe the intercepts as a series of "filters," beginning with "the ultimate intercept" being best clinical practices in the community that prevent persons with mental illness from becoming involved with the criminal legal system. Such community-based practices, including crisis lines and a crisis care continuum, are sometimes referred to as "intercept 0" (Policy Research Associates, 2017). This intercept is followed by subsequent intercepts: (a) law enforcement and emergency services; (b) post-arrest, including initial detention and initial hearings; (c) post-initial hearings, including jail, courts, forensic evaluations, and forensic commitments; (d) reentry from jails, state prisons, and forensic hospitalization; and (e) community corrections and community support (Munetz & Griffin, 2006). At each intercept, screening, assessment, and/or services may be used to engage persons with mental illness in treatment and connect them to resources in order to decrease time spent in the criminal legal system, deter criminogenic behavior, and reduce reoffending. It is best for these goals to be achieved through the joint efforts of professionals across disciplines, including courts and corrections, health and mental health, and human services. Examples of potential strategies include using crisis intervention teams in the community, pre- and post-arrest diversion programs, mental health and drug courts, specialized mental health caseloads for probation and parole officers, and transition planning for citizens reentering communities.

Throughout this book, we will discuss challenges for girls and women associated with their pathways through the legal system. In each section of the book, we include a chapter that draws on the sequential intercept model to discuss promising strategies designed for that specific stage of legal involvement. Yet, as we have stated, the model has applicability beyond mental health. We will also discuss how intercepts can serve as points for identifying and addressing other barriers such as substance abuse, experiences of trauma and adversity, and economic disadvantage. Much of the work to be done around these and other issues goes beyond work with individuals. It must include examination of our laws and operations of the criminal legal system. This requires advocacy, collective action, and systemic change. While we attempt to implement best practices to assist persons with individual struggles, we must also think critically to address systemic barriers that require changes in procedures, policies, and norms that have disparate impacts on persons of different racial and ethnic backgrounds, socioeconomic statuses, health and abilities, gender identities and sexual orientation, citizenship, and so on.

Organization of the Book

This book is divided into three sections. First, we will discuss women's and girls' experiences prior to entering the criminal legal system, focusing on exposure to trauma and adversity, mental health, and marginalization and discriminatory practices embedded in our criminal legal system and broader social systems. Next, we will summarize research on women's and girls' experiences in the courts and while incarcerated. Finally, we will present findings on women's and girls' experiences during the reentry process. In addition, we include excerpts from our interviews with women and girls in detention centers, jails, prisons, or post-release, to highlight their experiences in their own words. We will end each section with a brief chapter that focuses on points of intersection, where individuals working in the system can impact the pathways of women and girls.

Credits
Fig. 0.1: Source: https://www.bjs.gov/content/largechart.cfm.
Fig. 0.2: Source: https://www.prainc.com/wp-content/uploads/2018/06/PRA-SIM-Letter-Paper-2018.pdf.

SECTION I

POINTS OF ENTRY INTO THE SYSTEM

How do girls and women first become involved in the criminal legal system? The most intuitive response might be to respond, "They commit a crime," but the reality is not so simple. The boundaries between who commits a crime and who becomes a victim of crime are sometimes not so clear, and those who become involved with the system—as victims or offenders—may be dealing with challenges at multiple levels. At the individual level, a person may experience child maltreatment and/or may struggle with mental health issues. On an interpersonal level, they may be influenced by family dynamics, witnessing family or community violence, and antisocial peer networks. At the societal level, they may face subordination within gendered role expectations and/or they may experience discrimination in response to their race, ethnicity, class, ability, or sexual orientation. Thus, to understand how girls and women enter into the system, it helps to take a look at who is in the system and how these persons differ from those who are not in the system. These differences can be compared on multiple levels such as individual and interpersonal characteristics, as well as in their social positions. Here, we focus on a number of factors identified as central to girls' and women's involvement in the system.

Experiences of victimization or interpersonal violence have been identified as factors that contribute to girls' involvement in the juvenile legal system for status offenses (i.e., things that are illegal because of the person's status as a minor), such as running away from abusive homes. Research also shows that victimization is evident in women's use of violence against their abusive partners. Following publication of research on adverse childhood events, other forms of adversity also emerged as having an important role in the lives of system-involved girls and women. Mental health is another factor to consider, demonstrated by studies showing the high number of persons with serious mental illness in jails and prisons. Finally, race, ethnicity, class, and other social vulnerabilities have long been recognized as contributors to involvement in the criminal legal system. Most notably, modern-day racial disparities in the criminal legal system can be traced back to Jim Crow segregationist laws. But there is growing attention to the structural means by which these disparities are perpetuated, especially when faced with growing racial and class divides and human rights abuses in enforcement and correctional practices. With this comes the growing acknowledgement of the need for criminal legal reform, as well as mainstream recognition of the structural inequalities that organize and criminalize behaviors in schools, on the streets, and in communities.

As you read, you will begin to see that it is not simply a girl's or woman's choice to act in a certain manner that determines if she becomes system involved. Rather, one must also consider the ways that rules and laws are developed and enforced, how behaviors are labeled and punished, and how this differentially impacts persons who are positioned differently in society—whether that position is by virtue of their gender, class, race, sexual orientation, immigration status, or something else.

CHAPTER ONE

Girls' & Women's Experiences of Victimization and Adversity

Introduction

Research with system-involved girls and women has identified high rates of victimization and adversity that is linked to delinquent and criminal offending. This chapter will briefly review prevalence rates of girls' and women's exposure to different forms of interpersonal violence. We will introduce the concept of adverse childhood events (ACEs) and poly-victimization, as well as summarize findings from key studies suggesting victimization is specifically and directly a risk factor for entering the criminal legal system. We will consider how adversity experienced by marginalized populations and individuals with intersecting identities creates higher risk for entry into the system, with consideration of disparities in access to resources, criminalization of survival strategies, and other contributing factors.

Victimization and Survival

As we mentioned in the introduction, the feminist pathways perspective posits that victimization plays a key role in women's involvement in the justice system. One of the first researchers to explore victimization among offenders was Meda Chesney-Lind, credited as the mother of feminist criminology (Belknap, 2004). While pursuing her master's degree in sociology at the University of Hawaii, she began examining Honolulu court records that spanned from the 1920s to the 1950s. Chesney-Lind noticed that many of the charges appeared to be "policing girls' sexuality" (Belknap, 2004, p. 10). Girls were frequently charged for sexual immorality (e.g., sexual activity) and waywardness (e.g., willful disobedience), often at the request of parents who insisted on the arrests, with girls being subjected to court-ordered gynecological examinations to attest to condition of the hymen (essentially checking if girls had engaged in intercourse). As a result, Chesney-Lind recognized that behaviors such as running away from home were likely survival strategies used by the girls to flee abusive or neglectful home environments and that official statutes were being used to keep the girls under familial control in accord with the gendered expectations for girls to stay in the home. As runaways, girls were unable to enroll in school or take a job without being detected, so they were forced into the streets to engage in panhandling, petty theft, and prostitution to survive (Belknap, 2004; Chesney-Lind, 1989). Chesney-Lind pointed out that the major theories of delinquency focused on disadvantaged boys in public settings, systematically ignoring the relationship between girls' victimization and crime (Chesney-Lind, 1989). She likened her own difficult childhood to the experiences of such girls: "They were 'guilty' of the same crime as me: felony bad attitude, but *their* parents institutionalized *them*" (Belknap, 2004, p. 19).

Another researcher to examine victimization among system-involved women was Angela Browne. In the early 1980s, Browne was conducting research on battered women and working as a consultant on legal cases in which abused women were charged with the death or serious injury of their partners. She listened carefully to the stories shared by the women and brought attention to the severity of violence the women experienced before harming (or killing) their partners. In her book, *When Battered Women Kill* (1987), she documented the stories of 42 women from 15 states in the United States—describing the roots of violence in the women's childhoods, their experiences of courtship and early marriage, and the transition of their intimate relationships from affectionate to violent. In retelling the women's stories, which were corroborated by hospital and police records as well as testimony of relatives and other witnesses, Browne (1987) attempted to remain true to the women's perspectives on their own lives, stating "The decisions a woman makes in an abusive relationship are based on her perceptions of patterns and alternatives, so it is important to understand these perceptions as thoroughly as possible" (p. x). Browne characterized the violence these women experienced as escalating, frequent, and severe, with the women's partners often being under the influence of drugs or alcohol, sexually assaulting the women, and threatening to kill them. Browne (1987) concluded that these women "did not believe they could escape the abusive situation and survive, and now they could no longer survive within it either" (p. 130).

Studies such as those of Chesney-Lind (1989) and Browne (1987) underscored the relationship of girls' and women's delinquent and criminal offending to basic needs of survival. Such research also paved the way for theory on the criminalization of women's survival strategies. Criminalization is when a behavior is defined as illegal or when a person is labeled as a criminal. When we label a behavior (e.g., drug use) or a person (e.g., an immigrant) as criminal, we are choosing to address a problem through the criminal legal system rather than through other public service systems or strategies. If we look at laws in various parts of the United States and around the world, we can see that which is defined as a crime or criminal varies widely depending on social context and/or geographic location. As will be discussed throughout the book, many of the behaviors and persons viewed as criminal in the United States are those in pursuit of survival amid difficult circumstances. Furthermore, once behaviors or persons are deemed criminal, they may be differentially policed based on an individual's intersecting roles or positions in society. Specifically, persons of privilege may get a "pass" on some acts for which others may be penalized. To better understand this, let's begin with looking at the prevalence of victimization and other adversity among girls and women who are involved with the criminal legal system. After that, we will examine links between victimization and delinquent or criminal offending, as well as other intersecting factors that exacerbate risks for victimized persons to engage in criminalized behaviors.

Prevalence of Victimization and Adversity Among System-Involved Girls and Women

We described Angela Browne's (1987) work interviewing battered women who killed their partners. Noting the parallels between the long-term effects of victimization by family members and intimates (e.g., substance use, use of defensive violence) and the predominant reasons for women's incarceration (e.g., drug offenses and, to a lesser extent, violent offenses), Browne continued her research and led one of the first methodologically rigorous studies of the prevalence of violence in the lives of incarcerated women (Browne et al., 1999). The study, which involved interviews with 150 women sentenced to a maximum-security facility, revealed the severity and pervasiveness of violence in the women's lives. Seventy percent of the women experienced severe physical violence by caretakers in childhood or adolescence—that is, being kicked, bitten, hit with a fist or an object, beaten up, burned or scalded, threatened or assaulted with a knife or gun, or having their lives threatened. Fifty-nine percent experienced sexual abuse, including that which was noncontact (e.g., flashing, sexual invitations) or contact (e.g., oral sex, penetration), in childhood or adolescence by a person at least 5 years older at the time. Seventy-five percent experienced severe physical violence by intimate adult partners, and 77% experienced physical or sexual violence directed at them as adults by non-intimates (Browne et al., 1999). Browne and associates pointed out that violence in the lives of these women usually began early—before age 11—making it unlikely that experiences of victimization were precipitated by drug use or delinquent or criminal behavior.

GETTING REAL 1.1

He'd, like, get a hollow look in his eye, and then he'd just start pounding on me, yelling at me, beating me, um, and then he'd throw me down and rape me, kick me, stomp me into the floor.

Amanda, White, age 50, is a high school graduate, working part-time post-release. She has been incarcerated five times, most recently for drug possession and selling or manufacturing. During a research interview, Amanda explained she went to prison because she used drugs to cover up the pain of being abused physically and mentally. Amanda noted she is currently living in a woman's shelter and receiving a lot of support from her family, but she is not in touch with any of her old friends since she's been out, so that she can avoid the drugs. She is still waiting for a reentry mentor to be assigned to her—she's been out 5 months but there are not enough mentors to help all the women waiting. Before she went to prison, Amanda described being in a relationship with a partner who was violent pretty much daily. Her partner broke her back in their worst fight before she was incarcerated. Amanda says going to prison saved her life. Now that she is out, she says she is gaining strength every day. She says it has been really hard to get the assistance she needs, but she has a job she loves, and she thinks she's going to be okay.

More recent studies have demonstrated similarly high rates of victimization among women in prison. One of the authors of this book, Dana DeHart (2018), in a study of 60 women in a maximum-security facility, found that 72% of women had been maltreated as children, and 85% experienced intimate partner violence in teen or adult relationships. DeHart (2008) found that these women typically suffered more than one type of victimization, creating uniquely difficult situations with which the women struggled (e.g., witnessing family violence, experiencing sexual abuse, and being bullied at school). Such experiences of multiple *types* of victimization is referred to as poly-victimization and is associated with experiencing other lifetime adversities as well as greater psychological distress (Finkelhor et al., 2011) and poorer health (Felitti et al., 1998).

Among women in jails, who presumably are not as deeply enmeshed in the criminal legal system, rates of victimization are nevertheless also high. Authors of this book, Lynch, DeHart, and associates (2017) examined victimization among 491 jailed women from rural and urban locales across the United States. As can be seen in Figure 1.1, only 8% had no exposure to violence whereas 40% experienced child physical abuse, 47% experienced child sexual abuse, and 68% witnessed violence as children such as that between caregivers or severe violence in communities. In adulthood, 67% of the women experienced intimate partner violence, 45% experienced sexual assault, 38% had been robbed or attacked by strangers, and 61% witnessed violence in their homes or communities. On average, each woman experienced more than three types of violence.

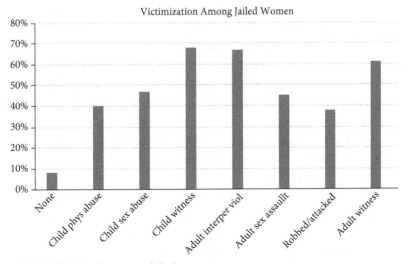

FIGURE 1.1 Victimization among jailed women.

Experiencing and witnessing interpersonal violence, however, are not the only forms of adversity prevalent in the life histories of incarcerated girls and women. A study conducted by the Kaiser Permanente medical group (Felitti et al., 1998) identified a number of victimization and non-victimization related adverse childhood experiences (ACEs) associated with enduring social and health outcomes over the life span—outcomes including as alcoholism, drug abuse, depression, suicide attempts, sexually transmitted diseases, and even chronic conditions such as heart disease, cancer, lung disease, and liver disease. The ACEs that precipitate these outcomes include victimization such as physical, sexual, and psychological abuse, but they also include dysfunction in the household of origin during childhood, such as growing up in a household with substance abuse, mental illness, family violence, or a household member who had been incarcerated. Researchers studying women's crime noticed that these factors appeared common within samples of offenders and began to add measures of non-victimization adversity to their studies. For example, in a study of 598 women in prison, Susan Sharp and associates (2012) found that most of the women experienced childhood physical abuse (52%) and sexual abuse (56%), but also high rates of childhood emotional neglect (70%), emotional abuse (63%), and physical neglect (47%). Their childhood households were also likely to include a family member who abused alcohol or other drugs (70%), a household member with a mental illness (46%), mothers experiencing domestic violence (34%), and a family member incarcerated in prison (27%) (Sharp et al., 2012). Sharp (2014) examined the distribution of adverse childhood experiences in this sample and found that the vast majority of women experienced more than one type of adversity, with at least half experiencing five or more types.

Let's pause for a moment here to consider how experiencing so much adversity might affect your beliefs about the world, your ability to be safe, and your ability to engage productively in tasks like school and work. How do you think experiencing high rates of interpersonal violence and adversity is likely to affect any individual? What are your thoughts about labeling behaviors such as running away, truancy, and substance use as criminal behaviors when you consider these as potential responses to victimization and adversity?

In Dana DeHart's research on women in prison—following from Browne et al. (1999)—she noticed that violence and adversity typically began very early in the lives of incarcerated women. To investigate further, DeHart developed another study that examined victimization and other adversity in the lives of girls who were incarcerated in long-term commitment facilities and group homes in the juvenile legal system. Even within this sample of 100 girls aged 12–17, victimization and adversity were pervasive (DeHart & Moran, 2015). Sixty-nine percent experienced caregiver maltreatment, including physical and psychological abuse, neglect, and parental kidnapping. Forty-two percent had already experienced dating violence, and 31% experienced gang or group attacks. The most predominant form of violence within this sample was sexual violence, experienced by 81% of girls, including assaults by known and unknown adults, assaults by peers, attempted rape, having been "flashed," verbal sexual harassment, and—most commonly—"consensual" sex with adults. The latter was experienced by 69% of the girls and was often characterized by large disparities in the ages of the girls and their adult partners. Witnessing violence was nearly universal among the girls, most of whom had seen or heard community shootings or riots or witnessed bad attacks involving weapons. Many had also witnessed assaults of caregivers or siblings, and more than one-third had witnessed a murder. Nearly half had a close friend or family member who was murdered. Many of the girls in this sample also experienced non-victimization adversity (DeHart, 2009), such as death or serious illness of a close friend or family member (84%), a caregiver incarcerated in jail or prison (54%), a caregiver whose drug or alcohol use caused problems (48%), or families that always argued or fought (44%).

Looking comparatively between girls and boys, in 2006, Belknap and Holsinger conducted focus groups and interviews with 441 detained youth. They observed that 75% of girls and two-thirds of boys experienced physical abuse from a family member. In addition, three-fifths of girls and one-fifth of boys reported sexual abuse, often by a family member. Many of the girls also reported experiences of sexual abuse from non-family members as well as family members. In the focus groups, more than half of the girls and two-fifths of the boys connected their experiences of physical and sexual violence to their entry into the criminal legal system. Girls were also more likely to report being abandoned or deserted by a parent, to dropping out of school because they could not "keep up," to have attempted suicide, and to report they would rather live in a corrections institution then in their homes. The authors of this study note the high rates of violence exposure for both boys and girls in the system but suggest that the extent of girls' sexual violence experiences as well as their additional experiences of adversity such as parent loss, dropping out of school, and their preference for living in correctional facilities (versus current living situation) suggests that girls' and boys' pathways may differ in important ways and require different forms of support to change their paths.

GETTING REAL 1.2

The police officer took me to the hospital, and I was there all night. And they had a rape counselor there and gave me an exam. … The police took the report down, and then they took me back to school, and I just wanted to forget about it. I couldn't deal with it no more, so I just—I stopped talking to the police, and I stopped taking the calls from the counselor. I didn't want to talk about it. I just quit school and came back. I told my family I got beat up, because when I came back, I had a big scrape, and I had a black eye, and my lip was swollen. I just told them I got in a fight and I got in trouble for my drinking.

Enola was a 38-year-old American Indian woman serving a 1-year sentence for a DUI and parole violation. She described many experiences of interpersonal violence in her lifetime during a research interview about how others had responded to her when she disclosed her experiences of abuse. Enola reported she and her sister were sexually abused when she was about 6 by her stepfather. Many years later, she tried to tell her mother about the abuse but her mother said they would "talk about it later," and they never did. At age 16, she was in a car accident that took about a year and three surgeries to recover from. When she was 18, Enola was raped when she accepted a ride home from her brother-in-law. She explained she was blacked out from drinking, and when she woke up, he was having sex with her. A week later, she told her cousin, and then she and her cousin beat her brother-in-law up to get him back. Two years later, her brother-in-law killed himself. Enola's first romantic relationship was when she was 16 and lasted until she was 19. He beat her up a lot. The next guy she was with broke into her place through the window when she tried to break up with him, he broke her jaw and forced her to have sex. She started drinking a lot again after that and told the bartenders what happened to her, and her ex got his ass kicked. Then she moved away, started going to college, and a guy raped her. She had gone for a ride with a group of people and she didn't know where she was, but she ran to a house and the people there called the police, and the police helped her. They took her to the hospital. After that, she just wanted to forget about what happened, but the police and a rape counselor kept calling her, so she quit school and went back home. She said she thinks a lot of what has happened to her is her fault because of her drinking. Enola estimates she has been incarcerated in jail or prison about 20 times.

In these and other studies examining prevalence of victimization and other adversity among offenders, statistical estimates of prevalence may fluctuate with variations in sampling sources (e.g., probation, jails, prisons), populations (e.g., women, girls), and measurement techniques (e.g., how "abuse" is operationalized or defined). Yet, even when the same measures are used to compare samples of incarcerated versus non-incarcerated populations, women who are incarcerated demonstrate more extensive histories of victimization and adversity than women who are not in the system. Radatz and Wright (2017) examined victimization and traumatic life events in the life histories of 424 women, some of whom were incarcerated and some who were not. The non-incarcerated women were from a high-risk sample and included women from shelters and who utilized social services. Despite the risk status of the non-incarcerated women, the incarcerated women still experienced more victimization and other traumatic events than those who were not incarcerated. These differences were particularly pronounced for intimate partner violence, including physical violence and controlling behavior, as well as traumatic events such as life-threatening accidents, man-made disasters, and sudden death of a loved one. The incarcerated women also were more likely than the non-incarcerated to report alcohol or drug problems as well as attempted suicide. Poly-victimized women were more likely to report such problems.

Pathways From Victimization and Adversity to Offending

Much of the research on the association between victimization and girls' and women's crime involves pathways or typologies of offending. Mary Gilfus (1992) described women's pathways to street crime in terms of a transition from victims to survivors to offenders. Her research utilized life-history interviews with 20 incarcerated women, with particular attention to women's interpretations of female sex roles and gendered victimization in setting the stage for criminal activities. Gilfus described not only the victimization that led girls and women to the streets and their use of crime to survive on the streets, but also subsequent victimization, sexual exploitation, and gendered roles within a subculture where violence was pervasive and street crimes were typically controlled by males. Here we see intersections between gender and access to resources. Girls' and women's engagement in crime was often interpreted by the women as an extension of their caretaking for male partners, for whom they supplied drug money through prostitution with the men serving in the role of pimps. In this case, women engaged in sex work as a means of survival.

Gilfus noted the blurring of boundaries between victim and offender in the criminalization of girls' and women's sex work. This blurring of boundaries continues today, as sexually trafficked persons, including minors who are trafficked, are still sometimes treated as criminals; for example, they may be arrested for prostitution and/or detained involuntarily in secure facilities while those who traffic them or solicit their services may elude prosecution. Godsoe (2015) has noted that U.S. prostitution laws have not yet progressed into alignment with anti-trafficking laws, complicating the issue of criminalization of girls' and women's sexuality and survival strategies. In other words, trafficked individuals may be arrested and charged for criminal behaviors such as prostitution even when their actions were not voluntary but rather behaviors they engaged in to stay alive.

Kathleen Daly (1992), in her study of 40 women defendants in felony court, also focused on the gendered contexts of victimization and survival on the streets. Daly (1992) characterized the link between childhood victimization and adult criminal activities as a "black box" (p. 15) warranting further research. Using pre-sentence investigation reports and court transcripts, Daly developed biographies of each of the 40 women, identifying common themes in their life experiences, relating this to established links between child maltreatment and criminalization, and organizing the women's biographies to describe typical pathways that bring women to felony court. The most frequent pathway to felony court was described by Daly as "harmed and harming women." Daly (1992) noted that the subgroup name "inadequately conveys the physically and emotional harmful experiences the women experienced while growing up, and the diverse and complex ways in which these experiences are reproduced in the women's harming behavior toward others" (pp. 28–29). These women typically had chaotic childhoods, with childhood maltreatment and parents who were addicted to drugs. In adolescence and adulthood, they turned to alcohol and drugs to cope as well as behavioral acting out. The next most common pathway, "street women," were pushed out of their homes or ran away to escape abuse, turning to petty crime on the streets such as prostitution, theft, and drug dealing. Third were the "battered women," who experienced relationships with violent men; these women would not have been involved with the felony court were it not for the women's defensive, retaliatory, or preemptive violence directed toward their abusive partners. The final two groups experienced less extreme victimization; "drug-connected women" were involved in drugs via their relationship partners or family members, and "other" women committed crimes due to immediate economic circumstances or greed. Based on these findings, Daly emphasized that not all women involved in the justice system came the route of "street women";

rather, a more multidimensional portrait of women's pathways to crime was needed—particularly when considering the diversity of the crimes with which women are charged, ranging from petty to more serious violent offenses. Daly's descriptions highlighted the salience of victimization and survival in the pathways to felony court—evinced through criminalized behaviors of acting out, running away, sex work, and fighting back, among other things. This is a good time to stop and think for a moment about why we label these behaviors as criminal. What other systemic responses could we have to these types of behaviors?

DeHart's (2008) qualitative interviews with 60 women in a maximum-security facility highlights incarcerated women's own perspectives on the ways that victimization intersected with other life factors to bring the women to prison. The women described ways that victimization led directly to crime, as in cases where children were mis-socialized by their caregivers by being told to steal or being provided with drugs, when parents sexually exploited girls into commercial sex work, when battered women used lethal force against abusive partners, and when girls or women were otherwise coerced or provoked into criminal activity. The women also described ways in which victimization's impact created ripple effects on their physical or mental health, finances, or social and spiritual well-being—pushing the girls and women away from mainstream avenues of success and toward antisocial peer networks and illegitimate means for survival. Victimization's impact included pain, disability, mental disorders, substance dependence, sexually transmitted diseases, unwanted pregnancies or infertility, poor academic performance, job loss, property damage, household disruption, loss of family and friends, and loss of faith. In the face of unrelenting trauma, social stigma, and barriers at each turn in life, girls and women gravitated toward others who were living on the margins of society, surviving using the only means left. DeHart lists a number of pathways from child maltreatment to crime, intimate partner violence to crime, property loss to crime, as well as pathways from crime back to victimization as when women and girls find themselves in risky situations due to criminal activity. DeHart notes that the cycle of victimization to crime to more victimization can leave women struggling to keep their heads above water. She emphasizes the importance of viewing women's behavioral choices within the broader frame of life circumstances, particularly as these are shaped by overwhelming contexts of victimization and other adversity.

Roos and associates (2016) examined the association between victimization and incarceration in a nationally representative sample of 34,653 persons aged 20 and older. These authors concluded that childhood maltreatment confers specific risk for incarceration beyond caregiver maladjustment, with the latter operationalized to include a caregiver's substance use, incarceration, mental illness, and suicidal behavior. They found that those individuals with more severe poly-victimization and parental substance use had the highest risk of incarceration. Others who experienced different forms of maltreatment, including acts of omission (i.e., neglect), were also at increased risk. Persons who experienced only caregiver maladjustment in the absence of maltreatment were not at increased risk for incarceration, and the authors suggest that it is the nature of the caregiving—not the nature of the caregiver—that confers risk. The association between maltreatment and risk for incarceration was robust and persisted even after controlling for substance use disorders. The authors suggest that other pathways between victimization and criminal behavior might include biological changes to the brain, such as changes in physiological arousal and stress responses that increase risky behavior or maladaptive coping.

One compelling study to provide evidence of the link between victimization and offending is a prospective longitudinal study conducted by Cathy Widom (2000). This type of study follows people over time and allows us to draw stronger conclusions about the association between victimization and offending. Widom and Maxfield (2001) identified 908 abused and neglected girls and boys between the ages of 0 and 11 based on court records as well as a matched control group of 667 youths the same ages with similar socioeconomic conditions. The study followed the cohort—from between 1967 and 1971—until they were adults in their 30s. Widom notes that all the participants in this study were predominantly lower class, with less access to resources, thus the results may represent intersection of victimization and class as predictors of offending. She found that 20% of the abused or neglected girls were arrested as youth compared to 11% of the matched control group and 28.5% of the abused and neglected girls were arrested as adults compared to 15.9% of the matched controls. Essentially, the abused and neglected girls were arrested at twice the rate of non-abused (control) girls across adolescence and adulthood.

GETTING REAL 1.3

My parents were very, very abusive, and I have a problem with that ... I have a fighting problem. It takes a lot to get me mad, and you've got to keep egging it and egging it and egging it before I actually do something, but I do act out physically, which is not good, and I think that that has a lot do with the way I was brought up.

> Marta is a 23-year-old Latina woman serving a 12-month prison sentence for parole violation. She was previously incarcerated for 36 months. Marta completed a pre-treatment research interview after requesting to participate in a treatment group for women with substance use and PTSD. She had a baby just as this prison sentence started, and she wants to participate in this treatment program because she has heard it is good. She wants to talk about things that have been hurtful to her so she can get over them. There are a lot of people depending on her. Marta uses prayer and working out to cope, but it is not enough. Marta reported having problems cutting down her drinking when things get really stressful. She explained she was abused by her parents when she was younger and that she believes that is why she gets in fights so easily. She mostly feels supported by her family now, especially her sister, who is caring for her child.

Further, about half (49%) of the abused and neglected girls and 36% of Widom's control group girls arrested for status offenses as youth went on to be arrested for other crimes as adults. This suggests that status offenses (e.g., running away, truancy) were entry points or represented increased risk for continued system involvement for these girls/women. This study illustrates that many youths who are abused and neglected (70%) do not go on to offend, but also that abuse and neglect experiences heighten the risk of offending. This is a critical point for us to consider. What could we do to further decrease victimized youth's risk of entering the criminal legal system?

Intersection of Victimization and Adversity With Race, Class, and Social Position

One of the most important things to keep in mind regarding routes into the criminal legal system is that multiple factors influence one's position in life and their passage through the system. While we have discussed intersections of gender with victimization and adversity, other determinants of social position intersect with victimization and adversity to impact whether women's behavior is policed and penalized. Regina Arnold (1992) conceptualized dimensions of victimization beyond family and gendered violence, noting the roles economic marginality, racism, and mis-education may play in pushing girls and women out of conventional institutions and into criminal subcultures. Specifically, Arnold discussed how active resistance to victimization, such as running away, stealing, and leaving school, are socially constructed as pre-criminal behavior. Arnold (1992) described how "females, as young girls, are labeled and processed as deviants—and subsequently as criminals—for refusing to accept or participate in their own victimization" (p. 154). She argues that this refusal results in structural dislocation—removal by choice or force—from the primary socializing institutions of family, education, and occupation. Association with deviant peers and entry into criminal life become rational choices for survival under such circumstances. Often girls and women use alcohol and drugs to numb themselves to the pain of their harsh realities. As victims of class, gender, and race oppression, these women are what Arnold (1992) refers to as victims of "triple jeopardy" (p. 163). In fact, the Girls Study Group, a group of researchers examining girls' pathways to delinquency, found consistent associations between childhood maltreatment and delinquent or criminal offending among both girls and boys. The researchers identified victimization as a central factor in girls' delinquency, noting that girls were at increased risk of victimization (especially sexual abuse and sexual assault). Economic conditions compounded this risk, with girls from disadvantaged neighborhoods being more likely to behave violently than others (Zahn et al., 2010).

One taxonomic approach that explicitly addresses the intersection of gender, race, and crime is outlined by Beth Richie (1995) in her book, *Compelled to Crime*. Richie was visiting the women's jail at Riker's Island Correctional Facility when she noticed that most of women there were women of color from low-income communities. "While the 'official' sources report that at least half of the women there are battered women," she reflected, "my experience as an activist and advocate in anti-violence programs had me convinced that far more than that have been abused by their partners" (Richie, 1995, p. 3). In her book she describes the inescapable despair in these women's lives, stemming from abuse, degradation, economic difficulties, and overt racism. Richie saw the link between the women's victimization and their survival through illegal activities, and she articulated this in terms of the logical extension of the women's racialized gender identities and culturally expected roles in violent relationships. Richie's mixed-methods research involved 37 incarcerated women, including Black and White women and those who had and had not experienced intimate partner violence. By contrasting the experiences of different groups of women and garnering detailed narratives of women's pathways, Richie (1995) was able to describe the "gender entrapment" of Black women who were "confined by social conditions in their communities, restrained by their families' circumstances, severely limited by abuse in their intimate relationships, and forced to make hard choices with very few options" (p. 5). Richie identified six pathways to crime for Black, battered women. These included women held hostage in severely violent relationships, women who projected violence at men based on the women's experiences in previous relationships, women who were sexually exploited following long histories of child sexual victimization, women who fought back against abusive partners, poor women who committed crimes out of economic motivation, and women who were addicted to drugs, often as a means to cope with adversity in their lives. Richie's analysis showed how race, gender, and violence intersect to create private and public conditions of subordination and make Black battered women vulnerable to participation in criminalized activities. The women in Richie's study were, quite simply, compelled to crime in order to survive victimization and other extreme circumstances within the confines of their racialized, gendered social positions.

Kolleen Duley (2007) articulated the connections between criminalization and ways in which racialized, classed, and gendered violence are tied to mass incarceration. Duley argued that viewing incarceration as individualized—stemming from a woman's personal life experiences rather than being connected to broader forces of social marginalization—pathologizes their experiences and obscures the political contexts that differentially oppress women of color. These contexts include things like the war on drugs, criminalization of immigration, and rampant policing of communities of color. If we ignore these contexts, we may erroneously perceive all offending as an individual failure rather than seeing the politically connected processes by which marginalized people are systematically disadvantaged and labeled as committing crimes. Disadvantaged communities may lack access to adequate schools and housing, employment, job security, health and mental health care, disability services, substance abuse treatment, resources for battered women, and other community supports, while at the same time suffering scrutiny and mistreatment from law enforcement and the courts. Accordingly, persons in disadvantaged communities may not look at police as protectors and may be reticent to utilize the criminal legal system to address social disorder. Duley characterized some crimes—such as drug use and sales—as common ways that marginalized persons may cope with loss of basic human rights in such communities. Criminalizing the most vulnerable and utilizing their prison-based labor for economic expansion of corporate interests, the current system confers further advantage on the most powerful at the expense of the most vulnerable.

SUMMARY

Here we have addressed some of the ways that girls' and women's attempts to survive and resist victimization, adversity, and racial- or class-based oppression may bring girls and women to be scrutinized by the criminal legal system. We described a number of studies that illustrate high rates of adversity and victimization among incarcerated women and girls, and we discussed the ways in which women's and girls' efforts to cope with these adversities (e.g., running away, substance use) may increase the risk of engaging in behaviors labeled as criminal. In many cases, women and girls are exposed to multiple forms of victimization or poly-victimization, and these cumulative exposures push them away from systems like schools and helping organizations, resulting in further isolation and risk of criminal behavior. Finally, women and girls are at differential risk for being penalized for their behaviors depending on their social identities (e.g., ethnicity, socioeconomic status). In the next chapter, we address the roles of mental and physical health in girls' and women's susceptibility to criminalization.

DISCUSSION QUESTIONS

1. What types of adversity are most common among incarcerated women and girls? How do their rates of exposure compare to other individuals with similar backgrounds but who are not incarcerated?
2. How does exposure to adversity increase the risk of entering the criminal legal system? What is the evidence that girls' and women's exposure to adversity and poly-victimization increases the likelihood of incarceration?
3. Several behaviors such as running away, truancy, sex work, and substance use are labeled as crimes but also as survival strategies. What are your thoughts about how the system labels these behaviors? Are there ways we could label and respond to these behaviors that do not criminalize them?
4. How do the social identities (e.g., ethnicity, class, sexual orientation, disability, immigration status) of women and girls influence risk of incarceration?

CHAPTER TWO

Mental and Physical Health of System-Involved Girls and Women

Introduction

Incarcerated women and girls have high rates of mental health problems compared to incarcerated men as well as girls and women in the general population. Women are also at greater risk of chronic health problems and reproductive health concerns than men. In this chapter, we will briefly discuss the most common mental and physical health difficulties experienced by system-involved women and girls. We will summarize the limited research on system-involved girls' and women's access to health care and discuss health disparities among marginalized populations. Next, we will present key findings from research illustrating links between victimization, adversity, and negative health outcomes among system-involved girls and women. We discuss ways in which health and mental health difficulties may intersect with women's entry into the criminal legal system, including deinstitutionalization and criminalization of mental health difficulties, substance abuse, and other physical/behavioral health issues.

Mental Health and Impairment

Before we describe incarcerated women's and girls' mental health, let's review a few key terms. Mental health is a term used to describe our well-being; how we think, feel, and act. When we are mentally healthy, we are better able to respond to and cope with stressful situations. A mental disorder, according to the Diagnostic and Statistical Manual of Mental Disorders (DSM), is "a syndrome characterized by clinically significant disturbance in an individual's cognition, emotion regulation, or behavior that reflects a dysfunction in psychological, biological, or developmental processes underlying mental functioning" (American Psychiatric Association, 2013, p. 20). Typically, to receive a diagnosis, an individual must be distressed, have impaired functioning, and exhibit a pattern of symptoms (e.g., sad mood most or all of the time, difficulty sleeping, agitation, difficulty concentrating) for a specified period of time such that they meet criteria for a mental disorder.

Mental disorders are common; they affect people of all ages, cultures, and socioeconomic statuses. Mental disorders can be persistent or intermittent. The National Institute of Mental Health (NIMH, 2020) reported that in 2017 that about 19% of adults in the United States experienced a mental disorder in their lifetime. Many adults with mental disorders are able to function without major difficulties. A mental disorder is labeled as severe or serious when the disorder substantially interferes with or limits one's ability to engage in major life activities such as working, maintaining social relationships, engaging in leisure activities, or caring for themselves. About 4% of adults have had a serious mental illness (SMI) in the United States in the past year. Women, younger adults, and multiethnic adults report higher rates of SMI (see Figure 2.1).

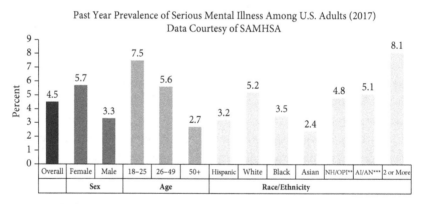

FIGURE 2.1 NIMH rates of serious mental illness.

Deinstitutionalization and Criminalization

Several theorists have argued that one reason there are such high rates of individuals with mental health problems, particularly serious mental illness, in the criminal legal system is due to the deinstitutionalization movement. This movement started with good intentions. In the late 1940s, increasing attention was called to the harsh, prison-like conditions in many facilities for individuals with serious mental disorders. In addition, new medications were becoming available that decreased the severity of psychotic symptoms like hallucinations, delusions, and mania, suggesting individuals could live in less restrictive environments. Communities developed new policies for treating the mentally ill, with the aim of increasing the availability of community-based mental health services and reducing the use of institutions to house individuals with mental illness (Primeau et al., 2013). However, many communities were not prepared for the cost of providing services, nor did they have sufficient numbers of trained providers.

In a 2010 report on mentally ill individuals and incarceration, Torrey and associates noted that there are approximately three times as many individuals with serious mental illness in corrections settings than in mental hospitals in the United States. To look more closely at the relationship between psychiatric facilities and the incarceration of mentally ill individuals, Primeau et al. (2013) examined records from psychiatric hospitals between 1978 and 2010 and incarceration rates in Pennsylvania. They found a significant negative correlation or association between psychiatric facilities availability and incarceration such that as the number of psychiatric hospital beds went down, the number of incarcerated individuals increased. The authors controlled for a number of important factors, including poverty rate, population changes, and unemployment rate in their analyses, and found that 6.8% of the incarceration rate was explained by reductions in psychiatric facilities.

Deinstitutionalization is one explanation for the increased numbers of people who are mentally ill in the criminal legal system. Another related explanation concerns our strategies for how to manage the behavior of mentally ill persons in our communities. For example, individuals with mental illness are often charged with disturbing the peace, disorderly conduct, or drug- or alcohol-related charges (Brandt, 2012). As we mentioned before, it is critical that we consider what behaviors are labeled criminal acts. When an individual is arrested and processed in the criminal legal system for behaviors directly associated with their mental illness, this is "criminalization" of mental illness. Within the criminal legal system and even upon reentry back into communities, if mental illness is not addressed, the individuals are likely to cycle in and out of the criminal legal system (Blevins & Soderstrom, 2015; O'Keefe & Schnell, 2007). Now that we have briefly discussed ways in which institutional and social policies impact our criminal legal responses to individuals who have mental health problems, we will review the rates of mental health disorders for system-involved women and girls.

Mental Health Problems Among System-Involved Women and Girls

Incarcerated women have high rates of mental health problems and disorders. In 2017, the Bureau of Justice Statistics published a report on the number of persons in jails and prisons who had mental health problems based on a national survey administered to 106,532 persons incarcerated in prisons, jails, or special facilities (e.g., detention in military, immigration, Indian country facilities) (Bronson & Berzofsky, 2017). Survey respondents responded to six items assessing mental health symptoms (e.g., nervousness, hopelessness, depression). More women in jail (32%) and prison (20%) reported mental health problems in the past 30 days then men in jail (26%) or prison (14%). In total, adult prisoners are five times more likely to experience serious mental health problems than adults in the general population in the United States. This survey sheds light on the high levels of distress of incarcerated individuals but does not give us information about the specific disorders incarcerated women experience.

There have been a few studies with large samples of incarcerated women that provide more information about the types of disorders women experience, the prevalence of these disorders, and women's treatment needs. One of the earliest studies was carried out in Cook County Illinois with 1272 women in jail by Anna Teplin and her colleagues (1996). They reported 80% of the women met criteria for a mental disorder. The most common disorders were drug or alcohol disorders and post-traumatic stress disorder (PTSD).

GETTING REAL 2.1

I was using drugs and alcohol to self-medicate myself because I hadn't been properly diagnosed. And, ah, that path that I chose, drug and alcohol use, led me to prison
...

Sandy, a White woman who is aged 42, has her GED and is a parent of two children. She last worked 3 years before her most recent arrest. She was incarcerated for 14 months for a parole violation and is now back in the community participating in an aftercare program. She has been incarcerated twice before. We interviewed her to learn about her access to services, trauma exposure, and mental health post-release. Sandy explained that before her arrests, she was using alcohol and drugs so she wouldn't feel anything, to manage her depression, and that her drug use is why she went to prison. Sandy believes if her mental health problems had been correctly diagnosed and treated and she had gone to a drug treatment program, she would not have ended up in prison. Now, post-release, Sandy described participating in two weekly treatment classes as part of her reentry plan. She also has a supervision officer, but she has had a lot of trouble communicating with her. Sandy explained she thinks her supervision officer has too big a caseload and can't get back to her even though she needs help with things like moving. Sandy explained she had a couple of really violent partners before she was incarcerated. Her most recent partner before she was incarcerated tried to choke her a lot. She called the cops many times. The worst fight was when he tried to drown her. That's when she left him. Today she wouldn't tolerate that kind of violence. She's more careful now. She also has a good support network of friends now that she didn't have before, and some of her family is really supportive. In the past, her relationships were based on using drugs and alcohol. Now she has been diagnosed with depression and is taking medication for it. She said she's doing good now.

Trestman and his colleagues (2007) conducted structured diagnostic interviews with 307 men and 201 women randomly selected from new admissions to jails in Connecticut, allowing comparisons of rates by gender. Women met criteria for a psychological disorder in their lifetime at higher rates (77%) than men (65%), but as you can see, the majority of these men and women in jail had experienced a psychological disorder and at higher rates than we see for adults in the general population. The most commonly reported disorder was major depressive disorder for women (49%) and men (21%). Another frequently occurring disorder was PTSD with 42% of women and 20% of men in jail meeting lifetime criteria. Latinx and White women reported depression at higher rates than Black women. There were not ethnic differences in the prevalence of PTSD. Women also met criteria for antisocial personality disorder (27%) and borderline personality disorder (23%) at high rates, though men met criteria for antisocial personality disorder at higher rates (39.5%). Importantly, more than half the women

(56%) met criteria for multiple lifetime disorders, suggesting the need for treatment programs that can address multiple disorders.

A more recent survey of 491 women in jails provides further insight into the rates of serious mental disorders and impairment among women in jail (Lynch et al., 2014). This multi-site study was conducted by the authors of this book, Shannon Lynch and Dana DeHart, and two colleagues, Joanne Belknap and Bonnie Green. The project was funded by the Bureau of Justice Assistance. The study included women randomly selected from jails in four regions of the country. We assessed the lifetime and current year (12 month) prevalence of serious mental illnesses such as major depressive disorder, bipolar disorder, PTSD and psychotic disorders, as well as substance use disorders. As can be seen in Figure 2.2, we found high rates of lifetime disorders among the women: substance use disorder (82%), PTSD (53%), major depression (28%), bipolar disorder (15%), and schizophrenia spectrum disorders (4%). It is important to stop for a moment and consider these rates in comparison to the prevalence of major depression (20%), PTSD (9.7%), bipolar disorder (4.5%), and substance use disorder (29.6%) found in women in the general population (Kessler et al., 2005). We will talk more about this later, but as you will see, the risk of PTSD and substance use is significantly associated with poly-victimization and adversity experienced by women in the system.

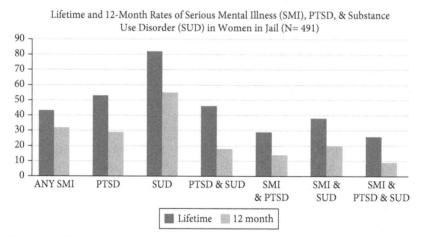

FIGURE 2.2 Lifetime and 12-month rates of serious mental illness (SMI), PTSD, and substance use disorder (SUD) in women in jail (N = 491).

Lynch and colleagues (2014) also reported on the rates of current year disorders and impairment in incarcerated women. More than one in four women (28%) met current criteria for PTSD, over half met criteria for current substance use disorder (53%), and 25% of the women reported severe functional impairment in their ability to carry out daily tasks. Finally, about one woman in ten (9%) met current criteria for PTSD, substance use disorder, and a serious mental illness concurrently. These rates of mental health disorders and impairment suggest that many incarcerated women have notable mental health treatment needs. In this study, there were not significant differences in mental health problems by ethnicity of the women, but women located in western regions of the United States such as Idaho and Colorado reported higher rates of disorders. What are some reasons that women in the western regions of the country may experience higher rates of mental health disorders? How might access to treatment resources in rural areas affect rates of mental health problems?

One possible argument for high rates of disorders among women in jails is that being incarcerated increases psychological distress. While this is likely true, many offenders indicate mental health problems prior to incarceration. For example, a study by Schnittker et al. (2012) compared data from 5,692 individuals who participated in the National Comorbidity Survey Replication. Their sample included people who had never been incarcerated, were previously incarcerated, or were currently incarcerated. These authors reported that mental illness frequently occurred prior to incarceration in this representative sample. Further, while the types of psychological problems and onset or start of mental health problems were similar for never incarcerated and incarcerated individuals, those who had been incarcerated reported much higher rates of childhood adversities than individuals who had not been incarcerated. Schnittker and colleagues commented that higher rates of exposure to adverse events among the incarcerated participants was notable and hypothesized that this was an important difference between incarcerated and non-incarcerated survey participants. Another way to assess the association between mental health problems and incarceration is to follow people over time. In a longitudinal study that followed over 14,000 adolescents into adulthood, those who had been incarcerated for more than 1 month as youths reported higher incidence of impaired functioning, depression, and suicidal thoughts than the non-incarcerated youth (Barnert et al., 2017). These studies suggest that individuals experience mental health problems both before and after incarceration.

The issue of mental health problems among incarcerated persons becomes even more complex when considering mental health of incarcerated transgender persons, who are often imprisoned in facilities aligned with their biological sex at birth rather than their current gender identity. In a study of 315 transgender persons in one state's prison facilities, Sexton et al. (2010) found that 66% had experienced a mental health problem since their incarceration, and 71% had experienced a mental health problem in their lifetimes. These persons also faced other risks, including very high rates of physical (88%) and sexual (75%) assault, including events that occurred both before and during incarceration. Later in this book, we further address some of the ways that transgender persons may be subjected to unique risks in enforcement (Chapter 3) and confinement (Chapter 6) across the criminal legal system.

There is also a growing body of research suggesting that system-involved youth experience high rates of mental health problems. In 2013, Abram and her colleagues published data on the prevalence of PTSD and co-occurring disorders among detained youth. This study included 898 randomly selected youth who were detained in the Chicago Cook County Detention Center. This sample was selected from a larger group of over 1,800 youths to be representative in regard to gender (40.8% girls) and ethnicity (54.6% African American, 28.1% Latinx, 17.1% non-Latinx White). Using diagnostic structured interviews, the researchers found that 14.7% of the girls and 10.9% of boys met criteria for current post-traumatic stress disorder (PTSD). There were not significant differences by gender or ethnicity in the prevalence of PTSD. The majority of the youth with PTSD (93%) also had at least one additional disorder, most often a drug use disorder. More than half of the youth without PTSD (64%) had a mood, anxiety, or substance use disorder. In this sample, boys were at greater risk of reporting two or more disorders. Thus, it is clear that both youth and adults in the system experience higher rates of mental health problems and disorders than individuals in the general population. Further, in most studies, women and girls report higher rates of disorders than do men and boys.

As you read these statistics, you might pause and wonder why we should be concerned about the rates of mental health disorders among women and girls in the legal system. One issue to consider is to what extent these mental health difficulties are risk factors that increase the likelihood of people entering the system. Lau and her colleagues (2018) took an interesting approach to this question. They examined records of 12,476 youth arrested for the first time in Indiana. A little over a quarter (28.5%) of the youths had obtained services for psychiatric problems before their first arrest. They found that youth who had sought out mental health services were younger at the time of their arrest. In addition, Black youth were also younger at first arrest. Younger individuals were less likely to be released and more likely to be detained or placed on probation. They did not identify differences by gender. This study suggests that youth with psychological problems as well as minority youth may enter the system earlier. Further, only 3% of the youth who had previously sought behavioral health services such as substance use treatment were referred for treatment after their arrest. This suggests we may be missing important opportunities to intervene in and influence youths' pathways into the legal system.

In summary, as we reduce the availability of mental health services, we see increases in the rate of incarceration. The incarceration of individuals who have mental health problems suggests that our community systems of care are insufficient to meet the needs of individuals with mental disorders. This raises a number of questions. What is the best or most effective way to respond to mental health problems of community members? Who is most affected when there are insufficient services? How many individuals are arrested because of behaviors that are due to mental health problems but labeled as criminal acts? Is incarceration the best response in these cases? These questions are important to consider because we know that correctional facilities have limited resources. Most facilities are not constructed with the intention of housing individuals with mental health problems (e.g., the facilities are not built with spaces to manage individuals who are psychotic, self-harming, or suicidal) nor are corrections personnel trained as mental health professionals.

Physical Health Problems Among System-Involved Women and Girls

There has been less attention to the physical health problems of system-involved women and girls in the research literature. The Bureau of Justice Statistics published a special report focused on medical problems of incarcerated persons (Maruschak et al., 2015). This report indicates 40% of individuals in state and federal prisoners and jails report having current chronic health conditions such as cancer, high blood pressure, diabetes, heart problems, arthritis, asthma, and cirrhosis of the liver. In addition, 21% reported having infectious diseases such as tuberculosis, and Hepatitis B and C, as well as other sexually transmitted diseases. Incarcerated individuals were more likely to have these health problems than individuals in the general population. For example, 44% reported ever having chronic health conditions compared to 31% of the general population, and 21% of had infectious diseases compared to 4.8% of the general population. As can be seen in Figure 2.3, women reported higher rates of chronic conditions in prisons (63%) and jails (67%) and infectious diseases in prison (25%) and in jails (20%) compared to men's reports of chronic conditions in prison (50%) and jails (48%) and infectious diseases in prison (21%) and jails (13%). Latinx persons were least likely to report chronic health or infectious diseases compared to White and Black persons who were incarcerated. The report does not compare rates across gender and ethnic categories, so we do not know if ethnicity and gender intersect to confer greater risk.

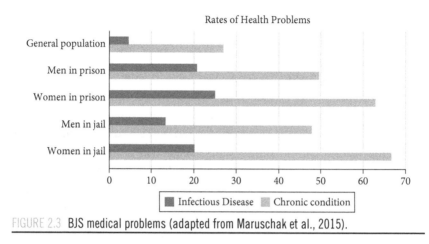

FIGURE 2.3 BJS medical problems (adapted from Maruschak et al., 2015).

Binswanger and colleagues (2010) reviewed surveys administered to 6,982 individuals in jail to assess rates of medical, psychiatric, and substance use disorders and made specific comparisons across gender. There were 1,998 women in the sample. The women had higher rates of medical (56.8%) and psychological disorders (43.6%) than the men (40% and 21.6%, respectively). Women reported the following rates of medical diagnoses: cancer (8.3%), hepatitis (9.6%), hypertension (21.9%), arthritis (20.2%), and asthma (24.4%). In this survey, women also reported a greater burden of chronic medical conditions than men in jail, suggesting the need for health services during incarceration and post-release access to medical care. For example, women were up to seven times more likely to have cancer than men. The authors note common forms of cancer included cervical cancer among women, but only 20% of the women reported a cervical exam during their incarceration. This again illustrates opportunities to provide more effective screening and treatment that might positively affect women's outcomes.

Health problems among the incarcerated are not limited to the aforementioned conditions. One health concern receiving increasing attention for incarcerated women is traumatic brain injury (TBI). The Centers for Disease Control and Prevention (no date) indicate that persons in jails and prisons report high likelihood of having experienced TBI, with rates from different studies ranging from 25–87% among incarcerated persons relative to 8.5% in the general population. These persons may also experience co-occurring serious mental illness, substance use, and/or PTSD, and there are indications that TBI may be an important factor for those committing violent crimes. Additional research is needed to elucidate prevalence and risks of TBI among women and girls involved in the criminal legal system.

Another area receiving increased attention is women's and girls' pregnancies and deliveries while incarcerated. According to the National Task Force on the Use of Restraints with Pregnant Women under Correctional Custody, 5% of women entering jails and 4% of women entering state prisons are pregnant at the time of intake. A best practices statement was published in 2012 by this task force and provides a rationale for prohibiting some forms of restraint (e.g., abdominal restraints) as well as guiding principles if restraints are necessary (e.g., when using wrist restraints, a woman should be able to protect herself and her fetus during a fall forward). In addition, this document indicates all facilities should have written procedures to guide officers' actions (e.g., transport to the hospital and labor and delivery). However, the National Resource Center on Justice Involved Women (no date) notes the use of restraints with this population is an ongoing critical issue. "The First Step Act" included a ban on the use of restraints with federal prisoners, but use across state and county facilities is variable (Atkins, 2019). A 2017 report by the American Psychological Association suggests 37 states and Washington D.C. prohibit or limit the use of restraints or shackles during labor and delivery. Finally, health care providers and advocates note that there is little information about pregnant women's health during incarceration, and data is needed to better inform policy and treatment services (Atkins, 2019).

There is even less information on the physical health of girls in the juvenile legal system. A 2006 review of the medical status of youth in the legal system indicates similar levels of medical problems in youth as we have seen in adult populations, with as many as 46% of youth being diagnosed with a medical problem during a detention stay (Golzari et al., 2006). Many of the most common problems with which youth presented were not physical health issues but rather were psychological distress, substance use, and trauma exposure. In addition, Golzari and colleagues note that dental problems, asthma or respiratory problems, and sexually transmitted diseases were among the more common physical health concerns reported across studies with system-involved youth. They also indicate that there are comparatively few studies that have examined whether access to treatment decreases recidivism among youth, but note there are some examples of studies in which reoffending was reduced when youth participated in treatment and/or community services. This review did not address differences in physical health by gender or ethnicity nor intersecting identities.

Treatment Access and Health Disparities

In 2017, the Bureau of Justice Statistics report by Bronson and Berzofsky indicated that almost three quarters of individuals in jail and prison had received mental health care prior to their most recent incarceration. The most common forms of treatment were prescription medication and counseling. Another Bureau of Justice Statistics report (Maruschak et al., 2015) that focused on medical problems suggests that 80% of persons in prison and 46% of those in jails access at least some health care while incarcerated. A little over half of these individuals reported being somewhat (43.8%) or very satisfied (12.6%) with the health care services they received, but over half (53%) also indicated that the services they received while incarcerated were worse than services prior to incarceration.

It is important to consider the quality of care that individuals receive and whether care is addressing their problems or symptoms. In the study by the authors of this book and their colleagues with 491 women in jail, approximately half of the women received substance use treatment or mental health treatment prior to incarceration (Lynch et al., 2012). However, approximately 30% of the women who obtained treatment disagreed that their symptoms and coping improved. Thus, while many incarcerated individuals seem to have some access to health care, it is not clear they are obtaining care that helps them improve or manage their health problems. You might recall the study by Lau and her colleagues (2017), described earlier in this chapter, that examined records of 12,476 youth arrested for the first time in Indiana. About 70% of this sample reported they accessed no mental health services prior to first arrest. The authors also note that about 2% of youth received a referral to behavioral health services after their arrest, suggesting a lack of communication between corrections and mental health systems.

In short, we are left with more questions than answers about the extent to which incarcerated women and girls are able to access health care for medical or psychological problems and what the quality of that care is. We do know that social identities such as ethnicity, income, education level, gender, employment status, and sexual orientation are associated with health disparities or inequalities in the United States (Centers for Disease Control and Prevention (CDC), 2013). For example, individuals who have lower socioeconomic status are at greater risk of death and illness and have less access to care and lower quality care in the United States (CDC, 2011). Studies of health disparities help us to consider how intersecting identities are associated with health status and access to health care. According to the Centers for Disease Control and Prevention, individuals with low income and educational levels are most likely to be Latinx, American Indian, or Alaska Natives. We also see double the number of individuals with disabilities living at or below the poverty level compared to individuals without disabilities. Another example related to income concerns the greater numbers of Latinx and non-Latinx Blacks without health insurance compared to Asian Pacific Islanders and non-Latinx Whites. Thus, we can see that ethnic identity and ability status interacts with SES to increase risk of poor health. But it is also important that we consider how identities are linked with opportunities, such as where we go to school or live. For example, poor quality housing is associated with negative health outcomes such as cancer, heart disease, and asthma (CDC, 2011). We can immediately guess that individuals with fewer resources are more likely to have this housing, but we see inequity in adequate housing differing by ethnicity as well. Specifically, non-Latinx Blacks, Latinx persons, and then American Indians and Alaska Natives were living in poor quality housing at the highest rates, thus increasing their risk of these health conditions. These are only a few examples of disparities in health that are associated with social identities. We do not have this level of data for system-involved women and girls, but we do know that incarcerated individuals typically have lower education and lower income, and that ethnic minorities are overrepresented in the corrections system (Nellis, 2016).

Links Between Adversity, Victimization, and Health

Thus far we have reviewed psychological and physical health of incarcerated women and girls and treatment access, and we have started to consider how social identities are associated with negative health outcomes. An additional clear risk for women's physical and psychological health is victimization (Priester et al., 2016), which—as discussed in Chapter 1—is very prevalent among system-involved women and girls. Priester and her colleagues conducted a review of the existing research literature and summarized the findings of studies examining links between victimization and health. Specifically, the review identified studies on psychological and physical health outcomes of individuals with experiences of childhood physical and sexual abuse as well as adult experiences of partner violence and sexual and physical assaults. They note that depression, post-traumatic stress disorder, suicide, and substance use are commonly associated with these forms of victimization experiences in the general population. Further, there are clear links between victimization experiences and reproductive, neurochemical, gastrointestinal, and cardiopulmonary health outcomes.

One of the most influential studies that has helped us to connect experiences of adversity and traumatic experiences such as child abuse and neglect to psychological and physical health outcomes is the ACEs study, which we introduced in Chapter 1. In 1998, Vincent Felitti and several colleagues published a study that included exposure rates for childhood emotion, physical and sexual abuse, and household dysfunction (e.g., living with adults who were violent, used substances, were mentally ill, or incarcerated) for 9,508 individuals who had completed surveys and a standardized medical examination. Over half of the sample reported at least one adverse event. Study participants who reported four or more forms of childhood exposure to adversity, compared to individuals without any exposures, had four to twelve times the risk of alcoholism, depression, drug abuse, depression, and suicide. In general, as their number of adverse exposures increased, individuals' risk for health problems such as sexually transmitted diseases, heart disease, cancer, skeletal fractures, and liver disease increased. This study brought increased attention and awareness to the links between experiences of interpersonal violence or victimization and health outcomes in the general public.

There are also a growing number of studies examining the links between victimization and health outcomes specifically among system-involved women and girls. One of the first studies to assess this association in a large sample of women was carried out by Messina and Grella in 2006. They conducted in-depth interviews with 491 incarcerated women and noted increased risk of a number of mental and physical health outcomes associated with experiences of childhood victimization. The women in their study reported the following rates of victimization: physical neglect (19.5%), physical abuse (30.6%), sexual abuse (45.1%), and witnessing family violence (47.6%). About 16% of the women reported no experiences of childhood violence, while 20% reported experiences of five or more forms of childhood victimization. They found that as the number of traumatic exposures increased, the odds of seeking services for mental health problems and incidence of physical health problems increased substantially. For example, women with 7 or more traumatic experiences were 980% more likely to seek mental health services. Women with an increase of one traumatic event were 21% more likely to have alcohol problems, 23% more likely to have a sexually transmitted disease, and 15% more likely to report gynecological problems and poorer overall health. This study illustrates higher risk of a range of health problems associated with victimization in incarcerated women, similar to the ACEs study findings.

We talked before about a study conducted by the authors of this book, Dana DeHart and Shannon Lynch, along with their colleagues Joanne

Belknap and Bonnie Green, to examine women's pathways to the criminal legal system. We interviewed 491 women in jail in four regions of the country using structured diagnostic interviews and detailed trauma assessments. We have examined the associations between victimization and mental health a few different ways using this data. First, we found that cumulative childhood victimization and adult victimization were each strongly associated with women's overall mental health severity and substance use (Lynch et al., 2017). In addition, we looked specifically at the extent to which experiences of interpersonal violence in this sample was associated with individual diagnoses of major depressive disorder, PTSD, bipolar disorder, and substance use disorder (Green et al., 2016). Experiences of interpersonal violence significantly predicted each of these disorders. We found few ethnic differences, with the exception that being Latinx or non-Latinx White increased the likelihood of major depression.

The ACEs study also increased awareness of the increased risk of suicide after trauma exposure. A few studies have examined this association specifically in incarcerated women. First, it is important to note that in general, women commit suicide at lower rates than men. Thus, in the general population, being female is considered a protective factor against completing a suicide. However, this does not hold true for incarcerated women. Incarcerated women complete suicides at higher rates than incarcerated men or individuals in the general population (McCullumsmith et al., 2013). Further, suicide is a leading cause of death for incarcerated women and men. DeCou et al. (2016) examined the associations between exposure to physical and sexual victimization and suicidality in 224 women in prison. It is important to note that this was a sample of women seeking trauma treatment while incarcerated, so they all had some trauma exposure. Almost half of the women (49%) reported a prior suicide attempt. The women's experiences of sexual and physical violence were significantly associated with suicidality, but only for non-Latinx White women. For women who were Latinx or American Indian, there was not a significant association, suggesting that women of color in this sample were at decreased risk of suicide. Tripodi and Pettus-Davis (2013) also examined victimization and suicidality among 125 incarcerated women. They reported that women with experiences of sexual abuse or both physical and sexual abuse were more likely to have attempted suicide than women without these exposures. Let's pause for a moment and consider the implications of high rates of mental health problems and suicide in system-involved women and girls. In the fourth chapter, we will discuss points of decision making in the system that may offer alternative pathways for women and girls, but we encourage you to think now about what types of information professionals should know about health and mental health to make informed decisions and help identify nonlegal pathways for women and girls who are struggling.

Mental Health and Offending

First, it should be clear at this point that system-involved individuals experience mental health problems at higher rates than individuals in the general population. Next, we also know that individuals with mental disorders or mental health problems are more likely to be re-arrested. For example, in the 2017 Bureau of Justice Statistics report on mental health problems of incarcerated persons (Bronson & Berzofsky, 2017), those with mental health problems were more likely to have been arrested multiple times. Almost half (49%) of individuals in prison and more than half of those in jail (56%) or arrested 11 or more times had a history of mental health problems compared to 27% of individuals in prison and 31% of individuals in jail arrested for the first time. However, there is not information about gender or ethnic differences in this report. There are a few studies that have examined how victimization and adversity and mental health all intersect in women's lives and increase risk of entering the criminal legal system.

Bringing It All Together: Victimization, Adversity, Mental Health, and Offending

Considering together what we have discussed in Chapter 1 and the material discussed in this chapter, there are several studies that specifically look at how victimization, adversity, and mental health all intersect to create pathways to offending for women and girls. In our pathways study of 491 women in jails, Lynch and associates (2017) found that both childhood trauma and adversity and adult trauma were significantly and indirectly associated with women's crime (i.e., number of convictions) via pathways of trauma through mental health and substance use disorders. In other words, as childhood and/or adult victimization increased, women's mental health problems including substance use increased, and so did the number of arrests. Further, women with less victimization also had fewer mental health difficulties and fewer arrests. In narrative accounts for a subset of the same women (DeHart et al., 2014), the women described how mental health problems such as depression often stemmed from victimization and loss, and that the women coped with these problems by using alcohol and drugs (often described as self-medication), which in turn led to their entry into crime. Women also described running away as a means of coping with abuse in their homes of origin. In both these cases, we can see that the systemic decision to label drug use or running away as a criminal behavior (and to respond with punitive consequences) criminalizes girls' and women's attempts to manage distress related to victimization. For some women in the sample, the ties between victimization and offending were quite direct, in that the women described responding to violence with violence (either defensive or retaliatory), and they also described some instances in which they were coerced by violent men into committing crimes such as commercial sex work and drug sales. In particular, witnessing violence, caregiver violence, and intimate partner violence each put women at increased risk for specific types of crime. Similarly, DeHart and Moran (2015) found that, in their sample of girls in the juvenile legal system, witnessing violence, caregiver violence, and sexual violence played important roles in predicting criminal/delinquent behavior of the girls.

Salisbury and Van Voorhis (2009) examined recidivism among 313 women on probation and identified three different pathways to incarceration for these women, some of which involved this complex intersection of victimization, adversity, and mental health. First, the authors described a pathway through which childhood victimization contributed to offending by way of mental health disorders and substance abuse. Next, women also fit a relational pathway through which women's relationships with violent partners contributed to offending via victimization, lower self-efficacy, mental health problems, and substance abuse. Finally, there was a third social capital pathway through which criminal behavior was influenced by problems in relationships, low family support, lack of access to education, and low self-efficacy. Thus, two of the three identified pathways highlight how experiences of victimization and mental health problems co-occur and appear to influence women's entry into the system. The third pathway highlights how lack of resources and disorganization in one's family (i.e., adversity) confers risk. Through this research, Salisbury and Van Voorhis demonstrated that women's repeated offending, not just entry into crime, was notably influenced by factors such as childhood and adult victimization, mental health, conflicted intimate relationships, and poor familial support systems.

Brennan et al. (2012) utilized a similar a taxonomic approach to identify pathways to women's crime. Their research provided support for past qualitative typologies while expanding and adding depth through sophisticated statistical modeling. Specifically, these researchers used data from a sample of 718 serious and habitual offenders in a women's prison, using newer quantitative measures that measure both gender-neutral and gender-responsive factors that may be associated with women's crime. As you may recall, gender-neutral factors are those that have been found to be associated with risks and needs in samples of both men and women, such as antisocial peer networks, substance abuse, education, employment, and criminal history. Gender-responsive factors, in contrast, have been identified as primary risks or needs in samples of women but not men. These include factors such as victimization and other trauma, family and relationship conflict, parenting issues, and mental health. The researchers used a "person-centered" approach of clustering cases to identify commonalties within subtypes. They also used replication across methods and samples to test the stability of their findings. What emerged was a more nuanced understanding of potential pathways to offending, including eight reliable pathways that were nested within four broad categories. For the present purposes, we will focus on the broader categories. The first category included "normal" functioning drug-dependent women; these women exemplified less victimization, fewer mental health issues, and less marginalization, yet they showed chronic substance abuse problems. The second category included victimized/battered women, particularly those who had more severe physical and sexual abuse histories both in childhood and adulthood. This second group of women also experienced high rates of depression symptoms and substance use. Third, the socialized/subcultural group showed greater marginalization as well as educational and vocational deficits, but they had less victimization and fewer mental health issues; they were often from high-crime neighborhoods and engaged more in trafficking aspects of the drug trade. Finally, the aggressive/antisocial group of women displayed more mental health issues, came from abusive and high-crime families and relationships, showed low self-efficacy and greater hostility, and were often homeless or survived via street crime. Brennan and associates noted the advantage of using a person-centered pathways approach, in that relationships between factors such as victimization, mental disorders, and crime may hold only for certain types of offenses. That is, the pathways approach does not presume that a single, general theory of crime applies to all types of offenses. This has implications for prevention and intervention, in that different individual-level and societal-level approaches may have more or less impact depending on which pathway is likely to shape a girl's or woman's route through the criminal legal system.

SUMMARY

At this point you have reviewed summaries of the literature on victimization and mental health of incarcerated women. It should be clear that system-involved women have high rates of mental health disorders, particularly depression, PTSD and substance use disorders, and medical problems. Further, these health problems are strongly associated with women's and girls' experiences of victimization. In addition, while women appear to have at least some access to physical and mental healthcare, it is unclear that they obtain quality care that improves their conditions. We also know that women and girls who are ethnic minorities, with low SES, and/or persons with disabilities are more likely to have mental and physical health problems and have less access to health care. Much of this research has been conducted with women while they were incarcerated but represents their lifetime exposure to violence and mental health histories. Thus, we urge you to think about how exposure to victimization and to health problems prior to incarceration are linked and how individuals' social identities and lack of access to resources may increase the negative impact of these experiences and influence entry into the criminal legal system.

DISCUSSION QUESTIONS

1. Some individuals are arrested due to behaviors that are associated with mental health problems but labeled as criminal acts. Is incarceration the best response in these cases? What else could we do?
2. What types of mental and physical health problems are most common in incarcerated women and girls? How much do we know about their health problems? What type of treatment do they receive?
3. What is the evidence that trauma, adversity, and mental health are associated with entering the criminal legal system?
4. How does the research on health disparities inform our understanding of incarcerated women's health? What are potential points of intervention to improve women's health prior to incarceration?

Credits
Fig. 2.1: Source: https://www.nimh.nih.gov/health/statistics/mental-illness.shtml.

CHAPTER THREE

Social Context and Vulnerabilities of System-Involved Girls and Women

Introduction

In this chapter, we discuss how disparities of social context influence girls' and women's entry into the criminal legal system. We begin with discussion of the historical roots of racial disparities in criminal legal involvement. We summarize studies that demonstrate disparate risk of entering the criminal legal system for marginalized women and girls such as persons of color, immigrants, and/or persons from lower socioeconomic statuses. We also address institutional responses to delinquent youth as well as the role of contextual influences such as neighborhood disadvantage.

The Historical Roots of Racial Disparities in the Criminal Legal System

As we will detail, racial disparities in criminal legal involvement have been well documented. Understanding these disparities as they relate to girls' and women's pathways into the criminal legal system requires consideration of the historical framework of racial injustice in the development and enforcement of laws. Police interactions with communities of color are built on a different foundation than police interactions with White communities (Oluo, 2018). While major cities, particularly in the Northern United States, established municipal police in the mid-1800s, the historical origins of policing in the South, where nearly all Blacks lived at the time, were rooted in slave patrols tasked with catching and re-enslaving runaway slaves, providing an organized form of terror to deter slave revolts, and exercising discipline for slave workers who violated plantation rules (Blackmon, 2008; Oluo, 2018; Potter, 2013). Indeed, many behaviors that were freely enacted by Whites were illegal for slaves per the "Slave Codes"—rules based on the idea that slaves were property rather than persons (Encyclopædia Britannica, 2018). Prohibited behaviors included actions such as learning to read, leaving the master's property without a pass, smoking in public, or walking with a cane. While there was a single offense—first degree murder—that could result in the death penalty for a White resident of Virginia, there were 73 that could result in the same penalty for a slave (Kennedy, 2011). The former slave patrols evolved into a police force charged with enforcing "Black Codes" (Encyclopædia Britannica, 2018), including Jim Crow segregation laws, as well as controlling freed slaves who worked as laborers in agriculture and industry (Potter, 2013). In the South, policing by its very design served to maintain White domination and to prevent Black access to equal rights and protections.

In the book *Slavery by Another Name: The Re-Enslavement of Black Americans from the Civil War to World War II*, Blackmon (2008) details the mechanisms by which racism and capricious enforcement of laws fueled the debt servitude of African Americans—a system through which Blacks were compelled to work in order to pay off debts that resulted from criminal offenses. After the Civil War, White southerners were faced with freed slaves among them—persons whom the Whites did not want to recognize as equals and upon whose labor White farms and businesses depended (Blackmon, 2008). By the early 1900s, offenses such as vagrancy were selectively enforced to penalize Black men who were unable to demonstrate current employment; sentences were extended when the men were unable to pay associated fees to sheriffs, deputies, court clerks, and witnesses. Those persons who were criminalized were then subjected to involuntary servitude by means of agreements between governments and farms, mines, lumber camps, quarries, and factories—with both the government and private entities reaping financial benefits. The men were often kept under lock and key. They risked whipping and other torture as discipline for failure to perform labor to the specified levels, and the toll of hard labor, physical abuses, and rampant disease led to countless deaths. Their sentences could be extended by new accusations, such as eating food to which they were not entitled or having departed at the end of the contract in clothing owned by the employer.

Men were not the only ones impacted by these convict labor arrangements. Black women—accused of crimes such as larceny, debt, or prostitution—were put into service as cooks or washer women and often subjected to sexual exploitation. Further, it was common for women to be accused of crimes and locked up when they showed up seeking freedom for their husbands and male relatives (Blackmon, 2008). In her book *Chained in Silence: Black Women and Convict Labor in the New South*, Talitha LeFlouria (2015) provides detailed accounts of Black women's experiences. She describes Black women prisoners as "everywhere, yet nowhere … scattered in the railroad camps, prison mines, lumber mills, brickyards, turpentine camps, plantations, kitchens, stockades, washhouses, and chain gangs. Yet their lives are nearly impossible to trace in writing from the post-Civil War era" (LeFlouria, p. 189). She notes that women were often subjected to the same hard-labor assignments as men, and "as if the unremitting slog of hard labor in the state's camps was not unbearable enough, female inmates were … left vulnerable to the predations of White whipping bosses (overseers), guards, camp doctors, and lessees" (LeFlouria, p. 12).

This system was permissible under the Thirteenth Amendment to the Constitution, adopted in 1865 to abolish slavery, but which allowed involuntary labor as punishment for committing a crime. The accumulated evidence—often in the form of letters, photographs, and documented court proceedings—points to a system through which Whites could capriciously accuse Blacks of having committed crimes, and White members of communities developed reciprocal relationships with one another to exploit Black debt servitude. As described by Blackmon (2008), arrests rates appeared to correspond more to rises in the need for cheap labor than to demonstrable criminal acts, and the South's judicial system had as "one of its primary purposes the coercion of African Americans to comply with the social customs and labor demands of Whites" (p. 6). These practices were widespread in the South in the early 1900s and continued into the 1940s, with some reports to federal investigators in the 1950s (Blackmon, 2008).

But even as the civil rights era eradicated some of these abuses, racially disparate treatment persisted in a variety of forms. In her book, *The New Jim Crow*, Michelle Alexander (2012) describes the remnants of the Jim Crow South in the "Southern Strategy" (p. 44), popularized during the 1960s and 1970s. This strategy was employed by politicians via coded rhetoric to appeal to poor and working-class Whites through racial fears and resentments and perpetuated a race-based criminal legal system (Alexander, 2012). As described by a Nixon aide in discussing antiwar leftists and Blacks as enemies of the administration, "We knew we couldn't make it illegal to be either against the war or Black, but by getting the public to associate the hippies with marijuana and Blacks with heroin, and then criminalizing both heavily, we could disrupt those communities. … Did we know we were lying about the drugs? Of course, we did" (LoBianco, 2016, paragraph 3). Using imagery of slums, street crime, urban riots, civil unrest, and cities in which women felt unsafe after dark, law-and-order rhetoric set a foundation for tough-on-crime policies that would for decades disparately impact African Americans (Newell, 2013). Such policies included no-knock drug busts (associated with death and injury of residents, pets, and officers), preventive detention of defendants deemed dangerous (prior to conviction), expansion of bail (which disproportionately impacts the poor), forfeiture of assets for accused drug offenders even if unconvicted (which incentivizes arrests by generating revenue for police), and mandatory minimum prison terms for certain crimes (Hattery & Smith, 2018; *Washington Post*, 1971). Mandatory minimum sentences for violent and drug offenses, for instance, are notable in dispensing severe penalties even for low-level offenses. Samuel Kelton Roberts, who has written extensively about the intersection of substance use and public policy, has characterized drug epidemics as "diseases of despair" stemming from social and economic conditions. Roberts notes, "But of course, we didn't treat them as such. We had mandatory minimum sentencing" (Brown, 2018, paragraph 11). The 1986 Anti-Drug Abuse Act, in particular, imposes a 5-year minimum prison term for simple posses-sion of crack cocaine, while the maximum sentence for simple possession of any other drug (including powder cocaine) is 1 year. Despite evidence that an estimated two-thirds of crack cocaine users are White, African Americans represent over 80% of defendants subject to the act's more severe penalties (Newell, 2013). Some argue that the "Southern Strategy" continues to be employed by politicians, as in recent polarizing rhetoric around migration and crime (Jones, 2016). Importantly, Congress passed the Fair Sentencing Act (FSA) in 2010. The FSA reduced the disparity in sentences for crack cocaine to powder cocaine from a 100:1 to an 18:1 drug quantity ratio. While this was an important step in the right direction, the 18:1 ratio demonstrates continuing disparities in punishments that disproportionately affect people of color.

Contrary to the assertions of those who use the "Southern Strategy," Alexander (2012) argues that the idea that there are major characterolog-ical differences between those who are criminals and those who are not is fiction. She posits, "Our racially biased system of mass incarceration exploits the fact that all people break the law and make mistakes at various points in their lives and with varying degrees of justification. Screwing up—failing to live by one's highest ideals and values—is part of what makes us human" (Alexander, 2012, p. 216). Yet, persons of color are differentially funneled into the criminal legal system through selective arrest, charging, conviction, and relegation to an undercaste via collateral consequences of conviction (Alexander, 2012). In *Stamped from the Beginning: The Defini-tive History of Racist Ideas in America*, Kendi (2016) describes race-based rationalizations that perpetuate oppression of African Americans. While negative behaviors of Whites are *individualized*—perceived as what is wrong with that one person—negative behaviors of Blacks are *generalized*—viewed as indicative of what is wrong with a race. Kendi describes perpetuation of such attributions through sensationalistic news accounts that connect crime to Blackness and poverty—and most recently, immigration. This, in turn, feeds greater suspicion of African Americans, persons of lower socioeconomic statuses, immigrants, and so on. Accordingly, poor neighborhoods and neighborhoods of color are policed more heavily, more arrests occur, and the cycle continues.

Although the Civil Rights Act of 1964 legislated against clear intention to discriminate (i.e., discriminatory racial language), it failed to address policies that may have appeared to be race neutral but which had discriminatory outcomes (Kendi, 2016). This focus on intent and not outcomes is an important limitation that impacts the criminal legal system and its disparate impact on persons of color. As Kendi (2017) notes, "Racial disparities persisted after the law was passed because discriminatory policies persisted under a patina of colorblindness" (p. 1). Oluo (2018) explains that systemic racism occurs when there exists a broad pattern of events that disproportionately or differently affects persons of color, independent of the racial intent of individual actors involved; she argues, "Those who demand the smoking gun of a racial slur or swastika or burning cross before they will believe that an individual encounter with the police might be about race are ignoring what we know and what the numbers are bearing out: something is going on and it is not right … all across the country, in every type of neighborhood, people of color are being disproportionately criminalized" (p. 86).

Evidence of Racial Disparities in the Criminal Legal System

In the book *Policing Black Bodies: How Black Lives Are Surveilled and How to Work for Change*, Angela Hattery and Earl Smith (2018) summarize extensive evidence of racial disparities through all stages in the criminal legal system. With particular attention to entry into the justice system, these authors detail racial biases that exist within recent criminal legal practice that disproportionately affect African Americans. For instance, New York's stop-and-frisk law, which allowed police to detain, question, and search persons who appeared to be suspicious, overwhelmingly impacted African American and Latinx citizens, with those two populations representing about 83% of stops between 2004 and 2012; further, 88% of the 4.4 million stops revealed no evidence of wrongdoing (Editorial Board, 2013; Goldstein, 2013). A judge, citing lack of objective rationale for stops as well as racial discrimination in stops she called "demeaning and humiliating," ruled the law unconstitutional in 2013 (Takei, 2018). In another example, a report by the U.S. Department of Justice (DOJ) examining events following riots in Ferguson, Missouri, identified police violations of the First, Fourth, and Fourteenth Amendments to the Constitution. Arrest warrants and increased patrols in the predominantly African American community were being used not to protect citizens, but rather to generate revenue for the Ferguson Police Department (Hattery & Smith, 2018; U.S. DOJ, 2015). This has negative consequences not just for individuals arrested and their families, but also for broader communities. A study that examined finances and crime data in 6,000 cities (Goldstein et al., 2018) found a strong link between revenue collection and clearance rates—indicating that those police departments that collect more revenue from crime actually have lower rates in clearing violent and property crime cases; that is, police departments that collect more fines solve fewer crimes. Contributing factors may include, among other things, how police focus their time and resources as well as reduced public confidence in police, and hence reduced likelihood of cooperation (Goldstein et al., 2018).

Consider data on overrepresentation of minorities in routine police stops. Whites represent about 76.6% of the United States population relative to 13.4% Blacks and 18.1% Latinx (U.S. Census, n.d.). In a nationally representative sample of persons in the United States, Davis et al. (2018) examined contact with police in 2015. Whites were more likely to experience police contact (23%) than Blacks (20%), Latinx (17%), or persons of other races and ethnicities (18%) and were more likely to actually be the initiators of this contact (12%) than either Blacks (9%) or Latinx (9%). Yet, when it came to being pulled over in traffic stops or stopped on the street, Blacks were the most likely to be stopped. That is, despite representing a much smaller percentage of the total U.S. population, in 2015 9.8% of Blacks experienced traffic stops relative to 8.6% of Whites and 7.6% of Latinx. Additionally, 1.5% of Blacks experienced street stops relative to less than 1% of Whites and Latinx. Blacks and Latinx were also less likely than Whites to perceive such stops as legitimate and were less likely to be given reasons for stops. In addition, both Blacks and Latinx were more likely to experience threat or use of force in their contacts with police (Davis et al., 2018). A similar study found that Whites were less likely to be searched during traffic stops (2%) than were Blacks (6%) and Latinx (7%) (Langton & Durose, 2016). Alexander (2012) describes pretext stops—when officers use minor violations as an excuse to search for drugs without evidence—as a common tool used by law enforcement officers. While these aspects of enforcement can sometimes appear subtle, there can be deadly consequences, as is evidenced in cases highlighted by the #BlackLivesMatter movement. Similarly, Kimberlé Crenshaw—who originally coined the term "intersectionality" decades ago—has noted the under-examined impact on lives of women and girls. Citing cases such as Rekia Boyd, Tanisha Anderson, and Aiyana Stanley-Jones, Crenshaw created the #SayHerName campaign to increase awareness of police violence against Black women. She also notes issues including mental disorders and disability as compounding the dangers girls and women face in relation to law enforcement (Khaleeli, 2016). How does this information inform your understanding of current policies and procedures where you are located? What are your thoughts about how local law enforcement policies might impact community relations with police officers?

In the evidence brief *An Unjust Burden: The Disparate Treatment of Black Americans in the Criminal Justice System*, Hinton et al. (2018) lay out specific evidence of disparate treatment of Blacks at various stages of criminal legal involvement. They note that war-on-drugs policies like drug-free zones (which more heavily penalize drug crimes proximate to schools, parks, and public housing) and hot-spots policing (which increase patrols in areas determined to have high-crime concentrations) disproportionately impact Black and Latinx people, both due to increased representation of Blacks and Latinx in the high-density areas targeted by these policies and due to biases in arrests in these areas. For instance, Beckett et al. (2006), in an examination of multiple data sources on drug practices, found that Blacks represented 47% of persons delivering crack cocaine, with 41% of deliveries of crack cocaine performed by Whites; yet, Blacks represented 79% of those arrested for such deliveries relative to 8.6% of arrests being Whites. The study also indicated that White drug dealers were involved in the bulk of transactions for heroin, methamphetamine, ecstasy, and powder cocaine, with crack cocaine being the only drug that involved a predominance of Black dealers. The focus on enforcement for crack cocaine and not other drugs contributed to the racial disparities in drug arrests overall.

In a meta-analysis that examined data from a large number of existing studies conducted in the United States, Kochel et al. (2011) found consistent evidence that, among crime suspects, persons of color are more likely to be arrested than Whites, even when controlling for factors such as nature and severity of the crime, quality of evidence at the scene, presence of witnesses, suspect use of alcohol or drugs, and prior arrest record of the suspect. The analysis used 27 independent data sets ranging from the year 1966 to 2004, with strong coverage of years across the nearly 4 decades.

These researchers note that the findings hold over time, setting, and data collection methods. The authors conclude, that "the extant research does not demonstrate the causes of this racial disparity, nor does it point to clear policy response for dealing with it. What it does establish is that where there is smoke, there is indeed fire regarding racial disparity in the arrest practices of American police" (Kochel et al., 2011, p. 499). The collective evidence is extensive, as summarized in a *Washington Post* article that detailing findings from over 100 studies (Balko, 2018). Taken together, research indicates that, as Oluo (2018) asserts, police are often positioned as more of a threat to communities of color than as stewards of community safety and order.

Other Marginalized Groups Disparately Impacted by the Criminal Legal System

While disparate criminal legal outcomes for persons of color are well documented in the research evidence, there are other marginalized groups at risk for experiencing disparate impact of the criminal legal system. For example, immigrants, transgender persons, and persons from impoverished backgrounds face increased risk of being swept into the U.S. criminal legal system. Let's begin by examining involvement of immigrants in the United States legal system. Both voluntary and involuntary immigration have been part of the history and founding of the United States, and there is considerable evidence that immigration contributes not only to strong and diverse social experiences within the country, but also to safer communities and a stronger economy (Ghandnoosh et al., 2017). Bersani and Piquero (2016) found that first-generation immigrants are less likely to commit crimes than their U.S.-born peers, and that this difference is not attributable to self-reporting biases; beyond their study that involved 10 waves of data among 1,300 males and females, the authors point to a century of rigorous research supporting this pattern (Cepeda, 2016). Yet, efforts to link crime and immigration, particularly in the political realm, persist. This creates dire consequences for families and communities when manifested in public policy. In 2009, U.S. Immigration and Customs Enforcement (ICE) was provided with an immigrant-detention quota via a directive from Congress for ICE to fill 34,000 beds in 250 detention facilities across the nation with immigrant detainees each day. This policy, which is likely to contribute to arrests, is an extension of decades of anti-immigration enforcement policies being enacted with increasing regularity, despite a majority of detainees having no prior criminal record (Robbins, 2013). Ewing, et al. (2015) note that growth in policies that promote immigrant arrest and detention may stem in part from lobbying of private prison industry interests in the criminal legal system. In the United States, we appear to be redefining what it means to be a "criminal alien" in broader terms that subject more and more immigrants to be defined as criminals and thereby arrested, detained, and deported. This includes criminalizing persons who commit minor infractions (e.g., misdemeanors) that would be of little or no consequence for non-immigrants in the United States, criminalizing those who pled guilty to such offenses prior to the offense having been defined as deportable, and criminalizing even those immigrants who are lawful permanent residents and who have U.S.-based families. Ewing and associates (2015) liken these policies to criminalization of immigrants themselves, just by virtue of their status as immigrants. Such criminalization practices are eerily reminiscent of the slave codes and Black codes by which African Americans were criminalized for behaviors freely enacted by Whites across the southern United States from the 1600s through the Civil Rights era. The criminalization of immigration-related behaviors, in a convergence of immigration and criminal law, has sometimes been referred to a "crimmigration" (Stumpf, 2006). Beyond immediate consequences for persons who are criminalized, there are additional consequences for public safety when immigrants fear coming forward to report or cooperate in criminal investigations. Most recently, there have been cases in which immigrants who are victims or witnesses have been confronted with deportation when coming forward to testify against their batterers, sexual abusers, and other violent criminals (see, for example, Bravo et al., 2018).

Lesbian, bisexual, gay, and transgender persons have faced similar consequences of arrest in cases in which they were the victims of violent assaults and acted in self-defense, including defending themselves against street harassment and hate-based physical assaults, as well as defending themselves against intimate partner violence (Stahl, 2018). Beyond discriminatory laws and differential enforcement, another contributor to gay, lesbian, bisexual, and transgender involvement in the criminal legal system may be participation in survival economies due to marginalized social and professional status. For instance, a majority of transgender persons report family rejection, and one in five report homelessness as a consequence of housing discrimination or family rejection, with nearly a third of those who report homelessness also reporting having been turned away from a shelter due to being transgender (Grant et al., 2011; Ray, 2006). Bullying and discrimination can also result in increased school dropout, limited employment options or unemployment (Grant et al., 2011; Kosciw et al., 2013), lack of health insurance coverage and health care, or other factors that push sexual minorities into survival-based economies. Transgender persons may, in particular, face difficulties in accessing identity documents necessary to drive, obtain a credit card, apply for a job or school loans, vote, or travel (CAPMAP, 2016). Use and sales of illegal drugs may thereby serve as mechanisms for coping with marginalization, and commercial sex work may become a means of generating income (Fitzgerald et al., 2015).

Persons with lower incomes also are disparately impacted by the criminal legal system. In the United States, persons living in poverty are more likely than those who are not poor to be fined, arrested, and incarcerated for minor offenses (Dolan & Carr, 2015). Extreme poverty, specifically homelessness, is criminalized via laws against life-sustaining activities; these laws, common across the United States, prohibit public sitting, sleeping, sheltering, and panhandling. Some cities even have laws against sharing food with a homeless person (NLCHP, 2014). Often, those who are poor or homeless are differentially targeted for enforcement. Law enforcement officers have, in some cases, used food stamp records to find and arrest people with outstanding warrants (Ocen, 2012). If an individual is not able to afford fines and fees and fails to appear for court, that person may be subject to further warrants and arrest. The individual may accrue further debt, with fees for public defender services, room and board during lockup, probation and parole supervision, drug and alcohol treatment, and DNA samples (Anderson et al., 2014). Abin-Lackey (2014) has noted that probationers usually end up paying more in additional fees than the actual debt owed for the crime committed. Pause here for a moment and consider how those individuals with the fewest resources appear in many ways to be the most vulnerable to enforcement. What types of changes would we need to make to the system to decrease these disparities?

Youth Legal Involvement and the School-to-Prison Pipeline

These disparities of enforcement and impact do not begin with the adult criminal legal system. Rather, criminal legal involvement is an extension of patterns that may be established early in the lives of persons who have been marginalized from the mainstream. Common pathways described in the literature involve juvenile legal and educational systems. Nanda (2012) has described the intersection of race and gender as these coalesce in the juvenile legal system. Noting that the juvenile legal system was designed around the assumption that children are different than adults and should be treated differently by the courts, with a wide latitude for discretion in judicial decision making about whether a child should be punished for an offense or if some other form of intervention may be more appropriate, Nanda explains how this "blind discretion" is differentially applied to boys and girls, White children, and children of color, rendering Black and immigrant children more vulnerable to social control. This occurs at multiple points in the legal process, given policies that allow discretion by police officers, probation officers, district attorneys, and judges—and result in children of color arrested, charged, detained, and sentenced more severely than White children. As racial and gender stereotypes come together, some children may be penalized more heavily than others, depending on the offense and the decision maker's perspective. Nanda notes a lack of research specifically examining how stereotypes distort assessments of youth as they come into contact with police, prosecutors, and so on.

GETTING REAL 3.1

I'm here [detention] for a probation violation, for fighting with a girl. She had stole[n] my flat iron. I had let the situation go for a while. Then the girl started talking trash about me on the bus. I, I couldn't take it anymore. I got up and started hitting her. I was on probation for another fight. A girl had called me nigger and threw rocks at my cousin's house. So I got in a fight with her.

Jasmine, African American, aged 17, was interviewed at a detention center. She was originally detained for assault and battery. She was at a group home going to an alternative school when she got in the fight on the bus. She had attempted to run away from the group home prior to the fight. Jasmine's mom has been in and out of jail and prison all her life, and her dad drinks heavily. Jasmine was in a group home as an infant after her brother fell out of a two-story window. He wasn't hurt, but they took the five kids away. Her dad could only get his three back, so she lived with her father and two brothers after that. She was on Honor Roll up through fourth grade, then her grades started going down. In fourth grade, her uncle sexually abused her. She used to have nightmares about it, and when people talk about rape, she would get upset. She still has to sleep with the light on if she's by herself. Last time she was at the Department of Juvenile Justice, she had to just put her head under the covers to sleep, and she felt like someone was standing over her—like it was him. After about fifth grade, her dad would hit her whenever her stepmom told a lie about her or whenever Jasmine got in any kind of trouble. Jasmine started fighting from fifth grade on and has been in too many fights to count.

She also started dating in fifth grade. She dated both boys and girls. From seventh grade on, she used to go in the store and steal candy and clothes with her cousins. In ninth grade, she was placed in a group home due to neglect. There wasn't food in the house. Now she is in detention and in her third year of ninth grade.

There is an established literature demonstrating racial disparities in school disciplinary practices, with a sharply increasing discipline gap in the past 4 decades between Black students and their White counterparts. The result is that Black students are more likely to experience sanctions such as suspension and expulsion, even when their levels of misbehavior are similar to White peers (Bottiani et al., 2017). In a study of nearly one million students in Texas schools, Fabelo and associates (2011) used school disciplinary and juvenile criminal records to examine the discipline gap and its impact of school removals on academic performance and youth criminal involvement. While 54% of students experienced in-school suspension, 15% were assigned to disciplinary alternative education programs, 8% were placed in juvenile legal alternative education programs, and only 3% of disciplinary actions were for conduct mandated to result in suspension or expulsion under state law. Rather, the overwhelming majority of disciplinary actions were discretionary—based on decisions of school officials and primarily in response to local school conduct codes. African American students—both male and female—and students with particular educational disabilities were disproportionately likely to be removed from classrooms for disciplinary reasons. The researchers controlled for a variety of demographic and other variables to isolate the effects of race on disciplinary actions and found that African American students had a 31% higher likelihood of school disciplinary action relative to identical White and Latinx students. Of particular concern, the researchers found that students who were suspended or expelled were more likely to be held back a grade, drop out, and become system involved. Specifically addressing the impact of school disciplinary practices for African American girls, Morris and Perry (2017) found that Black girls were three times more likely than White girls to receive referrals for discipline—a much wider gap than that between White girls and Black boys or White boys. The referrals were frequently for subjective infractions (e.g., disruptive behavior) that may be influenced by gendered interpretations of femininity. Morris and Perry argue that Black girls are differentially penalized for violating gender norms or commonly held ideas about how girls and women should act.

In another examination of discipline disparities, Poteat et al. (2016) used cross-sectional data from 869 gay, lesbian, bisexual, and questioning youth and 869 demographically matched heterosexual youth and found that the sexual minority youth were more likely to report school suspension and juvenile legal involvement than their heterosexual counterparts. The discipline gap was not attributable to differential behavior; rather, when there were high rates of infractions by any youth, the sexual minority youth were more likely to experience punitive discipline. The overall pattern of research findings is that students who are White, heterosexual, wealthy, or otherwise privileged are more likely to get a "pass" on behaviors for which students of color, poor, or marginalized students may be disciplined and/or arrested.

Some researchers have termed the path from the education system to the juvenile or adult criminal legal system the school-to-prison pipeline, noting that school discipline is disproportionately applied to the most vulnerable and that consequences often do not fit the offense (McCarter, 2017). McGrew (2016) cautions that thinking of disciplinary gaps only in terms of a school-to-prison pipeline can artificially situate conversations around the pervasive, racialized, and structural problem involving social control of minorities as a mere problem in schools. That is, trying to address school discipline gaps without understanding their position within broader social practices and historical contexts is akin to treating symptoms while ignoring root causes. To truly grasp the complexity of factors that are pushing vulnerable populations into the criminal legal system, we must shift the lens from viewing these persons as individuals at risk who need intervention and instead recognize that they are most vulnerable because the design of our social institutions disparately impacts them (McGrew, 2016). This can have social and emotional effects that last a lifetime. Oluo (2018), in describing the use of school resource officers in relegating childhood discipline to the legal system, frankly describes the impact on Black children: "When our kids spend eight hours a day in a system that is looking for reasons to punish them, remove them, criminalize them—our kids do not get to be kids. Our kids do not get to be rambunctious, they do not get to be exuberant, they do not get to be rebellious, they do not get to be defiant. Our kids do not get to fuck up the way other kids get to: our kids will not get to look back fondly on their teenage hijinks—because these get them expelled or locked away" (p. 133).

The Role of Neighborhood Disadvantage

As we have illustrated, there exists credible evidence of systematic racism, classism, heterosexism, and other biases in the U.S. criminal legal system. In light of this, what about real differences in crime between minority and majority groups? While some of this may be, as previously addressed, a matter of what is defined as a crime and enforced, there do exist some real differences in levels of serious crime (e.g., acts of violence) across different sectors of society. For instance, research indicates that community context can affect development of antisocial behavior through a number of different mechanisms, as reviewed by Ingoldsby and Shaw (2002). The first involves demographic and structural composition of neighborhoods. Factors such as housing policies contribute to greater racial and ethnic segregation of neighborhoods and development of isolated areas of concentrated poverty. These conditions heighten racial tensions and reduce access to resources, employment, and role models—presumably contributing to the development of antisocial behavior and delinquent or criminal offending. A related mechanism involves social disorganization and social control in neighborhoods characterized by economic decline, population turnover, and few family resources. In disadvantaged communities, community members may be less trusting of their neighbors, may be less likely to look out for one another, and may be less likely to collectively act to deter crime and delinquency. These norms may promote antisocial behavior as acceptable and unlikely to result in sanctions. A third mechanism involves community violence exposure, which—like direct victimization—can have effects via increased desensitization and reduced empathy for others, increased anger, and modeling of antisocial responses as a form of problem solving. Finally, the fourth mechanism described by Ingoldsby and Shaw involves parenting practices and social networks. Specifically, parents who live in isolated or disorganized neighborhoods may be less able to provide positive opportunities for children, instead facing frustration, exercising less supervision over children's neighborhood activities, and using more punitive discipline, thereby contributing to children's aggression and association with deviant peers.

Yet, some such factors can be traced back to social inequities similar to those discussed throughout this chapter. In his memoir, Ta-Nehisi Coates (2015) describes in visceral terms the experience of oppression and its connection to crime and vulnerability: "To be Black in the Baltimore of my youth was to be naked before the elements of the world, before all the guns, fists, knives, crack, rape, and disease. The nakedness is not an error, nor pathology. The nakedness is the correct and intended result of policy, the predictable upshot of people forced for centuries to live under fear. The law did not protect us" (p. 17). He goes on to describe the further assault of being policed via criminal legal policies such as stop-and-frisk, while those with privilege are protected through social safety nets and ancestral wealth. In fact, there have been many critiques of the "broken windows" theory (Wilson & Kelling, 1982) that gave rise to enforcement of "quality-of-life" policing of petty crime in the interest of social order (for critique, see Thatcher, 2004). In other words, locations with broken windows, graffiti, or other signs of being under-resourced were targeted for increased police presence and supervision. Such policing disproportionately impacts poor and minority persons and also magnifies the likelihood that women will be arrested—both due to women's greater risk of housing insecurity (Ocen, 2012) and women's increased involvement in minor offenses such as drug possession (Schwartz & Steffenmeier, 2008)—a type of activity often targeted by such policing (Swavola et al., 2016).

Jody Miller describes how neighborhood disadvantage leads to increased risk of violence for Black girls in her 2008 book *Getting Played: African American Girls, Urban Inequality, and Gendered Violence*. Similar to Coates's observations in Baltimore, Miller describes residents in Chicago communities making connections between community violence and neighborhood disadvantage. Residents linked deterioration in their neighborhoods to increased presence of criminal networks that brought in drugs and then, subsequently, escalation of violence such as shootings. Miller also notes that often disadvantaged communities are clustered together such that youth label their neighborhood experience as typical and do not see other ways of operating. Finally, Miller notes community members report both lack of police response in high-risk situations as well as experiences of harassment by police. In short, police are not viewed as sources of public safety.

Crenshaw (2013) provides numerous examples of under-protection and over-policing of marginalized groups. She underscores the danger of focusing on individuals and families as the source of disadvantage, rather than developing contextual understanding of inequality as a function of broader societal processes that structure relations between the marginalized and the mainstream. Hayes (2017) further details the problematic nature of linking law enforcement to factors such as neighborhood disorder rather than public safety, in that what is perceived as orderly is highly subjective—bringing in outsiders to police the communities of others, positioning persons in power to monitor and control the behaviors of marginalized groups, and using crime and punitive enforcement as political tools to further segregate and oppress. Hayes argues that our punitive approaches to address disorder derive from socially and politically constructed menus of options, through which we have focused on referral of issues to the criminal legal system rather than using other means to address the root causes of harm. In the next chapter, we will summarize research, practices, and policies that may inform new ways to address the human struggles addressed herein. That is, we will look at tools both within and beyond the criminal legal system, as these may help ameliorate some of the inequities currently seen in criminal legal practice.

SUMMARY

In this chapter, we discussed the historical roots of the criminal legal system and its disparate impact on African Americans and other persons of color. Black and Latinx persons are more likely to be stopped, searched, arrested, and exposed to police use of force than are Whites. Other marginalized groups such as immigrants, transgender persons, and persons with lower incomes are likely to experience criminalization of their behaviors, and some may be pushed into survival economies due to disenfranchisement from the mainstream. The ways that crimes are defined, enforced, and punished shape who is impacted most in our society, and disparate impacts begin even in childhood with differential discipline enacted in schools. Impacts continue throughout life, influencing entry into juvenile and adult criminal legal systems. Beyond disparate application and enforcement of laws, social context can also serve as a contributor to delinquent and criminal offending via isolation from resources and increased segregation in poor neighborhoods. Understanding the pathways that girls and women take into the criminal legal system necessitates consideration of the historical and structural operations of the system in the United States.

DISCUSSION QUESTIONS

1. How does the history of how police units were formed in the South help us to understand current community-police tensions in communities of color?

2. Much of the content of this chapter provides examples of how policies and laws disparately affect individuals with different social identities. One example described was the 1986 Anti-Drug Abuse Act, which stipulated a 5-year minimum prison term for simple possession of crack cocaine versus the maximum sentence for simple possession of any other drug (including powder cocaine), which was 1 year. How does this law demonstrate systemic discrimination against specific populations?

3. What is the school-to-prison pipeline? What are some examples of how disciplinary strategies in schools affect youths' entry into the juvenile legal system?

4. There are several examples in this chapter of systemic biases in policing and the legal system. Identify and discuss at least two examples of bias based on access to resources, economic disadvantage, race or ethnicity, or geographic location.

CHAPTER FOUR

Practice and Policy Implications at Systemic Entry Points

Introduction

In this chapter, we describe ways that the sequential intercept model can be used at entry points into the system to identify resource needs of marginalized persons and, when appropriate, link persons with services or interventions. We note the importance of coordinated approaches across systems of legal intervention, victim/witness advocacy, human services, and health/mental health care. Examples are provided of specific strategies that may be used by first responders in crisis response, law enforcement, and services for children and youth. While many of these strategies were initially conceptualized to address the needs of persons with mental disorders or behavioral health issues, the integrated and multi-systemic approaches described here have potential to ameliorate other forms of disadvantage and/or marginalization. We will also highlight how a trauma-informed approach may be integrated into these intercepts given the prevalence of victimization in this population.

Importance of Coordinated Approaches to Addressing Intersectional Impacts

In the introduction of this book, we described stages of legal processing and the sequential intercept model. In simply reflecting on each stage of processing, there are professionals who make decisions that can impact girls' and women's pathways through the system. Swavola et al. (2016) describe how this can occur. For instance, law enforcement officers can choose to arrest, release, or book persons into custody; prosecutors determine whether to charge and with what offenses; officers of the court can hold, release, accelerate, or delay processing; and probation and parole officers can determine how closely to monitor individuals and how to respond to alleged violations. Swavola and associates note that strategies to address involvement in the legal system will fall short if they do not address each of these decision points. There is also complexity that extends outside of the criminal legal realm into human services and other systems.

As discussed in Chapters 1, 2, and 3, girls' and women's entry into the justice system often intersects with backgrounds of trauma and adversity, mental and physical health struggles, and experiences of systemic bias affecting persons of color, immigrants, sexual minorities, transgender persons, persons with lower incomes, and other marginalized groups. The multifaceted nature of combined risks, needs, and challenges necessitates responses that bridge systems, including the legal system, human services, and public health, as well as others. Many of the issues addressed in the first three chapters point to the need for broad social change to truly address root causes and eradicate inequities that impact girls' and women's entry into the system. Yet, such change is rarely achieved in rapid, sweeping transformations of our systems and social norms. While research on root causes, identification of solutions, and systemic advocacy is underway, we must also implement incremental approaches that alleviate immediate conditions experienced by girls and women as they come into contact with the legal system. Thus, we must balance prevention and risk-reduction efforts to address challenges for individuals and refine system-level protocols, while remaining mindful of the larger social forces that have created the conditions in which the individuals, families, and communities live. We must understand that such social forces often push individuals into difficult situations in which survival strategies may come into conflict with the law. Ideally, professionals can work across disciplines to examine micro-level (individual, family) challenges while also engaging in collective dialogue and action to address macro-level (community, system) factors that impact girls and women. A multifaceted approach can achieve tangible short-term gains while also striving toward social justice for girls and women of diverse backgrounds and experiences.

Sequential Intercept Model: Entry Into the System

Within the sequential intercept model, as refined by Abreu and associates (2017), intercept 0 refers to the front end of the criminal legal system, before an individual has been placed under arrest by law enforcement. Specifically, this includes first responders and behavioral health crisis care, including but not limited to mobile crisis outreach teams, crisis respite services, emergency medical services, and fire departments. These responders have potential to keep persons from ever coming in contact with the criminal legal system. There are also some law enforcement responses that fall within intercept 0, as the response stems from officers' roles as legal protectors of those unable to protect themselves (e.g., vulnerable populations such as dependent children, persons with mental disorders, or persons with physical or mental disabilities). In this role, officers may take part in transport or crisis responses as well as exercise alternatives to arrest for individuals whose criminal involvement may stem from behavioral health issues. Such alternative responses may include crisis intervention teams, serial inebriate programs (for repeated public intoxication), homeless outreach teams, and law-enforcement-assisted diversion. In contrast to this guardian role, officers also have a role involving use of police powers to enforce state laws. This role falls more under intercept 1, which ends when the individual is placed under arrest. In this way, law enforcement responses bridge intercept 0 and intercept 1, as do responses of 911 dispatchers (Abreu et al., 2017). Ideally, law enforcement officers and other first responders partner with behavioral health providers to form an integrated network of community support at these points of interception.

Crisis Response at Intercept 0

Many persons may come into contact with the criminal legal system because a crisis has occurred. This can become a dangerous situation for many reasons, as the heightened distress of a crisis situation can affect poor decision making by the person experiencing the crisis, by bystanders, and by first responders to the scene. Crisis phone lines may serve as one part of the intercept 0 response that help diffuse such situations and prevent contact with the criminal legal system. Crisis phone lines include hotlines, which usually provide 24-hour emergency services such as support and assistance with coping, as well as referral to community-based services. There are also warm lines, which are operated by peer support specialists under more limited response hours (Abreu et al., 2017). These phone lines can be used in attempts to resolve the crisis through de-escalation rather than bringing in law enforcement or other first responders. We are also seeing increased offerings in the form of online chat crisis services (e.g., thehotline.org) or crisis support via texting (e.g., crisistextline.org). If needed, on-scene support may be dispatched. This might include a mobile crisis outreach team composed of behavioral health practitioners or emergency department diversion with triage services, embedded mobile crisis (practitioners working with police), or peer specialist support. Beyond serving as partners for on-scene responses, law enforcement officers may assist in transporting those in crisis to locations such as 23-hour crisis stabilization beds, short-term crisis residential stabilization services, community-based walk-in services, or crisis respite centers (Abreu et al., 2017; Substance Abuse and Mental Health Services Administration (SAMHSA), 2017).

By utilizing the continuum of behavioral health services, responders can attempt to resolve the crisis without involving law enforcement on the front end. Crisis care may include assessment, short-term treatment, treatment engagement, and recovery support. If needed, law enforcement may be engaged in a supportive partnership role with behavioral health practitioners, but officers and dispatchers should be trained and equipped to respond appropriately to the complex situations that might evolve when behavioral health and/or trauma-related distress is an issue. Training should include skills related to recognizing and responding to signs of traumatic distress and mental disorders. This includes eliciting information on mental health indicators as well as tracking calls and responses. Crisis partnerships with law enforcement also necessitate protocols for centralized drop-off sites that include adequate security, evaluations for involuntary commitment, and no-refusal policies for persons brought in by officers (Abreu et al., 2017; SAMHSA, 2017). Rural communities can face particular challenges around limited resources, fewer community agencies and support services, and long distances between providers and communities. Sites such as Rural Health Information Hub (ruralhealthinfo. org) provide examples of how rural communities have worked to develop and offer crisis-intervention services.

Specialized Law Enforcement and Dispatch Response at Intercept 1

As noted, some of the law enforcement and dispatch responses bridge both intercept 0 and intercept 1 of the sequential intercept model. One of the most essential components of assuring safe and effective responses to marginalized persons involves training responders to recognize traumatic distress, mental illness, and behavioral health issues such as substance abuse or co-occurring disorders. Dispatcher training can be used to educate 911 responders to recognize signs of mental or behavioral health crises so that information may be passed on to responders, including crisis intervention teams comprising both law enforcement and behavioral health providers. Similarly, law enforcement can be trained for specialized police responses to persons in behavioral health crisis. For instance, in some locales, law enforcement, court personnel, and first/rescue personnel receive training in trauma-informed approaches and crisis and mental health first-aid training to facilitate a warm hand-off to a crisis response center with behavioral health providers on site. This facilitates intervention and risk assessment, screening, case management, peer support, and integrated health care for those in need (SAMHSA, 2017). Stepping Up is a federal initiative to help counties determine strategies to prevent incarceration of persons with mental disorders. Its website (stepuptogether.org) provides information regarding the self-assessment tool for counties to evaluate their approach and develop a collaborative framework for partnerships between law enforcement and behavioral health providers. The goals include increasing connection of communities to resources, reducing arrests, reducing repeated encounters with law enforcement, and reducing police use of force (SAMHSA, 2017).

Another promising response at intercept 1 is law enforcement–assisted diversion. The program is designed for persons who have mental health and substance use disorders and who commit specific offenses such as low-level drug offenses or sex work. Participants in the program can have cases diverted if they receive case management, behavioral health treatment, and other support services such as health care, job training, and housing assistance (Abreu et al., 2017).

GETTING REAL 4.1

The officer who busted me is a new guy who views things as "his way or no way." He wouldn't listen like most officers do. He just wanted a bust and didn't care that I had tried AA and NA.

Thelma, White, aged 45, is incarcerated on three charges: probation violation, possession of drugs, and shoplifting. During a research interview, she explained she's been shooting heroin for 23 years and has been in and out of prison most of her life since her 20s. Every offense was related to drugs. She would shoplift and sell the clothes she took in order to get drug money. She was shoplifting all day, every day, sometimes traveling back and forth between different cities to do so. Thelma came from a well-to-do family, and her parents drank in a "5:00-p.m. cocktail hour" way until her teens—at which point they were getting falling-down drunk. By the time she was 16, Thelma was hiding their jiggers and monogrammed bottles to try to prevent them from drinking. Her mom and dad's relationship was falling apart, and the house was filled with tension. Around the same time, Thelma was sent to boarding school because of desegregation, as her family wanted to take her out of the public school. She was kicked out for smoking pot. Thelma's mom wanted the kids to act a certain way, and Thelma's brother and sister did, but Thelma didn't. Her mom would tell her, "You'll never amount to anything." Her mother was disgusted and disappointed in her, and Thelma thought that if she was going to be labelled a disappointment, she might as well become one. Thelma went "buck wild." She spent the money her parents gave her on drugs, and she dropped out of high school as a junior. She got a GED, and her mom pressured her to go to college, so she enrolled in an art school so she could get what she wanted from her parents. In college, she tried heroin, and she also liked opiates, valium, soper, and ludes. She liked downers because she felt sure of herself and invincible. When Thelma was 19, her mom died, and her dad "bottomed out." He died a few years later, and this was a real change for her. She had to survive on her own, and she was lonely and scared. She went out looking for guys and made a lot of bad choices. Her boyfriends were often violent, and the police "didn't do a damn thing." With her parents dead, the money also stopped, so she had to find a "new hustle" to get money. That's where the shoplifting came in.

Additional recovery supports may be offered in serial inebriate programs for individuals, typically homeless individuals dependent on substances, who repeatedly come in contact with law enforcement, emergency departments, or detoxification centers (Abreu et al., 2017), or for persons with specific physical health and/or economic needs, such as pregnant women and parenting mothers. Some of these approaches integrate a variety of strategies for assisting persons who have mental, substance use, or co-occurring disorders, with services such as peer support, motivational interviewing, and behavior therapies (SAMHSA, 2019a).

Services for Children and Youth

There are also school-based responder models involving cross-system collaborative teams. Typically, these involve schools, behavioral health providers, and families as partners to promote family and youth engagement through planning and implementation of behavioral health response protocols. This includes screening and assessment for youth in schools, training for school personnel, formal policies on behavioral health issues, referral to community-based resources, memoranda of understanding between partners, and decision-making tools for determining appropriate responses. There are also mobile crisis services dispatched to schools or other locations via a crisis line, and case managers at courts and juvenile legal centers. School administrators have indicated that these programs decrease incidence of serious events occurring on school grounds (SAMHSA, 2017).

Specifically regarding the school-to-prison pipeline, service provision requires individualized assessment for root causes of behavioral problems, including engaging with families to understand whether issues are family driven or child driven and whether resources on trauma, mental helath, substance use disorders, disabilities, or poverty may be warranted. School staff should be trained to utilize strength-based approaches that recognize positive behaviors, while working with law enforcement and courts to limit use of arrest in schools. Overall, the goal should be to keep kids in the classroom while also reinforcing accountability. Suspension and other such strategies should be last resorts in response to severe issues (MST Services, 2018; RED, n.d.). Multisystemic therapy is an intensive, family-level intervention that has demonstrated positive results through provision of in-home and in-school therapeutic work with children and families (MST Services, 2018).

Policy Recommendations to Prevent Entry Into the System

While the aforementioned coordinated responses may help address individual or micro-level issues for vulnerable populations, broader macro-level policy approaches are required to truly address the root causes of disparate impact at the front end of the criminal legal system for marginalized populations. The YWCA (2017), an organization that promotes social justice and empowerment of women, has encouraged a multifaceted strategy to ending racial profiling and criminalization of communities of color. This includes updating federal racial profiling guidance to eradicate loopholes that allow racial profiling by the Federal Bureau of Investigation, Transportation Security Administration, Customs and Border Patrol, and state and local law enforcement. YWCA also calls for standards of mandatory training for law enforcement, immigration agents, and school resource officers on topics including hate crimes and gender-based crimes, implicit bias in enforcement, ineffectiveness of racial profiling, de-escalation techniques, and avoiding use of force. Data collection disaggregated by race, ethnicity, and gender must be publicly available in order to address continuing disparate use of stops, searches, arrests, and use of force by law enforcement, immigration, and school resource officers (Center for American Progress and Movement Advancement Project (CAPMAP), 2016; YWCA, 2017).

Additional consideration should be given to approaches suitable for addressing needs of other marginalized populations, such as persons struggling with housing instability and transgender youth or adults. For instance, congressional legislation could require that proposed new criminal law or penalties must include examination of potential disparate impact on marginalized populations (CAPMAP, 2016). Law enforcement can also eliminate revenue-generating quotas and instead use warnings, cite-and-release or issuance of desk-appearance tickets in lieu of custodial arrest, and diversion programs for lesser offenses (CAPMAP, 2016; Swavola et al., 2016).

School-based approaches might include review of current counseling and intervention strategies and promote staff training in signs of trauma, mental disorders, and suicidality, as well as in use of trauma-informed practices (Crenshaw et al., 2015). When graduated measures are necessary, these might include restorative and procedural justice as well as guidelines around appropriate use of expulsion and other discipline, following from more integrated behavioral approaches (Crenshaw et al., 2015; YWCA, 2017). School staff training and organizational protocols may be used to increase knowledge regarding the impact of trauma and the principles of trauma-informed care as well as increasing organizational capacity to ensure nondiscrimination toward youth from communities of color, youth with disabilities, and sexual minority youth. Antibullying policies should prohibit bullying based on sexual orientation and gender identity (CAPMAP, 2016). Protocols should be in place to assure that—whenever feasible—school disciplinary issues are handled by teachers, staff, and students via conflict resolution versus law enforcement responses (CAPMAP, 2016). The Department of Education and other institutions should participate in statistical reporting on disciplinary issues using disaggregated data, for example by ethnic identity or income level, so that we can identify underlying patterns that may warrant policy change or new protocol development (Crenshaw et al., 2015).

Within the child welfare and juvenile legal systems, policy development can be used to identify trauma early and enhance coordinated responses from a trauma-informed approach. This includes establishing human trafficking as a recognized form of maltreatment under child abuse reporting guidelines, implementing mandatory training for staff and foster parents on signs of trauma and exploitation, screening for abuse using trauma-informed tools, establishing referral networks for multisystem responses and comprehensive services that protect children and youth, and coordinating data tracking for accurate analysis of cases across systems (Administration for Children and Families (ACF), 2013).

SUMMARY

In this chapter, we describe strategies that recognize girls' and women's entry into the legal system as it intersects with backgrounds of trauma and adversity, mental and physical health struggles, and experiences of systemic bias. We discuss crisis responses at intercept 0 of the sequential intercept model, including hotlines, warm lines, and mobile crisis response. We also discuss responses that bridge intercept 0 and 1, such as law enforcement–assisted diversion and interdisciplinary response teams that may connect women and girls with behavioral health resources. Each of these approaches can be supported by training of staff and family members, tracking of disaggregated data across systems, and coordinated response protocols with warm hand offs for wrap-around services. The structural barriers faced by marginalized women and girls necessitate approaches that include supports as well as those that target root causes of systemic bias, including racial profiling and overutilization of law enforcement responses to behavioral crises.

DISCUSSION QUESTIONS

1. What are some steps law enforcement officers and community agencies can take at intercept 0 and 1 to decrease entry into the criminal legal system?
2. Why are we concerned about how police respond to crisis situations? What role do crisis lines and crisis intervention workers have in reducing entry into the criminal legal system?
3. This chapter offers several suggestions for training of police officers in responding to individuals with behavioral health concerns. How might this change officers' responses and options when addressing an individual in crisis? What resources in the community are important to support this change in policing?

SECTION II

THE COURTS, DETENTION, AND INCARCERATION

The U.S. has the highest incarceration rate in the world, and the rate of incarceration of women, specifically, has increased notably in the past forty years. Why is that? As you read the chapters in Section II, we encourage you to consider further the types of behaviors that are considered criminal, the ways in which individuals move through the court system, and what our societal aims are when we sentence women and girls to secure confinement. It is also critical that we evaluate how our reliance on secure confinement in the U.S. affects the families and communities of individuals who are incarcerated.

First, we present data on the rates of incarceration of women and girls, describe the most common charges, sentence lengths, and penalties. For example, women are most often charged with drug or property offenses while girls are often charged with larceny-theft, simple assault, and disorderly conduct. We also highlight decision points during the court process that increase the vulnerability of marginalized girls and women to disparities in conviction and sentencing. For example, although White and Black women tend to receive shorter sentences then White men in the system, immigrants' sentences are often longer. As we examine charges and sentences, it is critical to keep in mind that prosecutors have substantial discretion in reducing or increasing the severity of the charges, including determining whether to bring a charge that has a minimum sentence length associated with it, identifying specific fees or bail amounts, or recommending the person be referred to a diversion program. We see even greater discretion when we consider the court process for juvenile offenders. In short, there are many potential points for intervention and change of women's and girls' pathways through criminal court proceedings.

Next, we focus on women's and girls'experiences during incarceration. In particular, we present research findings detailing their experiences of victimization and witnessing violence, mental and physical health problems while they are confined, and some of the barriers encountered by women and girls in obtaining services. We also discuss the physical and emotional safety of women and girls in secure confinement and draw your attention to common correctional procedures that may exacerbate retraumatization and distress. As you read about the research on women's and girls' reactions to being observed during personal hygiene processes or when they are moved from one unit to another, consider how facilities might implement some of the trauma-informed practices we have discussed to improve women's and girls' safety while still maintaining a secure environment. It is also important that we consider whether correctional facilities have adequate resources and staff to provide mental and physical health treatment to women and girls, what policies and programs are needed to improve the health of incarcerated persons, and how this might reduce recidivism.

We also discuss how incarceration affects the family members and communities of individuals. A 2019 study with a large, nationally representative sample of over 4,000 people found that almost half had an immediate or close family member who had been incarcerated (Enns et al., 2019). It is clear rates of incarceration in the U.S. are affecting the lives of many people. Research with women in jail and prison suggests that incarceration results in the separation of parents from children, affects how family members communicate with one another, and the financial stability of families. In addition, there is growing recognition of the impact of parental and caregiver incarceration on the emotional, cognitive, and behavioral development of children. In particular, it is clear that incarceration of a parent increases the risk a child will enter the criminal legal system. Finally, the families of incarcerated individuals report negative impact on themselves and their communities in regard to increased stigma, decreased financial support, and high rates of stress in communities with higher numbers of inidviduals who are cycling in and out of the system.

We close this section by once again drawing on the sequential intercept model as a framework to discuss interventions in court-based and corrections settings as well as policy recommendations. These include bail and financial penalty reforms, use of holistic defense strategies, mental health screening, post-arrest diversion programs, trauma-informed correctional practices, use of peer navigators, alternatives to incarceration, and justice reinvestment.

CHAPTER FIVE

Girls' and Women's Experiences With Courts, Penalties, and Sentencing

Introduction

In Section I, we discussed the ways that victimization, adversity, mental and physical health, race, class, and social position intersect with entry into the criminal legal system. In particular, we noted how these experiences create vulnerabilities as well as how systems are constructed in ways that disparately impact specific populations based on these factors. As girls and women come into contact with the courts, many such disparities are exacerbated. In this chapter, we discuss rates of incarceration of women and girls, typical charges, sentences, and penalties. We also discuss how basic processes of the court system include decision points that may leave marginalized girls and women vulnerable to disparities in conviction and sentencing. We highlight issues including prosecutorial discretion, cash bail and other legal financial obligations, and community supervision via probation.

Rates of Incarceration, Charges, and Sentences

In this chapter we will describe the process of entering the criminal legal system. Here, we give you a basic sense of how many women and girls are system involved, for what reasons, and average lengths of time women or girls are detained or incarcerated. The Bureau of Justice Statistics (BJS) provides counts of the number of adults in the corrections system (e.g., on probation or parole, and in jails, state, and federal prisons), as well as types of offenses. It is important to note that counts are typically provided for males versus females and for individuals by ethnicity, but very rarely is information available, for example, to compare the experiences of women of different ethnicities or any other social identities. The BJS reported that there were over 6.6 million adults supervised within the U.S. adult correctional system in 2016 (Kaeble & Cowhig, 2018). This is about 2.6% of the adult population or 2,640 per every 100,000 adults in the United States. The most common form of correctional supervision is probation (55%), followed by incarceration in prison (23%). Women make up approximately one quarter of the individuals on probation (Kaeble, 2018) and about 111,000 women are in state or federal correctional facilities. It is important to note that about a quarter of non-citizens who are incarcerated in state or federal prisons are women. Finally, recent reports of youth in the system indicate that 269,900 girls were arrested in 2015, accounting for almost one third of all arrests of individuals under 18 (Ehrmann et al., 2019).

The United States has the highest incarceration rate in the world, followed by China and Russia. Although the overall rate of incarceration has decreased in recent years, the Sentencing Project estimates that the number of incarcerated women increased 750% between 1980 and 2017 (Figure 5.1).

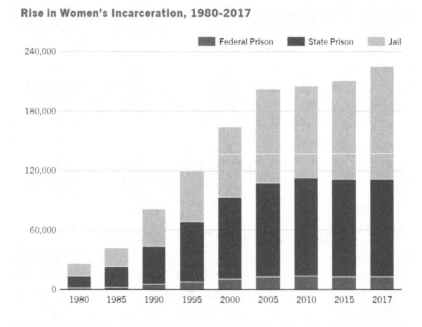

Rise in Women's Incarceration, 1980-2017

Sources: Bureau of Justice Statistics: Historical Corrections Statistics in the United States, 1850-1984; Prison and Jail Inmates at Midyear Series (1997-2017), Prisoners Series (1986-2018). Washington, DC.

FIGURE 5.1 Rate of incarceration.

Similarly, although the rate of incarceration of Black women overall has decreased by 53%, Black women are still incarcerated at twice the rate of White women, and Latinx at a rate 1.3 times that of White women (Sentencing Project, 2019). Between 2000 and 2017, the rate of incarceration of White women increased by 44% and Latinx women by 10%. When we consider system-involved girls, we see similar overrepresentation of girls who are ethnic minorities. American Indian girls are four times and Black girls are 3.5 times more likely to be incarcerated than White girls. Over half (54%) of girls in the juvenile legal system are ethnic minorities (Ehrmann et al., 2019).

Women are most often convicted of drug offenses or property crimes. For example, in 2017, 25% of women were incarcerated in state prisons for drug offenses and 26% for property offenses compared to 14% of men for each of these offenses (Bronson & Carson, 2019). A little over one-third of women are incarcerated for violent crimes (37%), for example, murder (12%) or assault (8%). When we examine federal statistics, over half of the women who were convicted were charged with drug trafficking offenses. It is important to note that the most recent available data indicates immigration charges represented 45% of federal cases in 2016 (Motivans, 2019).

Girls are most often charged with larceny-theft (24%), simple assault (18%), and disorderly conduct (9%) (Ehrmann et al., 2019). Arrests of boys outnumber girls for most types of offenses, with the exception of prostitution. A 2019 Juvenile Statistics Report indicated that more than three-fourths of 600 youth arrested for prostitution were girls. Girls are also more frequently incarcerated for lower-level or status offenses such as running away (Sentencing Project, 2019). Just over half of charges against girls are handled informally or without a petition. Approximately one-fifth of cases that are reviewed or adjudicated in juvenile court result in out-of-home placement while two-thirds result in formal probation (see Figure 5.2) (Ehrmann et al., 2019).

When adults are incarcerated, their average sentence served is 2.6 years in state prisons (Kaeble, 2018). Individuals convicted of drug offenses serve an average of 38% of their sentence in prison. As we note later, many factors influence how long sentences are and the amount of a sentence served in prison versus under community supervision. According to the U.S. Sentencing Commission (2018), between 2011 and 2016, women received sentences that were an average of 25 to 30% shorter than men's sentences. White and Black women's sentences were an average of 30% shorter than White men, while Latinas' sentences averaged about 18% shorter. However, individuals with immigrant status tended to receive longer sentences. We also see evidence of intersectionality of identities influencing sentencing. Steffensmeier

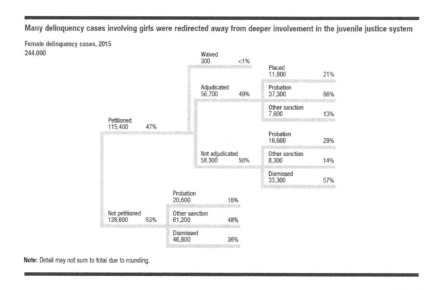

Many delinquency cases involving girls were redirected away from deeper involvement in the juvenile justice system

Female delinquency cases, 2015
244,000

Waived
300   <1%

Placed
11,800   21%

Adjudicated
56,700   49%

Probation
37,300   66%

Other sanction
7,600   13%

Petitioned
115,400   47%

Probation
16,600   29%

Not adjudicated
58,300   50%

Other sanction
8,300   14%

Dismissed
33,300   57%

Probation
20,600   16%

Not petitioned
128,600   53%

Other sanction
61,200   48%

Dismissed
46,800   36%

Note: Detail may not sum to total due to rounding.

FIGURE 5.2 Girls' placement rates, 2015. This chart illustrates the rate of formal and informal sanctions for system-involved girls.

and colleagues (2017) looked at sentences of 470,000 individuals in Pennsylvania for felony and misdemeanor convictions over seven years (2003–2010) and found women received shorter sentences than men and across ethnic groups, and that, in particular, younger women (age 18–20) were less likely to be incarcerated and received shorter sentences. Further, Black and Latinx males received the harshest sentences regardless of age.

Prosecutorial Discretion at Critical Decision Points

As described by the VERA Institute of Justice's 2018 publication, *Unlocking the Black Box of Prosecution*, if an individual is arrested and taken into custody, there are a number of critical decision points as the case moves through the criminal legal system. The prosecutor (sometimes a law enforcement officer in lower courts) makes determinations at these decision points that influence how the case is processed, and these decisions can also impact future decisions by law enforcement, judges, and juries. First, the prosecutor decides whether to prosecute the case at all and, if so, what charges to file. This may involve keeping the original charges suggested by law enforcement, dismissing them, or changing them—all based on the evidence, applicable laws, the policies of that particular prosecutor's office, and the prosecutor's own discretion. Factors such as the individual's prior record, severity of the offense, and community politics may all come into play in these decisions (VERA, 2018). Prosecutorial adjustments to the charges originally suggested by law enforcement may include reductions, as in the case of plea bargains, or may be increases, as in the practice of "overcharging"—tacking on additional counts or overstating a charge as a means to pressure the defendant to plea down to a more appropriate charge that is supported by the evidence (Graham, 2013). Prosecutors have power to influence judicial discretion in sentencing through the use of specific charges, as when a prosecutor chooses to put forth a charge that carries a mandatory minimum sentence. The charge levied against the defendant has impact beyond sentence length and type of sentence and can affect the amount of bail, fines, and fees as well as life-altering consequences such as deportation for immigrant defendants (VERA, 2018).

GETTING REAL 5.1

They could have sent me to rehab instead of sending me to jail. My lawyer tried to argue that I had no previous record. I was homeless. I didn't have a steady job. But the state's attorney said I was a crackhead and that this was homicide because I killed the fetus.

Donna, Black, aged 24, was charged with homicide by child abuse. She smoked crack while pregnant, and her child died. She received a sentence of 18 to life. She had no prior criminal record. When Donna was 5, her mother was checked into an institution for mental problems. Donna was placed in a foster home until her stepfather picked her up a year later. She loves her stepfather and his girlfriend, and the household didn't have any alcohol, drug use, or violence. She was frustrated with school and sometimes skipped with a friend, but realized that she had to go to get an education. She got in fights at school—one girl called her a "nigger" and spit in her cereal, and Donna had to go to in-school suspension for beating the girl up. On Donna's 16th birthday, her biological father came by and gave her two sacks of marijuana and smoked it with her. Ever since then, she smoked it every day. She tried crack when she was 20, after her mother was killed. Her aunt gave her some and told her to smoke it to take away the pain and the bad feelings. Donna didn't know any better, so she did. After the first hit, it was like she was chasing the dragon, always doing something to get the next hit. She'd turn tricks or go with her aunt to the store while her aunt would steal. Then one day her water broke, and it was the color of port wine.

The second decision point in which the prosecutor exercises substantial discretion is in choosing whether to recommend cash bail for temporary release of the defendant from jail. Bail is a sum of cash paid to the court that will be released back to the person who posted it upon case completion; bail is intended to ensure the individual will return for the court date in order to have the funds returned. If a defendant or her family does not have financial means for bail, she must stay in jail or seek paid bail-bonds services—costing a percentage beyond the amount paid to the court. Those unable to pay for bail or bond services and who thereby remain incarcerated are more likely to plead guilty (often to hasten release from jail) and more likely to receive harsher sentences (VERA, 2018).

GETTING REAL 5.2

When I got out of prison, the judge got me for failure to comply for not showing up for a court date when I was in prison. He fined me $700. I couldn't afford that and got behind in my payments. I got locked up again, and my stepfather paid the rest of the fine. Then my PO got me for failure to report— I didn't have a car, and I couldn't make it there. I got locked up again, and more money in bond and fines.

Anna, White, aged 34, was charged with grand larceny as her most serious offense, but she had other charges, like burglary. She's blocked out a lot of her childhood. Her father owned a mechanic's shop, and lots of her father's friends hung around drinking. She started getting sexually abused at age 5 or 6. She didn't know how to talk to anyone about it, but it made her feel not safe. Anna's dad made good money, so they were spoiled as far as some things—motorcycles, go-carts, camping. But her mom was always up under her dad in the shop and didn't tell him what the kids needed. Anna had maybe two pairs of pants to wear the whole time she was in school. Her dad had a bad temper, and Donna's mom tells her now that he used violence. About a year and half before he died, he started drinking a lot more and doing pills. Alcohol and drugs were everywhere, not just out back in the shop. Anna would go in his room and see coke, bags of marijuana. She figured if he could do it, she could do it too. Anna hung out with the druggies. After her father got killed when she was 15, it got a lot worse.

A third aspect of prosecutorial discretion—pre-charge and post-charge diversion programs—may be available through some prosecutor's offices. These programs offer service alternatives to incarceration for low-level offenses if the individuals successfully complete requirements such as substance abuse treatment, counseling, or other programming. For pre-charge programs, the individual may be able to avoid the charge altogether (similar to deferred prosecution), while for post-charge, diversion can result in dismissal or expungement of charges. However, some of these programs require additional monetary fees be paid by the individual, and some require daily or weekly program participation that may be difficult to achieve for an individual who is trying to meet other employment, family, educational, or financial obligations—increasing risk of incarceration due to failure in the program (Harris, 2016; VERA, 2018). As you read this, it is important to consider how individuals with fewer resources navigate or get stuck at these decision points in the system—including paying fines, alternate program fees, bail, and so on—compared to individuals with greater resources.

Two additional aspects of discretion include turning over evidence in the discovery process and avoiding delays in case processing. Prosecutors exercise discretion during the evidence discovery process as well. While the law requires that prosecutors inform the defense attorney of evidence favorable to the defense prior to a trial, the prosecution has some latitude in determining what meets this requirement and how early to turn it over to the defense. In terms of delays, prosecutor readiness at each step of case processing can impact whether a case progresses quickly or drags out over a long period of time (VERA, 2018).

A majority of cases are resolved through plea bargains, with prosecutors having almost complete discretion over the types of plea bargains offered, terms and conditions of the plea, how long the defendant has to accept the offer, and the accompanying sentencing recommendations. Finally, even in the absence of a plea bargain, prosecutor recommendations for sentencing are weighed heavily in judicial decisions regarding release or incarceration as well as sentence length (VERA, 2018).

More About Financial Legal Obligations

In her 2016 book, *A Pound of Flesh: Monetary Sanctions as Punishment for the Poor*, Alexis Harris details the multitude of ways that legal financial obligations are applied in association with court systems. When Dr. Harris became a professor, her research interests led her to examine the practice of courts imposing penalties in addition to jail or prison time—fines as penalties attached to a specific conviction, court fees for use of the criminal legal system, interest arising from unpaid legal debts, surcharges that support court or state functions, restitution to compensate victims, and collection charges associated with the overall process administered by the courts or their collectors. Furthermore, it is common for indigent defendants to be charged the cost of their appointed public defender, and persons who are incarcerated or under community supervision may be charged costs for these expenses on a daily, weekly, or monthly basis. Even seemingly beneficial programming can amount to substantial costs, as persons must pay for substance abuse treatment, including costs of room and board and drug testing. Beyond the prosecutor, other court personnel play a role in imposing, monitoring, and sanctioning compliance with financial legal obligations, including the judges who sentence the individual to a particular fee with its corresponding interest and court monitoring. County clerks may also be involved in determining an individual's ability to pay, monitoring payments, and applying sanctions for payment failure, insufficiency, or lateness of payments (Harris, 2016).

Based on court data as well as research interviews both with persons convicted of felonies and with professionals who work in the criminal legal system, Harris describes devastating impacts of legal financial obligations, concluding that "the imposition of fines and fees creates a two-tiered system of punishment: one for those with financial means and one for those who are poor" (Kindle location 252). Not only has the proportion of persons sentenced to financial legal obligations risen drastically in recent years, but courts have responded via establishment of collection units or partnerships with private collection agencies, and these agencies may tack on their own fees and surcharges (Harris, 2016). There is also substantial evidence that these financial legal obligations disparately impact poor persons and persons of color. These legal financial obligations linger beyond custodial sentences and community supervision to impact rights of individuals without financial means—potentially creating lifelong consequences. Until legal financial obligations are paid, the individual is still considered to be under criminal legal supervision. Debt accrues over time with interest, often exceeding the original fines and burgeoning into an insurmountable barrier for some. The resulting limitations on civil rights range from inability to own a gun to inability to vote or run for elected office until legal debts are paid. These debts cannot be eradicated through filing bankruptcy. In some cases, collectors of legal financial obligations address nonpayment by means such as wage garnishment, revocation of drivers' licenses, contacting family members, or incarceration (Harris, 2016). What are your thoughts about how these consequences impact individuals in the system? How could we create greater equity in the legal system?

Community Supervision, Pay Probation, & E-Carceration

In Chapter 3, we discussed in depth how racial injustice has long been part of the American criminal legal system—a pattern that persists today and which looms in the next generation of policies and practices. Alexander (2018) describes "e-carceration" as the "newest Jim Crow" (para. 1). As bail reform and other practices are coming into acceptance, new policies on detention include the use of computer software algorithms, which determine which persons present the highest risks to communities and should be detained rather than released. The algorithms derive from experience garnered over years of policing—thereby reflecting some of that same bias in formulas that are intended to be colorblind. The software technology is proprietary, so precise formulas are not transparent for public scrutiny to determine the extent to which they are based on factors correlated with race or those that may produce racially disparate outcomes. Those persons who are not detained may also be deemed risky enough to merit electronic monitoring, which is also the purview of corporate for-profit vendors. Such monitoring may seem to be a more humane alternative to prison, but this does not negate its role in extending the scope of monitoring and control of persons of color.

Another concerning practice in community supervision involves pay-only probation practices, described by Human Rights Watch (HRW, 2014) as legal financial penalties masquerading as behavioral oversight of probationers. Such practices have become widespread, with offenses that carry little or no incarcerative time on their own (e.g., speeding, driving without proof of insurance, noise violations) becoming incarcerative offenses if an individual does not make adequate payments toward court fines and probation company fees. Specifically, when courts impose legal financial obligations such as fines and fees, this can create a burden on smaller jurisdictions in which there is a lack of staffing and resources to monitor payment in the long term. Thus, "offender-funded" models of privatized probation have been developed, in which corporations offer the courts probation services in return for the ability to add supervision fees for monitoring those persons' payments. Yet, those persons sentenced to probation receive these sentences for the sole reason of being unable to pay their legal financial obligations. In addition to establishing payment plans for existing legal debts, probationers are charged a monthly supervision fee.

The primary "supervision" that is occurring is meeting for debt collection. The fiscal structure of these models—with poorer persons taking longer to pay down debt and thereby incurring more monthly fees—results in higher overall costs for the impoverished. The corporations that profit from these fees are often the designated authorities to determine an individual's ability to pay, and the companies function under limited oversight (HRW, 2014). Human Rights Watch has noted that these programs are most common in communities suffering from high unemployment, poverty, and economic distress. Some courts also impose conditions involving additional daily charges, such as GPS monitoring, mandatory drug testing, or alcohol monitoring devices (HRW, 2014). What does the research summarized here suggest is the potential impact of privatizing supervision and probation? What are your thoughts about how to correct this bias against individuals with fewer resources in the criminal legal system?

Juvenile Courts

Many of the factors already noted impact girls as well as women in their pathways through the court system. In her article "Blind Discretion: Girls of Color and Delinquency in the Juvenile Justice System," Jyoti Nanda (2012) discusses racial disparities in the juvenile legal system and describes the role of decision-makers' discretion in contributing to these disparities. Nanda points to the youth system's foundations in discretionary decision making—intended to ameliorate the harshness of the legal system and determine whether punitive responses are preferable to other interventions. This discretion derives from the court's role in protecting the best interests of the child, assuming lesser culpability of children in their actions, and favoring responses that are amenable to reforming the youths' behavior. While the flexibility of this discretion has certain strengths in allowing more merciful responses to children, it also has weaknesses in creating an entry point for personal prejudices as well as structural patterns of racism. Law enforcement officers have discretion to decide whether to give the youth a warning, direct them to a diversion program for informal processing, or process the youth formally via a notice to appear to a juvenile probation officer. In the latter case, the probation officer then uses discretion to dismiss, offer informal probation (in which conditions can be met to dismiss), or detain the youth.

If the youth is detained, the prosecutor then determines whether to decline prosecution or to file a petition or charge. A case can be adjudicated in either juvenile or adult court, based on the age of the child, crime characteristics, and prosecutorial discretion. A judge may then determine if the youth is responsible for the crime and impose a sentence. Punishments can include things ranging from probation to group camps or detention centers (Nanda, 2012). Minors are sometimes also sentenced to monetary sanctions, as described, with their parents bearing the burden of paying these costs or being held in contempt and possibly jailed (Harris, 2016). Nanda (2012) reviews extant research and details how both gender and race play a role in the youth's outcomes, typically with girls of color faring more poorly than White girls in terms of detention, adjudication, and sentencing outcomes as well as in having their needs met via programs and services.

Feld (2009) describes how parents' gendered expectations about girls' obedience and changes in enforcement—including increasing emphases on issues of domestic violence and school zero-tolerance policies—have resulted in increased arrest and confinement of girls. Specifically, girls relative to boys are more likely to engage in fights in home or school settings. Even when the girls do not instigate violent encounters, if there appears to be any mutuality, it may seem to enforcement officers that arrest of the youth is more efficient, given the need to shelter children if the caregiver is arrested. Over the years, there has been an increase in "overcharging" girls for status offenses (e.g., incorrigibility) and rendering these criminal offenses (e.g., simple or aggravated assault). Accordingly, Feld describes girls being confined proportionately more than boys, despite girls' less violent and less injurious offenses. Pasko (2017) notes that the increase in girls' confinement in recent decades disparately impacts ethnic minority girls and often impacts sexual or gender minorities. Pasko has noted that paternalistic use of courts and corrections to use confinement as a means to "protect" girls persists today. In her study of criminal legal and social service professionals, Pasko found that girls' character was often the focus of attention (e.g., girls as manipulative, deceitful, abusive) more so than the girls' histories of trauma, family disruption, and educational deficits. Thus, while professionals did not feel that girls posed a threat to communities, commitment to a facility was viewed as best for girls' "own good and protection" (Pasko, 2017, p. 9). Girls were overwhelmingly described as refusing to accept responsibility for their own behavior, unwilling to make different choices, unable to avoid unhealthy relationships or avoid risky situations, and unsuccessful in meeting conditions of probation. Commitment was often used as a means for professionals to restrict girls' participation in what were viewed as "undesirable" sexual relationships.

With regard to juvenile processing more generally, Petrosino and associates (2010) conducted a meta-analysis of 29 experiments or quasi-experiments over a 35-year period. Among the 7,304 youth studied, these researchers found that those youth who were formally processed via the criminal legal system experienced more negative crime/delinquency outcomes than youth who were diverted in lieu of services or those who were released without services. That is, those formally processed committed more crimes and worse crimes after having been processed. The findings indicate that youth processing through the system does not have a crime-deterrent effect as measured by prevalence, incidence, severity, or self-reported outcomes. Youth who were diverted with services experienced the least negative effects, indicating potential deterrent and/or rehabilitative effect of diversion with services as compared to formal processing. The researchers were careful to note that, because comparisons were between those processed versus those diverted or released, the findings did not support establishing diversion programs for youth who would not have been officially processed in the first place (e.g., net widening).

SUMMARY

Women and girls tend to enter the system for nonviolent offenses. Although the overall rate of incarceration of women and girls has decreased in the past 15 years, we still see differences in the types of sanctions and rates of incarceration that suggest we continue to engage in discriminatory practices that disadvantage individuals of color and individuals with fewer resources. Involvement with the justice system may result in substantial costs to individuals charged with crimes, often resulting in high financial penalties for those individuals with the most limited resources. Finally, much of this chapter illustrates that there are many points where justice officials have notable discretion in their decision making. Important questions for us to ask are "What criteria are being used to make these discretionary decisions?" and "What are the long-term consequences of these decisions?"

DISCUSSION QUESTIONS

1. What are the most common offenses committed by women and girls? What are the differences in rates of arrest of girls and women of different ethnicities? What are some possible explanations for these different rates?
2. What are examples of discretionary decision making as women and girls enter the criminal legal system? Who has discretion and at what times?

3. What are the financial costs of entering the criminal legal system? How do these costs differentially impact individuals with fewer resources?

4. What are the roles of private companies in furthering the financial burden of individuals in the criminal legal system? What are the implications of privatizing collections of fees?

CHAPTER SIX

Challenges of Secure Confinement

Introduction

This chapter addresses secure confinement and the challenges this poses for traumatized and/or marginalized populations. Issues include the recapitulation of trauma that may occur within secure settings, stigmatization of mental disorders within the secure setting, bullying and coercion by other prisoners and by correctional staff, physical health risks to prisoners, and access to resources for marginalized populations. We also address problems with coercive or punitive rehabilitation programs as well as the paradox of criminalizing yet infantilizing girls in secure residential facilities.

Secure Confinement in the Context of the Criminal Legal System

According to the Prison Policy Initiative, the U.S. incarcerates more women than any other country. For example, the state of Idaho incarcerates 209 women per 100,000 compared to 13 per 100,000 in Canada and the United Kingdom (Kajstura, 2018). As we noted in Chapter 5, about 111,000 women are in state or federal correctional facilities (Kaeble & Cowhig, 2018). Incarceration is costly for our country. Data from Wagner and Rabuy (2017) indicate that costs accrued collectively by both the government and by the families of those incarcerated reaches about $182 billion each year. While private companies bring in billions of dollars from government payments and from the items/services supplied to prison commissaries and communications systems, the correctional system is nevertheless primarily a public system (Wagner & Rabuy, 2017). Thus, for many reasons, including financial ones, it is critical that we consider the rationale for and impact of mass incarceration.

In recent years, Ancestry.com began posting generations of prison register entries online. Barry Godfrey and Steven Soper (2018), using these records, developed a compelling argument that the roots of mass incarceration in the United States—like the U.S.'s origins of policing (see Chapter 3)—have close connections to slavery and race in the South. These researchers examined over 25,000 register entries spanning a 200-year period beginning in 1817, examining rises and falls in secure confinement alongside historical events and practices such as convict leasing. The researchers found a significant increase in incarceration after the Civil War, when there was a substantial desire to incapacitate populations deemed "problematic." The researchers note that, at the time, a future governor of Georgia stated, "Emancipating negroes will require a system of penitentiaries" (paragraph 8). Andrea James (2019) describes the time period after the abolition of slavery when Black women arrested for crimes such as prostitution and vagrancy were forced to perform hard labor. Women worked alongside men on chain gangs, maintained the camps, prepared meals, and mended clothing, and they were beaten and raped. James describes modern-day prison labor, in which women who served time with her during her own incarceration performed labor such as driving prison vehicles and training officers on tasks, all for a wage that started at 12 cents an hour. James (2019) notes, "Officials trusted the women to keep the prison community functioning, but they did not trust them to serve their sentences in their own community" (p. 773).

Secure confinement includes jails, prisons, and residential facilities. While residential facilities are based in the community and focus on treatment services, jails and prisons serve primarily as a means of incapacitation (Hanser, 2018). Jails house persons awaiting trial or persons who have been convicted but will serve a year's time or less. Jails are often administered by local law enforcement or persons specifically employed by the county for jail administration. In contrast, prisons are used for longer-term confinement of persons serving more than a year's time. Prisons are typically administered by state departments of corrections or by the federal Bureau of Prisons (Sullivan, 2009). Prisons often face difficulties with staff morale, training, and turnover (Appelbaum et al., 2001; Brower, 2013; Finn, 2000), as well as shortages of resources for health and mental health, nutrition, and women's specific needs (Eliason et al., 2004; Ferszt & Clarke, 2012). Because of the shorter stays and varying funding streams for local or county jails, these facilities often lack even rudimentary programming relative to prisons. Thus, while theorists discuss correctional systems as serving multiple purposes, including incapacitation, retribution, rehabilitation, and deterrence, these systems are primarily designed to maintain the safety and security of officers and the public and do not adequately address rehabilitative needs (Kifer et al., 2003; Sullivan, 2009). Furthermore, secure confinement presents a number of challenges that may compound problems of those who are incarcerated, as well as create negative impacts on families and communities. As James notes, incarceration "is not an effective way to increase the well-being of the public, because it harms rather than heals the people we subject to it" (p. 782).

Physical and Sexual Victimization During Incarceration

Popular media have often portrayed the victimization that occurs in prisons, including physical and sexual victimization, both from other incarcerated persons and from correctional staff. Only in recent decades have systematic protective measures been enacted through legislation such as the Prison Rape Elimination Act (PREA) of 2003. The act created standards for elimination of prison rape, effective as of 2012. PREA provides analysis, training, and resources to protect individuals from prison rape (National PREA Resource Center, 2019). Wolff et al. (2009) examined prison victimization among 7,500 men and women incarcerated in a single state and identified 6-month victimization rates that far exceeded rates in the broader community. While rates of prisoner-on-prisoner physical victimization were the same for men and women (20.7%), men reported greater physical victimization by correctional staff (25.2%) relative to women (8.3%). For sexual victimization, prisoner-on-prisoner victimization rates were higher for women (21.3%) than men (4.3%), but staff-on-prisoner rates were about the same for men (7.6%) and women (7.7%). The researchers noted that women were more likely than men to report being touched or grabbed by other prisoners in a sexually threatening way. Overall, rates of either physical or sexual victimization by either prisoners or staff resulted in more than a third of men (38.4%) and women (36.9%) being victimized while incarcerated within the prior 6 months. Pause here for a moment and consider how these rates of victimization affect perceptions of safety of individuals who are incarcerated. The criminal legal system has increased attention to rates of victimization while incarcerated, but we still hear routinely about individuals in jails and prisons experiencing abuse. How do we decrease or stop this violence?

Barbara Owen (2017) describes the ways in which both overt experiences of victimization as well as typical daily operations in a prison (e.g., strip searches, showers at intake, and transitions from one unit to another) are examples of *gendered harms* that affect the emotional safety of women and girls in secure confinement. Owen notes that many of the policies and structured schedules implemented in secure settings may exacerbate trauma survivors' distress and contribute to women feeling less physically and emotionally safe. It is important to acknowledge the potential conflict between policies designed to increase security, with an emphasis on controlling behavior, and trauma-informed policies that emphasize safety, empowerment, and trust. However, there are growing numbers of secure facilities implementing trauma-informed policies while maintaining a secure environment.

Bullying and Indirect Victimization

Meghan Novisky and Robert Peralta (2020) conducted interviews with 30 previously incarcerated men and women to learn about their experiences of secondary victimization (i.e., witnessing violence) while incarcerated. Participants described violence as something that was inevitable in the prison environment and, by some descriptions, was unrelenting, occurring daily, and often including extreme acts. One man spoke of the impact of such witnessed violence in triggering trauma symptoms from his childhood victimization: "I can feel it trigger. You hear a loud noise, or you can hear feet scuffling, 'skeet, skeet, skeet,' 'doom, doom, doom' [walking/pounding noises]. You can hear them, their bodies, going against the wall and you know they're fighting. And it increases the heart rate [taps quickly on chest three times] and puts you on high alert. You might get the shakes, you know" (Novisky & Peralta, 2020, p. 17). While secondary victimization may be part of the landscape of incarceration, there are also more direct attacks to intimidate or control others while incarcerated.

In her book, *Bullying Among Prisoners: Evidence, Research, and Intervention Strategies*, Jane Ireland (2002) describes how bullying may include isolated, severe incidents as well as repeated acts. These can be direct forms of aggression or pressure or threats to engage in behaviors unwillingly. Some types of bullying are woven into the prison culture, such as "taxing" (theft of items under pretense of taking them for a tax) or "baroning" (providing goods and demanding payment with extortionate rates of interest). Bullying can be also be particularly pernicious when some bullies victimize others while remaining unidentified by using gossip, rumors, and ostracizing to intimidate and isolate. Based on years of research using multiple methods, Ireland concludes that women are at least as likely as men to engage in bullying behavior in prisons. Beyond these intentional acts of violence and coercion, there is substantial evidence that the institutional environment and procedures used by staff in correctional facilities can be traumatizing in their own right.

Recapitulation of Trauma

As we noted in Section I of this book, most incarcerated women and girls have experienced high rates of trauma and adversity, and many suffer from post-traumatic stress disorder. Similar to Owen's (2017) observations of factors detracting from women's sense of safety in secure confinement, Dirks (2004) summarizes some potential aspects of incarceration that can be traumatizing for women, particularly for persons with prior victimization histories. Among such factors are lack of privacy, invasive searches, use of restraints, reading of mail, and—for women's facilities in which men serve as officers—having body searches performed by males (Office of the Inspector General (OIG), 2018) and having to rely on men for basic needs including female hygiene items, phone calls, and visiting privileges (Dirks, 2004). Based on a sample of 100 system-involved girls, Schaffner (2006) describes recapitulation of trauma via activities such as bathing and using the toilet under surveillance, leaving girls feeling humiliated and invaded. Incarcerated persons also may experience distress in relation to crime anniversaries, parole hearings, and even institution-wide events such as lockdowns and executions. According to Benedict (2014), potential triggers that may remind incarcerated persons of past trauma include strip searches for contraband, transitioning incarcerated persons from one place to another inside a facility, being supervised by staff during personal hygiene or dressing, being extracted from one's cell, and being placed into segregated housing or into restraints. Noises present throughout jails and prisons—loud voices, banging doors, buzzers, and even visits with family and friends—can be stressful for incarcerated persons. While some institutional practices are necessary to maintain safety and security of facilities, there are steps that can be taken to reduce traumatic effects (see Chapter 8 for more on trauma-informed practices). As you read this material, what steps do you think could be taken to decrease recapitulation of trauma for system-involved women and girls?

Incarceration and Persons With Mental Disorders

As discussed in Chapter 2, serious mental illness is also common among persons who are incarcerated. Thus, experiences of trauma can be exacerbated by or feed into conditions of depression, anxiety, bipolar disorder, or schizophrenia spectrum disorders. Trauma treatment and programming was one of three key areas recently identified by the U.S. Department of Justice's Office of the Inspector General (2018) as an area of deficiency for women's prisons. Access to treatment in jail and prison settings is quite limited, leaving many women on their own in coping with trauma and mental disorders. In a recent focus group with incarcerated women at a state facility, one participant told Dr. DeHart, "I got here in June, and I didn't get to see a psychiatrist until July. They discussed my medication needs with me before they put me on the yard, and they brought me here because I required psych and needed meds. Here, it's like a jungle with banging and hollering, anyone who is like me—who has anxiety—will have issues with it." Appelbaum et al. (2001) have noted how stressful factors such as separation from family, limitations on privacy, fear of assault, boredom, and overcrowding can overwhelm coping skills of incarcerated persons with mental disorders, contributing to functional deterioration. Some of the challenges of secure confinement for those with mental disorders are described here.

- *Incarcerated persons with mental disorders may display behaviors that are out of their conscious control but which appear to be disorderly.* This might include things like (a) symptomatic behaviors that seem disruptive, such as unusual movements, gestures, or vocalizations; (b) aggressive or emotional outbursts stemming from a mental disorder; or (c) failure to follow directives, which may stem from inability to understand a request or enact the requested behavior (Blevins & Soderstrom, 2015).

- *Incarcerated persons with mental disorders are more likely than other incarcerated persons to be charged with disciplinary infractions.* A contributing factor may be those behaviors beyond the individual's control. In some cases, this results in administrative segregation of the individual, which can exacerbate an individual's distress and feelings of being unsafe. Further, disciplinary and parole boards often do not consider mental illness a mitigating factor for behavioral problems in prison, resulting in longer periods of incarceration (Blevins & Soderstrom, 2015; Torrey et al., 2010).

- *System-involved persons with mental disorders have higher recidivism rates.* Since correctional systems are typically not integrated with community mental health systems, persons with mental disorders who leave jails or prisons may not receive proper aftercare, which may be associated with reoffending and "cycling" in and out of jails and prisons (Torrey et al., 2010).

- *Incarcerated persons with mental disorders are at higher risk than other incarcerated persons for suicide and self-harming behavior.* Suicidal thoughts and behaviors may be associated with specific mental disorders such as depression, as well as with past trauma exposures or simply the stress of incarceration (Blevins & Soderstrom, 2015). Self-injuring behavior like cutting or headbanging may be a response to stress or a coping mechanism to exert control from a position of powerlessness (DeHart et al., 2009).
- *Behavior of an incarcerated person with a mental disorder may trigger disorderly behavior from others in response.* This might include things like other incarcerated persons lashing out against the mentally ill individual verbally or physically (Blevins & Soderstrom, 2015).
- *Other incarcerated persons may prey on the vulnerability of an incarcerated person with a mental disorder.* This might include unprovoked bullying, exclusion from social networks, or victimization of the mentally ill individual, who may be perceived as weak. Incarcerated persons with mental disorders are more likely than others to be physically and sexually assaulted while incarcerated, potentially exacerbating mental illness (Blevins & Soderstrom, 2015).
- *Incarcerated persons may malinger—fake or exaggerate—mental disorders in order to improve their conditions.* A valid concern is whether incarcerated persons are malingering, or intentionally producing false or over-exaggerated medical or mental health symptoms. Individuals may fake illness for legal reasons, such as avoiding responsibility, reducing or altering their sentencing, or obtaining benefits upon release. They may also fake illness to improve their living conditions while incarcerated, such as trying to get a transfer to a different location (e.g., hospital, infirmary, mental health unit), receive lighter work duty, obtain medications for recreational use or sale, or obtain other benefits. This puts a strain on budgets and resources, and some correctional staff are skeptical when confronted with health or mental health requests (Schoenly, 2010). However, it is important to note that faking mental illness, particularly at the stage of court proceeding—for example pleading not guilty by reason of insanity—is used infrequently (about 1% of cases) and is rarely successful (Schouten, 2012).

Considering these challenges, it is important to recognize that incarceration may worsen mental illness and may trigger symptoms such as delusions, hallucinations, mood swings, and disruptive behavior (Blevins

& Soderstrom, 2015). Further, aside from routine operations (e.g., custody reclassification, transfers), the most frequently cited reason for putting incarcerated women into segregation is due to mental health needs, and racial disparities put Black, Indigenous, and Latinx women at increased risk of placement in "ad-seg" or mental health segregation (Tasca & Turanovic, 2018). Lesbian, gay, and bisexual persons are also at increased risk of being placed in solitary confinement (28%) or segregation than heterosexual persons (18%), with such placements sometimes being done with the intent of "protection" (Beck, 2015). Similarly, in immigrant detention facilities, transgender persons, the elderly, those with disabilities, and those who complain about conditions have been subjected to segregated housing, and segregation has been used to alleviate overcrowding at some facilities (Southern Poverty Law Center (SPLC), 2016). Such restricted housing placements can have extremely negative effects on individuals without mental disorders, including depression, anxiety, rage, claustrophobia, hallucinations, and impaired ability to think; incarcerated persons with preexisting mental health problems may suffer even more damaging deterioration while in segregation (Fellner, 2006). Why do you think corrections environments rely on segregation to manage these problems and/or populations? What alternative strategies or programs do you think would shift our reliance on segregation as a behavior management strategy?

GETTING REAL 6.1

I was experiencing "emotional duress." They put me in a stripped cell with nothing but a mattress. … I felt like if anyone deserved to die, it was me. I used my teeth to rip the mattress rim off. I climbed on the toilet and looped the rim around a vent and around my neck and jumped. The next thing I remember is a blue balloon pumping over my mouth.

Becca, Black, aged 37, is serving a life sentence for killing her baby. Becca describes herself as a loner—she keeps her problems to herself. She didn't feel like she could talk to anybody. Her lawyer says he wishes she would have stayed in counseling as a kid, and she probably wouldn't be in prison today. She doesn't know the terminology, but she was diagnosed as psychotic, mixed personality disorder or something like that. Her counselor tried to explain it to her. Leading up to her crime, Becca had been living with her mother and having conflicts at home, so she left the state to "start over." She was raped, and she got pregnant. She doesn't know if the baby was his. The baby was sickly, and his medicine wasn't helping. Becca had lots going on, and she felt like she was going to snap. Her friend suggested she go to counseling, but Becca didn't go because she thought people would pick at her and say she's crazy. Two weeks later, it happened.

While research supports the provision of trauma programming early in the incarcerative period, many prisons are unable to provide trauma treatment until close to women's time of release due to staffing shortages at women's institutions (OIG, 2018). Consequently, if trauma and mental disorders are left unaddressed in the correctional setting, incarcerated women are at risk not only for deterioration and/or threats to physical health, but they also may cycle in and out of facilities, creating an emotional burden for prisoners and families, a safety risk for facilities and communities, and a cost burden for taxpayers.

Physical Health of Incarcerated Persons

Joanne Belknap and Elizabeth Whalley (2013) provide an integrative review of the health crisis facing incarcerated girls and women. They note that illicit drug use, tobacco use, involvement in sex work and with high-risk partners, stress, inadequate healthcare, and nutritional factors are some considerations that may place these girls and women at high risk for physical health issues. They summarize findings demonstrating incarcerated women's elevated rates of asthma, dental and vision problems, sexually transmitted infections, reproductive health problems such as ovarian cysts, high-risk pregnancies, cancers, tuberculosis, and Hepatitis C. Our own conversations with incarcerated women reflect many of these concerns, as well as highlight the difficulty of obtaining care during incarceration; specifically, women note that those with shorter sentences may have to wait until they are released to receive care if their conditions are not dire. Further, the women describe barriers in accessing the level of care needed while incarcerated (from DeHart's collected raw data). Similarly, medical neglect and poor nutrition (including serving spoiled or infested food) have been noted as recurring issues in immigrant detention facilities (SPLC, 2016). Across all types of girls' and women's facilities, issues such as unmanaged infectious diseases (e.g., influenza, tuberculosis, HIV, Hepatitis C), are problematic not only for the women and girls who are incarcerated, but also for those who are housed alongside them, visiting family members and service providers, frontline officers, and those in the communities to which they may return one day (Wodahl, 2006).

A 2018 report by U.S. DOJ's Office of the Inspector General revealed two key physical health needs that were not adequately addressed within Bureau of Prisons (BOP) programming and policy: pregnancy programming and feminine hygiene. The report notes lack of awareness of pregnancy programs among incarcerated persons and staff, as well as staff applying eligibility criteria more restrictively than intended. The result has been that just over one-third (37%) of pregnant incarcerated women sentenced to BOP facilities participated in pregnancy programs between 2012 and 2016. Regarding feminine hygiene, products have been distributed using varied methods across facilities, often in ways that do not assure access to sufficient hygiene products to meet women's individual needs. For instance, some facilities provide women a predetermined number of products for their entire cycle (e.g., 25 or 30 pads), while at others, women must visit a central location to obtain products. At some facilities, women were required to see a counselor or health care staff to obtain feminine hygiene products, which first requires permission from correctional officers to visit counseling/health services. These restrictive practices are purportedly attempts to prevent "misuse" of feminine hygiene products for purposes such as cleaning cells (OIG, 2018). We are aware from our own research that women describe having to improvise cleaning products from dishwashing liquid and shampoos to address mold, grime, and standing water in bathrooms and common areas—particularly in reference to foot fungus, Hepatitis C, and other health concerns. Thus, there may be plausible "misuse," but what are some other ways that these concerns could be addressed?

Again, similar issues are pervasive in immigrant detention, where availability of hygiene products (including feminine hygiene, toothbrushes, soap, and fresh clothing) and clean water have been woefully inadequate; the facilities—often repurposed from previously shuttered buildings— often present safety hazards, lack adequate temperature control, and may either fail to provide access to sunlight or, in the case of makeshift/tented facilities, may fail to protect inhabitants from the elements (SPLC, 2016).

Another important health concern that intersects with both mental and physical health of incarcerated women involves those who are older at the time of incarceration or who are serving lengthy prison terms. Aging of state prison populations has created unique barriers in health care, with the proportion of prisoners over 55 years old increasing 400% from 1993 to 2013 (Carson & Sabol, 2016). Incarcerated persons may experience rapid effects of aging given complex behavioral health issues (McKillop & Boucher, 2018), facing challenges such as Alzheimer's and dementia, ongoing depression and substance use disorders (as substance abuse continues while incarcerated when contraband is present), and chronic physical conditions such as cancer, diabetes, heart disease, liver disease, and HIV.

Incarceration and Sexual/Gender Minorities

As addressed in Chapter 3, sexual and gender minorities may be subject to greater surveillance and enforcement than persons identifying as heterosexual. Research has also demonstrated that sexual minorities are incarcerated at higher rates. Based on the National Inmate Survey with a probability sample of 106,532 persons incarcerated in prisons and jails in 2011–2012, 36% of women in jail and 42% of women in prisons identified as bisexual or lesbian or had engaged in sex with women prior to incarceration. Compared to incarcerated persons who identified as heterosexual, these women were more likely to have been sexually victimized as children, were sentenced for longer terms, and were more likely to be sexually victimized while incarcerated (Meyer et al., 2017). The same survey indicates that transgender persons who are incarcerated are at even higher risk of sexual victimization (Beck, 2014). The National Center for Transgender Equality (NCTE) (2018) describes risks faced by incarcerated gay, lesbian, bisexual, and transgender persons, particularly transgender females housed in male facilities. Like other incarcerated women, these women face risks of sexual victimization by both prisoners and staff. They may also be blamed for their own victimization, have grievances ignored, or may be subjected to unnecessary searches or placed in segregation as measures of "security" (NCTE, 2018). In some jails or prisons, transgender persons are housed based on their genital anatomy or gender at birth rather than gender identity, and these persons may be denied clothing and grooming items aligned with that identity or may be denied medical therapies deemed "cosmetic" by staff with inadequate training on transgender needs (NCTE, 2018).

Coercive Rehabilitation Programming

In secure facilities as well as in some unsecured but court-mandated programs, treatment programming runs the risk of becoming ineffective if participation is required and if therapeutic methods are coercive. Thus, even when therapies are provided in jails, prisons, and secure or mandated residential facilities, participants may be less than engaged or "going through the motions." Jill McCorkel (2013) describes in eloquent detail many of the problems of such programs in her examination of a privately run drug treatment program for women offered at a state prison. The program is explicitly directed toward "breaking" women from their "diseased" selves. In doing so, McCorkel notes, the program destabilizes women's understandings of their experiences of poverty, violence, and marginality, and—to paraphrase a program participant—robs the women of their dignity and self-respect. The program's "confrontational and coercive tactics effectively collapsed the distinction between treatment and punishment," containing the self just as prisons contain the body (McCorkel, 2013, Kindle location 58). McCorkel thereby characterizes such coercive rehabilitation as a gendered extension of tough-on-crime policies. Women's rejection of the program is often concealed as they "fake it to make it," undermining sincere efforts toward rehabilitation.

Similarly, residential programs for delinquent girls or those "in need of protection" often create analogous problems. As explained in Chapter 1, girls' delinquency has traditionally been conceptualized in ways that criminalize girls' efforts to cope with trauma and adversity. Thus, arrests for status offenses such as running away, substance use, and being "ungovernable" sometimes result in placement in secure facilities (Ehrmann et al., 2019). Girls who are trafficked may also be placed in secure facilities because of problems with substance abuse, mental disorders, pregnancy or having minor children, or other special needs that may render them ineligible for routine child placements (Florida Legislature Office of Program Policy Analysis and Government Accountability (FLOPPAGA), 2016). In a study of girls in secure facilities in England and Wales, Katie Ellis (2018) describes girls' rejection of the "vulnerable" label applied to them as well as rejection of the therapeutic child enrichment activities that were part of the program. Their lives, she notes, had been filled with adult activities, including sex, drugs, and alcohol. The girls found the therapy to be infantilizing and resented restrictions on their liberties. From the girls' perspectives, surviving their difficult life experiences, rather than making them vulnerable, demonstrated strength and independence. In order to get through the program, many girls "acted the part" of a good, girlish girl in order to appease the program staff. Ellis (2018) underscores the paradox of both criminalizing and infantilizing girls, which ultimately "disenfranchises girls from the services that are designed to help them" (p. 157).

SUMMARY

This chapter summarizes research on women's and girls' experiences during secure confinement. Existing research suggests that women and girls experience high rates of physical and sexual victimization while incarcerated, witness violence towards others, and are at risk of developing or exacerbating mental health problems. Correctional facilities have limited resources to provide treatment services, and many incarcerated women and girls may wait long periods of time for services or may have needs that are not addressed. In many instances, routine events during incarceration (e.g., searches, observation of hygiene behaviors) may retraumatize or trigger inidviduals. Individuals with mental disorders are more likely to act out while incarcerated, are at increased risk of self-harm and harm from others, and are more likely to be placed in segregation. Although there is limited research on incarcerated women's and girls' physical health, we know that they report elevated rates of a range of serious medical conditions, encounter numerous barriers to obtaining medical care while incarcerated, and that conditions in corrections facilities often heighten the risk of infectious diseases. We also know that individuals who are sexual or gender minorities are at greater risk of incarceration, often encounter significant barriers associated with their sexual and/or gender identities, and are placed in segregation at high rates. Similarly, we see evidence of racial disparities in the use of segregation to manage mental health problems and related behaviors for women and girls of color. The high rates of trauma exposure and mental and physical health needs in this population indicate clear need for evidence-based interventions to decrease health risks and recidivism.

DISCUSSION QUESTIONS

1. How can incarceration in a secure facility retraumatize individuals with histories of trauma and adversity? What practices are most likely to recapitulate traumatic experiences?
2. How are individuals who are mentally ill at risk while incarcerated? How might their behaviors be linked to their mental disorders?
3. Describe the risks to and/or differential treatment experienced by individuals who identify as lesbian, gay, bisexual, or transgender while incarcerated.
4. What are coercive treatments? How do women and girls respond to treatments that are coercive or infantilizing?

CHAPTER SEVEN

Impacts of Detention and Incarceration on Prisoners and Their Families

Introduction

In Chapter 6, we addressed challenges of secure confinement for prisoners. Yet, the impacts of incarceration extend beyond those immediate effects on prisoners. Specifically, girls' and women's separation from families and communities can have deleterious and lifelong consequences for family communication and cohesion, relationships with friends and community members, and health and well-being of those left behind. This chapter addresses separation from children and families, impacts on family communication, parenting from prison, second-generation impacts on child well-being, impacts on adult family health and finances, and impacts on communities.

Prevalence of Incarcerated Family Members

One of the most cited studies on prevalence of incarcerated parents and their children was conducted by Mumola (2000) using nationally representative data from the 1997 Survey of Inmates in State and Federal Correctional Facilities. According to that study, a majority of both state (55%) and federal (63%) prisoners had minor children, and more women (64%) than men (44%) lived with those children prior to prison admission. After incarceration of a mother, children most often lived with grandparents (53%), another parent (28%), other kin (26%), family friends (10%), or in a foster home (10%). A study by Glaze and Maruschak (2010) yielded similar findings using the later 2004 survey in the series and allowed researchers to project estimates of the number of children with a parent in prison in more recent years. Based on survey and incarcerative data, Glaze and Maruschak posit that the number of children with a mother in prison was likely to have more than doubled in the period from 1991 to 2007.

Taking another approach to understand the breadth of incarceration in separating families, Enns and associates (2019) used the Family History of Incarceration Survey with a nationally representative sample of 4,041 adults to examine the percentage of Americans who ever experienced incarceration of a family member. The study demonstrated that 45% of participants had experienced incarceration of an immediate family member, with Blacks, Latinx, and Indigenous women reporting higher rates than Whites. Experiencing incarceration of extended family members (47%) was similarly prevalent, and—collectively—having experienced either immediate or extended family incarceration impacted 64% of the sample. Lower percentages were evident when examining more restrictive criteria, such as incarceration of an immediate family member for more than 1 year (14%). These researchers identified cohort effects, with younger adults reporting much higher rates of parental incarceration than older cohorts—again, indicating that parental incarceration is a phenomenon increasing in frequency. This study is important in part because it illustrates the extent to which we rely on incarceration as a criminal legal strategy in the United States and demonstrates how common the experience of having an incarcerated family member is in this country. In other words, as the authors state, having a family member incarcerated is "a ubiquitous experience in the United States" (Enns et al., 2019, p. 10). How do you think this impacts us as a country? If incarceration is meant to serve as a deterrent to criminal behavior, is it working?

Visitation, Phone Calls, and Mail

The work of Mumola (2000) and Glaze and Maruschak (2010) revealed that most parents incarcerated in state prisons never had a personal visit after their admission. Among women in state prisons, contact by mail (50–66%) and phone (47–54%) is more common than in-person visits (23–24%) on at least a monthly basis (Glaze & Manuschak, 2010; Mumola, 2000). Rabuy and Kopf (2015) further analyzed the 2004 Survey of Inmates in State and Federal Correctional Facilities, identifying the top barrier to in-person visits by family as the distance required for travel to prisons, which are often located in isolated areas without ease of access to public transportation (Eason, 2017). Specifically, over 60% of those individuals in state prisons and over 80% of those in federal prisons are in facilities over 100 miles from their families (Mumola, 2000; Rabuy & Kopf, 2015). Because there are fewer facilities for women, it is particularly likely that women may be more geographically isolated from their families than are men, although women's facilities tend to offer more parent-child programming, video and audio recording, and child-friendly visiting areas (Cramer et al., 2017; Hoffman et al., 2010).

Beyond barriers due to distance and travel costs, Rabuy and Kopf (2015) describe prison visitation as "unnecessarily grueling and frustrating" (p. 1). In different states, prisons vary widely regarding how often visitation is allowed (e.g., once a week versus daily), length of visits, requirements for background checks and fees for visitors, enforcement of visitor dress codes, use of invasive searches of visitors, and displays of affection or emotion permitted during visitation (DeHart et al., 2018; Rabuy & Kopf, 2015). In some situations, non-contact visits may be utilized, allowing incarcerated persons to speak to loved ones across a plexiglass barrier using a handheld phone line, but these practices often lack privacy and can be confusing and traumatic for children (Cramer et al., 2017).

DeHart et al. (2018) conducted focus groups with 77 incarcerated men and women and interviews with 21 of their family members, including parents, spouses, siblings, and children. Both the prisoners and their families described the pain of being emotionally and physically separated from one another, including restrictions on touch during visitation and reduced intimacy of conversation due to privacy concerns on the phone and in person. Family members spoke of traveling long distances to visit, only to be turned away for failure to meet the prison's dress code. One family member even stated that she kept an extra sweater in her car to provide to other visitors when she saw that they were not going to be in compliance with requirements for longer sleeves to enter the prison. Both prisoners and families described changes to their family communication patterns that resulted from incarceration. For instance, prisoners—not wanting to create stress for family members—would hold back information about daily activities and events while incarcerated. They feared conversations that might create conflict with family members, because "they can hang up on you and not answer when you call back" (DeHart et al., 2018, p. 12). Incarcerated men and women avoided wasting conversation and instead tried to "pack meaning in" (DeHart et al., 2018, p. 13). Family members sometimes withheld information from their incarcerated loved one in order to avoid stress. Some of the incarcerated men and women were not told about family deaths, missed funerals, and felt like they were no longer a part of the family.

In some jurisdictions, video visitation has been implemented alongside in-person visits to increase accessibility of communication with loved ones. Cramer and associates (2017), underscoring benefits of visitation for child well-being and reducing recidivism, notes that use of video technology can alleviate some travel costs and may be a familiar interface for youth accustomed to Skype and FaceTime. However, practices vary from one facility to the next, and some facilities have utilized video visitation to supplant rather than supplement in-person contact. There can also be barriers to video conferencing, particularly when visitors must pay fees for video visitation to for-profit companies, when Web-based applications result in poor connection quality, or when visitors are required to drive to the facility (or other off-site locations) to use conferencing equipment (Cramer et al., 2017; Rabuy & Wagner, 2015). Technology for video conferencing is rapidly changing. Many individuals, even some of those living below poverty level, have access to Web-based communication services like Skype or FaceTime. What kinds of changes in policies or equipment would be necessary for jails and prisons to take advantage of these technological advances to increase visitation options?

Phone calls from correctional facilities are notoriously expensive, with some facilities charging over a dollar per minute for in-state calls. This places a burden on incarcerated persons and their loved ones, who must purchase phone cards to cover costs. While the situation has improved with recent caps placed on calls and fees by the Federal Communications Commission, there is notably less progress in county and city jails as opposed to state prisons. One reason for this is that jails may fail to negotiate contracts and sometimes rely on language provided by the contractors. These higher costs for calls can be of particular consequence for those detained, in that calls not only to family, but also to bail bondspersons, defense attorneys, landlords, creditors, and childcare providers may be costly and limited (Wagner & Jones, 2019).

Finally, communication of incarcerated persons with their families, friends, and professionals may be hampered by restrictive policies on mail. To curb drug smuggling in the form of liquids, gels, and powders that can be transferred via paper, many correctional facilities have adopted policies limiting the types of mail that can be received by incarcerated persons. This may include bans on greeting cards, colored paper, and even regular letters written on paper (Norwood, 2019; Prison Policy Initiative, 2013). Some jails, for instance, have postcard-only mail policies, which takes away all privacy of communications and costs more per word written than letters. It may also impede children's printed or drawn communications via mail (Norwood, 2019; Prison Policy Initiative, 2013). Some facilities send mail to outside vendors for scanning and storage, with prisoners only viewing digital copies (Norwood, 2019). Thus, the old adage of sealing a letter with a kiss (or a spray of perfume) is rendered moot. Lawyers have also objected to the practice of these policies, in that they infringe on confidentiality of client-attorney communication (Norwood, 2019). As an aside, these mail policies also affect prisoners' access to books, which are often restricted to particular vendors and/or which disallow books deemed obscene or inflammatory; these often include books on race and those that critique the criminal legal system (Gersten, 2019; Norwood, 2019).

Parenting From Prison

The physical separation of parents from families can have powerful effects on family dynamics and cohesion. Aside from those communication challenges mentioned, DeHart et al. (2018) also heard from incarcerated men and women that their parenting was inalterably compromised. DeHart and associates found that parents spoke of interference from ex-partners and relatives around caregiving for children. Children would be intentionally kept from talking to or visiting the prisoner, as well as being told not to end up a criminal like their mom or dad. Estranged partners and resentful family or friends can run interference as "gatekeepers," intercepting communication between parent and child and resisting efforts to coordinate transportation and accompaniment for visits (Ramirez-Barrett et al., 2006; Robertson, 2007). Even when active interference is not an issue, the costs of travel and communication, as well as the quality of communication via phone and in large group settings, may not support the parental role. For instance, one parent stated, "I end up parenting over speaker phone. I can't discipline 'em. I'm just a voice over the phone" (DeHart et al., 2018, p. 14). Journalist Keri Blakinger (2019), in describing her own time in prison in a Twitter thread, lamented the challenges of meaningful communication with visitors: "It's not just the journey. When your visitor gets to prison, often the visit is just sitting across a barren table for hours. It's so hard to nurture a relationship when all you can do is stare at each other across a table, under the watchful gaze of a guard. … I was grateful for visitors. But I also felt guilty for letting them take up a whole day in transit only to stare at me across a table. Sure, you can talk. But you do run out of shit to say—and this isn't how relationships work on the outside. In the real world, you DO things together, you have experiences in common, you have decisions to make and events to discuss. … It felt so hard to nurture relationships with so little nourishment."

While the quality of parent–child interaction is certainly impacted by incarceration, the very existence of the parent–child relationship may also be threatened. Kennedy (2012) notes that poor women and women of color are disproportionately affected by the intersection of punitive criminal legal policies and child welfare policies on permanence for children, in that women under correctional supervision may risk termination of parental rights because they must rely on relatives or the foster care system to care for children during incarceration. Specifically, federal guidelines limit the amount of time a child may remain in foster care before the state moves to sever parental rights. Further, kinship care may be financially and emotionally overwhelming for family caregivers, resulting in state intervention and, again, risk of terminating parental rights (Kennedy, 2012).

GETTING REAL 7.1

My children are my strength. DSS took them when I was arrested. Then they put them in foster care instead of [with] my family like they were supposed to. I wasn't allowed to contact them, but my family fought for them. …
I gave up my parental rights so that my brother could adopt them. I made mistakes I have to pay for, and I can't provide the home my children need. My brother can. I call once a month, and my family sends pictures.

Karen, White, aged 23. She is in prison for homicide by child abuse and unlawful neglect of a child. She's serving a 30-year sentence plus another 10 concurrently. During her interview, Karen explained her family was living with another family. Everyone had been sick, people were home constantly, and Karen had just had a baby. She was cooking and cleaning and reached a breaking point. The boy spat at her, and she slapped him. He went into a coma and died the next day. Karen had been adopted as a toddler, and when she was 11, her parents sat her and her sister down and explained that she was adopted. Karen took it personally. She had already been depressed and didn't have any friends. She ran away shortly after her parents told her. She figured her real parents didn't want her, so this family might not either. Karen stayed at a friend's house. After 3 days she was tired of it and called home. She got outpatient counseling for 6 or 8 months. She got pregnant and married at 16. Her husband cheated and was physically abusive. He expected her to cook and do anything he wanted. The real down part is when he raped her. She dropped out of school in 10th or 11th grade and has a GED now. Her husband couldn't hold a job, so they moved and moved. They moved in with the other family, and the other lady's husband went to prison on a probation violation. Before the crime, the only other trouble with the law for Karen had been driving without a license.

From state to state, policies differ regarding criteria for determining fitness of the parent to retain rights, including variation in whether courts can consider type of crime committed, length of incarceration, and parental efforts to communicate with children while incarcerated—the latter of which, as we noted, can be impeded by costs, geographic separation, gatekeepers, and other factors. Kennedy argues that these intersecting policies and termination of parental rights function to promote added retribution for the crime rather than help resolve crises facing families and communities.

Impact on Child Delinquency, Education, and Mental Health

Given the conditions described herein, it is not surprising that incarceration of parents may produce tangible impacts on the emotional, cognitive, and behavioral well-being of children. The National Institute of Justice produced a special issue of the *NIJ Journal* devoted to impact of incarceration on dependent children; in that issue, Martin (2017) describes the complexity of findings across a wide range of studies. Challenges of research in this area include differentiating impacts for children of incarcerated fathers versus mothers; in jails versus prisons; for boys versus girls; for children of different ethnic/racial backgrounds, varying ages, and living conditions; and in teasing out impacts of traumatic separation and communication barriers from those associated with changes in homes and caregivers, witnessing arrests and court proceedings, facing social stigma, and other factors. Martin notes, however, that there is substantial evidence that incarceration of a parent may increase risk of child criminal involvement. In a study of delinquent boys, Murray and Farrington (2005) found that parental incarceration conferred risk on children more than separation for other reasons, and that those children who were separated from parents by incarceration experienced more negative outcomes than those whose parents were incarcerated only before the child's birth. Similarly, Aaron and Dallaire (2010) found parental incarceration to predict delinquency outcomes even when accounting for other risk factors. In a meta-analysis of 40 studies that included 7,374 children with incarcerated parents and

37,325 comparison children in 50 samples, Murray et al.(2012) found effects for antisocial behavior to be those that held most consistently across studies. The researchers noted surprisingly little variation attributable to moderators such as child sex, whether mother or father was imprisoned, child age, type of antisocial outcome (e.g., crime or other outcome), or whether the event occurred in the United States. Other outcomes examined thus far have not yielded consistent effects in the literature. Martin's (2017) review identified frequent associations in studies of children's educational attainment and parental incarceration, but Martin states that more research is needed to provide a clear perspective. Murray et al.'s (2012) meta-analysis did not find consistent effects for educational performance or for mental health problems. They noted lack of rigor in many studies and a need for more prospective, longitudinal research.

Impact on Adult Family Members

Parents, siblings, adult children, and extended family also suffer impacts of incarceration. In DeHart et al.'s (2018) qualitative study, prisoners and their family members described effects of their loved ones' incarceration on mental health, physical health, and finances of families. Family members, for instance, spoke of profound hurt, family disruption, isolation and loneliness, and embarrassment. One mother spoke of her son's incarceration, "It's a void. I mean it's a space there that I know that he's supposed to be here, and he's not here" (DeHart et al., 2018, p. 14). Incarcerated men and women described their family members' substance use escalating since the incarceration, "My mom can't stay sober long enough to visit me" (DeHart et al., 2018, p. 15). Having been separated throughout her son's childhood, one incarcerated woman said, "He is not the kind, gentle, little boy I left. He is now a very angry man" (DeHart et al., 2018, p. 15). Family members also described gastrointestinal problems, high blood pressure, and rapid declines in health, which they associated with the stress of their loved one's incarceration. Family finances were affected by loss of income from the incarcerated loved one, having to take over household financial responsibilities, being forced to sell goods or property, and new costs generated by the incarceration (e.g., phone charges, canteen accounts, legal fees).

In a longitudinal study that included 138 mothers of incarcerated sons, Green and associates (2006) found that financial problems and increased burden of grandparenting mediated the relationship between a son's incarceration and his mother's psychological distress. Gueta (2017), examining 10 qualitative studies, suggests that parents of prisoners experience a kind of "imprisonment by association" (p. 767), manifest through the need to parent their incarcerated child from a distance, the burden of this caregiving, troubled parental identity due to the crimes of their children, and stigmatized social reactions to their child's incarceration. Guerta also discusses the ambiguous loss prevalent among family members impacted by incarceration, in that these family members experience substantial grief over the non-death loss of a loved one. Guerta also noted that some family members experience relief associated with incarceration when it alleviates concerns about a wayward offspring's well-being, as well as anxiety surrounding impending release from incarceration—both findings also present in DeHart et al.'s (2018) study. Thus, it is clear that families experience stress in response to their family member's incarceration. In some cases, they are concerned for the safety and well-being of their offspring, but in many cases, incarceration impairs their relationships, negatively impacts their health, and exposes them to negative reactions in their communities.

Impacts on Communities

Just as incarceration of a loved one may create a void in a family, it also may create a void in communities when persons are removed from neighborhoods and social networks. Todd Clear (2009) describes how those who are left behind in communities must take substantial efforts to either (a) maintain the social tie with their incarcerated loved one, or (b) learn to live without the resources/support that the incarcerated person previously provided. He has conducted studies demonstrating the destabilizing force that high levels of incarceration can exert on communities, weakening social ties, impacting labor markets, and disrupting families (Clear, 2009; Clear et al., 2001). As individuals move in and out of correctional facilities and back into communities, high-need returning citizens may require significant social and instrumental resources; they may also be distrusted by community members and business owners and be viewed as a source of stigma to communities (Clear et al., 2001). Particularly in high-incarceration communities, increased prison admissions may ultimately have an effect of increasing rather than decreasing crime (Clear, 2009; Clear et al., 2003).

DeHart et al.(2018), using in-person and phone interviews with families of incarcerated persons, found that family members described ways in which incarceration disrupted their social networks, with friends and community members shunning them after their loved one's incarceration.

Some family members self-isolated in order to avoid intrusive questions, and some felt hostility from former friends and from neighbors. In communities from which substantial percentages of residents are incarcerated, this may contribute to community-level stress that feeds into further incarceration via a variety of mechanisms (e.g., mental disorders, substance use, punitive policy and enforcement).

Von Hoffmann (2015) describes studies using rigorous epidemiological methods to examine impact of incarceration on communities. One study (Hatzenbuehler et al., 2015) found that, even after controlling for individual- and neighborhood-level factors (e.g., demographics, trauma exposure, violent crime rates), persons living in high-incarceration neighborhoods experienced more depressive and anxiety disorders than those in other neighborhoods. Another study (Kakade et al., 2012) posited that incarceration risk may be propagated through social networks, with incarceration being self-perpetuating in communities. Specifically, harsher sentences may have impacts that ripple through communities, impacting residents throughout.

Another impact of incarceration on communities occurs not in those communities from which incarcerated persons are removed, but in those where people are incarcerated. In his book, *Big House on the Prairie: The Rise of the Rural Ghetto and Prison Proliferation,* Eason (2017) describes geographic and demographic factors associated with prison building. He notes that prisons are often constructed in rural Southern towns with higher proportions of Blacks and Latinx, and that Southern towns are 12 times more likely to receive a prison than Midwestern or Northeastern towns. Yet, while persons of color may be a majority in such towns, they are often underrepresented in positions of power. While prisons are often constructed with support from townspeople and an expectation of bringing impoverished communities a "second chance" in the face of adversity, the actual impacts of having a prison in a community are complex. For instance, prisons may bring employment, but often those employed at a prison choose to live outside the community. Persons incarcerated in prisons are counted in the local population—something which apportions more resources to the prison community while removing resources from the incarcerated person's home community. Often, communities' expectations of gains from the prison may not be borne out in reality. Other times, these gains (e.g., in electoral representation) may come at the expense of prisoners and their home communities (e.g., prisoners are counted as residents of the prison community but usually cannot vote while incarcerated; NPR, 2019).

SUMMARY

A majority of those who are incarcerated have minor children who are impacted by that incarceration, with the most consistent documented outcome being children at increased risk of engaging in antisocial behavior. Further, it is not just the minor children of prisoners who are affected by the incarceration; parents, grandparents, siblings, and other family members are also affected. In short, substantial portions of persons in the general population have experienced the incarceration of a loved one. The separation of individuals who are incarcerated from their families is exacerbated by restrictive policies on visitation as well as high costs of phone calls, video visitation, and mail services. Geographic location of prisons also often presents a barrier to family cohesion, and prisons can create a range of impacts for communities. Impacts on delinquency, mental health, physical health, and finances can spill over into communities via weight on resources for social services, juvenile courts, schools, behavioral health, and primary care providers. Thus, impacts of incarceration spread beyond the incarcerated person to influence well-being of children, families, and entire communities.

DISCUSSION QUESTIONS

1. Are you surprised by findings suggesting as many as 40 to 60% of individuals, depending on race/ethnicity and education, have experienced having a family member incarcerated in the United States? What does that suggest about our criminal legal system?
2. How does incarceration of a parent impact their children? Who do children live with most often? What are the barriers to contact with their parent?
3. This chapter identifies many barriers to communication between incarcerated individuals and their families. What are your thoughts about the cost of calls or the refusal of visitors based on dress codes? What is the role of systemic policies in creating or decreasing barriers for communication between incarcerated individuals and family members?

CHAPTER EIGHT

Practice and Policy Implications at Detention and Incarceration

Introduction

In this chapter, we draw on the sequential intercept model as a framework for interventions in court-based and corrections settings. These include strategies used post-arrest in initial detention and court hearings as well as those for persons in specialty courts, jails, and prisons. Examples include bail and financial penalty reforms, use of holistic defense strategies, mental health screening, post-arrest diversion programs, trauma-informed correctional practices, use of peer navigators, alternatives to incarceration, and justice reinvestment. The interventions and policy reforms discussed here are not without controversy; as we discussed in Chapter 4, there are strong arguments toward transformative systemic reform, and some argue that focusing on refinements to the current system masks deeper social and systemic problems surrounding mass incarceration. Here, we have attempted to address a range of strategies so that these may be considered in layered and incremental approaches that provide some remediation of current conditions in the short term without losing sight of the longer-term goal of decarceration and reimagining criminal legal responses.

Bail Practices, Screening, and Diversion at Intercept 2

As we discussed in the introduction, intercept 2 of sequential intercept model focuses on initial detention and preliminary hearings (Munetz & Griffin, 2006). At this stage, a number of factors determine whether an individual will become further enmeshed in the criminal legal system, and several of these factors offer opportunities for legal reform or service intervention at intercept 2. In Chapter 5, we discussed the centrality of money bail in whether someone is detained. Of those arrested, charged, and booked, about 24% are released without financial conditions and 4% are held and denied bail. The remainder (72%) are released only if they pay money bail. About half of these people pay—sometimes at great expense beyond the price of bail itself, via use of a bail bondsperson. The remainder are incarcerated simply because they cannot afford to pay the price (Reaves, 2013). Accordingly, there is a growing movement toward bail reform. These reforms vary across jurisdictions, with some courts considering what the defendant is able to pay prior to setting bail. Other courts have eliminated bail for specific low-level crimes (e.g., selected drug and property offenses, prostitution), and some courts have done away with bail completely. Those who wish to stop the practice of money bail argue that any use of bail creates differential outcomes for those who can versus cannot pay, thereby allowing those with means to walk free and criminalizing others. Civil rights groups have presented legal challenges to money bail, arguing that bail systems are unconstitutional (e.g., violating due process and equal protection under the law), and some courts have ruled in their favor. Lawmakers have also enacted reforms in some states. Prosecutors can also use their power to advocate for bail reform, including use of early screening of cases as well as working toward the presumption that release should be recommended unless otherwise indicated (Brand & Pishko, 2018).

But how should courts decide who should be detained to serve the public interest? The American Bar Association approved a resolution that governments should favor release without money bonds, unless the courts determine that these financial conditions are the only type of conditions that will assure appearance in court; the resolution further states that no one should ever be detained solely based on their inability to pay (Brand & Pishko, 2018). Further, among the general public, about two-thirds of people believe that an individual should be released from jail before their trial as long as they are a low risk for committing a crime and are likely to show up for the trial (Kelly, 2017). Risk assessments are one method for determining whether detention is necessary. Risk assessments, however, have been criticized as overly reliant on past criminal history in that using criminal legal data as a proxy for crime, these tools may perpetuate racial disparities that result from over-policing and over-charging of crimes for communities of color (Glazer et al., 2017). Thus, if risk-assessment tools are used to determine whether someone is detained, the tool itself should not be the sole determinant, but rather a resource to be used in conjunction with careful deliberation. Arnold Ventures, with the National Partnership for Pre-Trial Justice (2020), has provided funding and development for public safety assessment measures that are intended to avoid reifying or exacerbating racial disparities in the criminal legal system. The Public Safety Assessment (PSA, available at psapre-trial.org) uses factors such as age, convictions, pending charges, and prior failures to appear in court to determine (a) whether there is a risk for new criminal activity and (b) whether there is a risk of failure to appear in court. The tool should be used within a broader decision framework and coordinated with local stakeholders to reflect local statutes, court rules, and policy orientations. Studies thus far have indicated that the PSA—when used along with other aspects of system reform—may be associated with decreased use of cash bail and increased pre-trial release without increasing new arrests, missed court dates, or racial disparities.

Gehring and Van Voorhis (2014) have noted that the focus of agencies on risk may preclude opportunities to identify needs. Certain types of needs, like severe mental illness or substance use disorders, may actually contribute to recidivism or to failure to appear in court. Such needs may take on heightened importance in working with women. There is considerable support for using mental health screenings in the early stages of legal processing in order to identify mental disorders. This can be done during court stages and is absolutely essential if individuals will be detained for any length of time (thus spanning intercepts 2 and 3). Mental health screens—in conjunction with crisis intervention, referral, and treatment—are crucial to meeting the legal mandate of correctional facilities to provide mental health care for incarcerated persons (Ford et al., 2007). Screens can be administered by non-clinical staff at booking and detention to identify serious issues that might require immediate attention (Policy Research Associates, 2017). How do you think screening policies are developed for different jurisdictions? One of the authors of this book lives in Idaho where the state legislature mandated that county assessments must be "free of bias" (HB No. 118, section 19-1910) as of July 2019. How much variation do you think there is in screening practices across our country?

Screening can contribute to suicide prevention, assure that the individual receives appropriate continuing care (e.g., medications), and help identify problems that may require additional non-emergency services (Scott, 2010). Martin and associates (2013) review a number of different screening tools that can be used in jails and prisons. The Correctional Mental Health Screen (Ford & Trestman, 2005), for instance, has an eight-item version for women that can be administered by correctional officers in less than 5 minutes. In accord with the sequential intercept model's recommended approach, mental health screening should be systematic and mandatory at intercept 2, with persons identified as having mental health issues being diverted to treatment, sometimes as a condition of deferred prosecution, sentencing, or probation (Policy Research Associates, 2017).

Aside from the recommended universal screening, periodic re-screening of incarcerated persons is also wise to identify any emergent or worsening conditions. Additional information on mental health of incarcerated persons is sometimes available from other sources, such as prior incarceration records, transfer documents, arrest reports, probation officers, or family and friends (Drapkin, 2009). The sequential intercept model underscores the need for data partnerships for sharing important health data between correctional facilities and community-based providers (Policy Research Associates, 2017). To address the needs of persons with mental disorders, it is extremely important that correctional staff be trained on issues of confidentiality of health data, as well as have basic education around interpersonal aspects of screening administration and an awareness of mental disorders and trauma among incarcerated women and girls. DeHart and Iachini (2019) have developed free online training materials on mental health of incarcerated persons and correctional officers, Mental Health in the Correctional System: Making Choices for Safety and Wellbeing (available at cmhtraining.sc.edu); the training is adaptable and can be integrated into existing training programs for correctional officers. For child-serving organizations, including juvenile justice settings, the Substance Abuse and Mental Health Services Administration (SAMHSA, 2012) has developed a resource guide that includes precautions and a listing of screening tools for serious mental illness, substance use disorders, trauma, and suicidality.

While screening for mental health and substance use are key, there are also more comprehensive screening instruments suitable for use from courts through later stages of processing. Krista Gehring and Patricia Van Voorhis (2014) developed an inventory to assess a range of needs for defendants. The Gender-Informed Needs Assessment (GINA) is a tool measuring residential stability and homelessness, family support, education, employment, finances, abuse and trauma, mental health, and substance use. It is typically used in conjunction with a risk assessment, and it allows staff to connect women to services and interventions, if the women wish to use these services. The GINA is the only assessment that takes gender into account, and the researchers identified distinct differences in the composition of needs for women versus men involved in the criminal legal system. Their research indicated that pre-trial needs were important in predicting outcomes of new arrests and failure to appear. For instance, gender-neutral needs like employment and finances, education, and substance use predicted new arrests for both men and women. These factors, plus mental health and homelessness, also predicted failure to appear in court. Abuse was an important predictor of both new arrests and failure to appear in court for women but not for men (Gehring & Van Voorhis, 2014). Researcher Krista Gehring indicated that in the first year of use of the GINA by Salt Lake County courts, addressing defendant needs improved pre-trial "success" rates from 30 to 48%, with those defendants who were at higher risk levels actually achieving greater success (K. Gehring, personal communication, January 7, 2020).

Assessing and addressing needs in this way is the central focus of a practice called holistic defense. Holistic defense services are those that address legal and nonlegal challenges in defendants' lives through provision of social services, with the intent to prevent individuals from becoming deeply enmeshed in the criminal legal system as well as to reduce collateral consequences of legal involvement (Giovani, 2012; National Legal Aid Defenders Association (NLADA), 2008). These practices are also sometimes termed holistic representation, client-centered advocacy, community-oriented defense, or comprehensive representation (Giovani, 2012) and are often carried out in partnership with public defenders' offices, circuit courts, or organizations that assist in defense of indigent persons. Holistic defense practices often involve social workers co-located in defense offices; these providers conduct assessments of needs in defendants' lives (e.g., treatment, housing, employment), link persons in need to community services, and examine suitability of diversion programs. What resources are necessary for programs like holistic defense programs? Are there corrections or court practices we could limit or eliminate to reallocate funds for programs like this?

Specialty Courts and Corrections Programming at Intercept 3

Intercept 3 of the sequential intercept model focuses on specialty courts, dispositional courts, and correctional settings (particularly jails, given that the model is intended to prevent individuals from becoming more deeply involved in the system) (Munetz & Griffin, 2006). Specialty courts are intended to address underlying problems that lead to involvement in the criminal legal system. Individuals are provided with the option to have their case handled in a specialty court, through which they may participate in services for the opportunity to have their sanctions reduced or eliminated. The courts typically have specialized staff and dedicated dockets, and service diversion may result in outcomes such as dismissed charges and sealed records (Lustbader, 2020; Scholars Strategy Network, 2016).

There are several types of specialty courts. Treatment courts include those such as mental health courts, drug courts, and homelessness courts; these provide service options to address serious mental illness, substance use, housing instability, and other factors that may be criminogenic (Lustbader, 2020). Accountability courts emphasize accountability for specific types of offenses. For instance, domestic violence courts might connect offenders to batterer intervention programs, while community courts focus on single neighborhood and on "quality-of-life crimes" such as shoplifting, graffiti, illegal vending, and prostitution (Bocanegra, 2017; Lang, 2011; Lustbader, 2020). Status courts address the needs of specific populations, including veterans' courts and girls' courts (Lustbader, 2020). Girls' courts, for instance, are informed by the unique needs, risks, pathways, and experiences of girls involved in the legal system, with the intent of creating a more gender-responsive, relationally guided system for girls (Curtis & Nadon, 2018); the courts may adopt a non-adversarial approach to promote public safety and due process, while offering and monitoring service access for trauma-informed care, substance use and recovery services, mental health treatment, and family engagement (Rubin, 2014).

GETTING REAL 8.1

Every time I was caught, they just threw me in jail and didn't ask any questions. A person's drug usage should be known—that's where half the crimes out there are coming from, and they (the authorities) know that. I made it known that I was on drugs—I told the judge that's why I robbed the place. Then they just put me in here and put me on more drugs (medications).

Chantelle is a Black woman, aged 24, who is in prison for a probation violation on her old armed robbery charge. When she violated, she had three pending armed robbery charges. They sentenced her to concurrent terms for a 5-year sentence. Chantelle thinks it's all due to crack. Her dad had been real abusive while she was growing up, and she was sexually abused by her uncle. Chantelle's parents started smoking it when she was 9. It got rough—she didn't know where her next meal was coming from, if she'd have clean clothes, and people were in and out of the house all the time. Things would go missing out of the house—the VCR, TV, even the washer dryer when they pawned it. There was also sexual abuse when her parents would take money, car keys, or whatever and let men have sex with Chantelle. Chantelle moved in with a 19-year-old dealer when she was 12. Her mother was murdered when Chantelle was 13. Within 3 or 4 months, Chantelle started smoking crack. Her aunt tried to get custody of her, but Chantelle kept running away. She wanted that high—nothing or nobody mattered. At age 17, she did her first felony—armed robbery. She turned 18 in prison. Her state of mind got even worse there. She did drugs inside, and she knew when she got out that she was going to get high. She maxed out her sentence and stayed clean for 15 days; then she was back at it again.

Specialty courts have been growing in use across the United States, but the courts do face some challenges. Critics have suggested that the courts are not fully "voluntary," in that defendants may feel that they have little choice but to participate if they want to access services or be perceived favorably within the system. This can undermine autonomy and result in coercive treatment like that discussed in Chapter 7 (Lustbader, 2020; Scholars Strategy Network, 2016). Further, the evidence supporting the effectiveness of these courts is limited. As voluntary programs administered by the courts, there may be selection biases in who is viewed as eligible to enroll and who chooses to participate. These potential biases make it difficult to determine whether success is due to participation or other pre-existing factors (Scholars Strategy Network, 2016). For some types of courts, like drug courts that have been in existence longer, rigorous experimental designs have supported efficacy of the courts in reducing future crime and contributing to cost savings in the long run (Scholars Strategy Network, 2016). Other courts, such as girls' courts, have shown success in reducing recidivism and increasing prosocial relationships (Davidson et al., 2011), but the body of research is less comprehensive. The courts do have appeal with judges and participants (Bocanegra, 2017; Lustbader, 2020; Scholars Strategy Network, 2016), potentially heightening perceptions of procedural justice for those involved. Yet, some argue that the proliferation of these courts may be taking the focus off a very real problem with the system that has criminalized social problems and overpoliced communities of color (Bocanegra, 2017; Lustbader, 2020).

Another consideration regarding services that are compelled by the courts involves costs. Recall in Chapter 5 that we discussed legal financial obligations, including costly treatment services, fines and fees, and pay community supervision. As bail reform, diversion programs, and specialty courts become more common, we should not lose sight of the costs that may be incurred for participants in such programs—particularly for indigent participants. Also, a consideration at the disposition stage of processing are monetary sanctions, which may be imposed along with other court requirements. Harris (2016) suggests a number of policy guidelines to ensure that the priority is on justice for victims and that punitive financial obligations do not create insurmountable debt for defendants. She recommends that (a) only defendants with ability to pay are sentenced to non-restitution sanctions, (b) state statutes define "indigent" and "current ability to pay" clearly, (c) only those with financial resources and incomes other than state/federal benefits are eligible for monetary sanctions, and (d) collection costs and interest are not applied to outstanding debt.

Finally, individuals who are incarcerated may also be in need of service interventions. At intercept 3, corrections-based treatment for mental health, trauma, and substance use may be warranted. For women, programs that address all of these issues may be particularly beneficial. For instance, the Trauma, Addiction, Mental Health, and Recovery (TAMAR) program is intended for incarcerated adults with histories of physical or sexual abuse, mental disorders, and substance abuse. The program consists of 20 sessions, providing trauma education to those who are incarcerated; the program also introduces corrections staff and community providers to trauma-informed principles (Policy Research Associates (PRA), 2012). Seeking Safety is a model that works with individuals or groups to help persons attain safety from trauma and/or substance abuse. It can be delivered by peers or professionals and does not require participants to disclose trauma narratives. It is also flexible regarding number of required sessions, the order of sessions is flexible or modular, and it has been used with a variety of populations, including incarcerated women (Lynch et al., 2012). Seeking Safety focuses on coping skills, integrated treatment of trauma and substance use, and addressing cognitive, behavioral, and interpersonal aspects of well-being. It has strong research support in addressing both PTSD and substance abuse (Najavits & Hien, 2013; Treatment Innovations, 2019). What obligation do corrections facilities have to provide treatment to incarcerated individuals? Many states have been sued for failing to provide appropriate, necessary treatment to prisoners. How might we convince policy makers and individuals who make county and state funding decisions that these types of programs are necessary?

Another promising corrections-based program is use of peer-support specialists to serve as a positive role model while providing support to incarcerated persons. These specialists can be trained in correctional settings or in the community, and they assist as individuals attempt to change negative attitudes and behaviors to engage in mental health or substance use treatment. In some programs, the specialists also provide resources on housing, employment, and educational opportunities (PRA, 2012).

In Massachusetts, Framingham prison implemented a peer support program that included a 2-day training for peer specialists, who then provided services in the facility via office hours, on-call hours, or on request. Peer support specialists received monthly supervision, individual support, and incentives for their work (Korn et al., 2015). Wellness self-management is an educational and skills training that has been used in New York state prisons to help incarcerated persons develop coping skills and social skills as well as manage mental disorders. The program involves 40 sessions on topics such as stress, substance use, recovery, building supports, proper medication use, reducing relapse, and self-advocacy (PRA, 2012). These programs all demonstrate promise for building skills and independence of incarcerated women, although the length and structure of some programs makes then better suited to prison settings than to jails.

Trauma-Informed Correctional Practices

When individuals are incarcerated or committed to secure facilities, universal precautions are recommended to prevent re-traumatization and reduce the likelihood of worsening mental health conditions. Such precautions may help incarcerated persons self-regulate psychologically and physically, become more stable and less likely to be triggered, and become more able to safely engage in programs and services. Such environments may also enhance job satisfaction and retention of correctional staff (Benedict, 2014). Women's facilities, in particular, have been implementing trauma-informed correctional practices to help alleviate some of the more depersonalizing and traumatizing aspects of incarceration. Training corrections staff on mental health and trauma is a key part of creating a trauma-informed setting, and programs like TAMAR and the online Mental Health in the Correctional System curriculum (both previously described) can be helpful in this respect. Trauma-informed correctional practices center around principles of safety, trust, choice, collaboration, and empowerment. While it may seem counter-intuitive to think of these concepts within a corrections setting, small adjustments to procedures can make a substantial difference to those who spend their daily lives in these facilities. Examples of trauma-informed strategies that can be employed by correctional staff include allowing choices (e.g., where to sit within a safe, secure space), using a tone of voice and pace of speaking that encourages relaxation, using nonthreatening body postures that are supportive and convey safety, and avoiding language that conveys control (e.g., instead of referring to "cells" or "shakedowns," using "rooms" or "safety checks"). Rather than referring to incarcerated persons as inmates and calling them by last names, titles of respect can be used to promote trust ("Ms. Smith"). During sensitive procedures such as pat-downs and searches, correctional officers may reduce trauma by telling the incarcerated person what is going to happen and why, reassuring the woman that the procedure will be conducted in a way that maximizes her safety, asking if she has any questions before the procedure begins, and using verbal cues throughout the procedure (e.g., "I'm going to place the items on the table")—just as a doctor typically does with a patient during sensitive procedures. Afterward, the officer may ask the woman how she is doing and thank her for her cooperation (Benedict, 2014). These procedures are at aimed at increasing women's physical and emotional safety.

Within trauma-informed environments, verbal de-escalation should be used as the first option when there is a conflict. This means that officers should use physical or chemical restraints only as a last resort after all less restrictive measures have been exhausted. When these are used, they should be used only for as long as needed to gain control and never used for punitive or disciplinary purposes (Drapkin, 2009). Restrictive housing—removing the incarcerated person from the general population and placing her in a locked cell for the majority of the day—should not be used at all for low-level offenses. Incarcerated persons should be housed in the least restrictive setting necessary to ensure safety, and specific reasons for placement in more restrictive settings should be documented. These placements should allow enhanced opportunities in the cell (e.g., reading), out-of-cell time for activities, and regular review of the placement to determine when it is no longer necessary (Human Resources Watch (HRW), 2015; U.S. Department of Justice (DOJ), 2016).

Family Visitation Practices

Cramer and associates (2017) suggest a number of improvements to support parent-child visitation in jails and prisons, citing the importance of such visitation for reducing stress, enhancing connection, and promoting emotional security. By embedding parent-child visitation practices within a broader family-strengthening program, parents, primary caregivers, and children can be educated regarding the importance of visits and may participate in these visits with accompanying therapy and coaching around contact and goal setting. These authors provide numerous examples of successful programs, including those for extended visitation of family members in on-site mobile homes, nursery programs that allow infants to spend several months with their mothers, child-friendly visitation rooms that are decorated and include toys and play areas, and wraparound services for mothers and children. In addition to therapeutic support, material supports such as transportation and childcare can improve accessibility of visitation for families. Further, correctional staff should be trained on the challenges families face during visitation as well as in techniques for communicating with children in age-appropriate ways (Cramer et al., 2017). Dehumanizing visitation policies, including strip and dog searches of visitors, should be ended, and for-profit and/or overly restrictive communication practices should be reduced and should not be used as replacements for in-person visits (Prison Policy Initiative (PPI), 2013; Rabuy & Kopf, 2015). To reduce phone costs, state prisons might be compelled to negotiate communications contracts that allow county jails to opt in to the state contract's terms (Wagner & Jones, 2019). The General Assembly of the Commonwealth of Pennsylvania (2011) further suggests scheduling phone calls based on availability of children and custodial caregivers, encouraging schools to provide report cards to incarcerated parents, and encouraging family-group conferencing for reentry planning. Because incarceration carries impacts across generations and among extended family, Gueta (2017) recommends development of multigenerational and multifamily groups for support and education. Researchers and administrators can also inform family visitation by improving data collection and analyses to better understand impacts of frequency, duration, and type of visitation on prisoner and family wellbeing (Cramer et al., 2017). Legislators and courts can make efforts to prohibit use of the statutory timeline to parental rights termination for incarcerated parents and to remove nonviolent incarceration from consideration in parental rights termination procedures (Kennedy, 2012). The San Francisco Partnership for Incarcerated Parents (2003) has published a Children of Incarcerated Parents Bill of Rights that addresses essential components of children's rights regarding their parents' incarceration. Examples include the right to be kept safe and informed regarding arrest, to be heard when decisions are made about the child, to speak with and touch the parent, to be supported around the parent's incarceration, and to have a lifelong relationship with the parent.

Transforming Justice

There is growing support for criminal legal reforms that will reduce incarceration and look to alternative ways to address social problems. Rabuy and Kopf (2015) argue that prison should be used only as a last resort (i.e., for threats to public safety) in cases involving caregivers of minor children, with alternatives like community custody being utilized instead. These authors also suggest sentencing and parole reforms—rather than prison expansion—be considered when facility overcrowding is an issue. Additional strategies include reducing the number of jail-able offenses via use of probation or other tactics to address low-level offenses (e.g., fare evasion, low-level marijuana offenses) and avoiding use of incarceration for technical violations (Jones, 2019). Ghandnoosh (2017) details strategies for shortening prison sentences. One example is establishing an upper limit on the length of prison sentences so that persons are not serving excessive sentences that amount to being sentenced to die in prison. Such reforms have been successfully implemented abroad, and some suggest caps of 20 years for any prison sentence. Other examples include reforming parole decisions so that these are based more on public safety risk and less on political considerations, as well as implementing compassionate release of medically infirm or elderly prisoners.

In 2019, the Stoneleigh Foundation and the Maternity Care Coalition (2019) brought together stakeholders to examine multigenerational impacts of incarceration on women, girls, and communities. These organizations released an executive summary, with recommendations including eliminating cash bail from pregnant women and parenting mothers, including medication-assisted therapy and home visitation programs as diversion options, stopping the detention of girls for their own safety when the offense is not a risk to the public, leveraging youth services to fight homelessness, and increasing use of restorative justice options. Indeed, restorative justice—with its focus on accountability rather than punishment—has gained popularity among reformers. Danielle Sered developed the organization Common Justice as an alternative to incarceration and victim service program addressing violent felonies in adult courts. She posits that our central focus on incarceration, including seeking alternatives to incarceration, limits our potential to see more transformative options for addressing harms and needs in society. In The Appeal Podcast, "Imagining a Post-Incarceration World" (Sered & Johnson, 2019), she describes how prison takes away the dignity and resources that individuals need to cognitively and emotionally process what they have done, own up to the harms they have caused, and take responsibility for addressing the crime's impacts on victims and communities. She advocates for transformative approaches that go beyond simple restorative justice to work outside of the existing criminal legal system to find solutions. Community-led solutions, investing in communities hardest hit by crime and social injustice (including prevention, intervention, and family reunification), and reduced reliance on incarceration and community supervision may help to alleviate collateral consequences of crime and incarceration for families and communities (Bocanegra, 2017; James, 2019).

SUMMARY

There are a number of reforms that can be implemented in the courts to reduce mass incarceration and to more humanely address the harms and needs stemming from criminal or delinquent activity. Bail reform is essential to reducing racial and class-based disparities in incarceration. Identifying risk and needs assessment instruments that do not reify or exacerbate racial disparities is also important to prevent further enmeshment in the justice system, particularly for those with substance use disorders or severe mental illness. Screening for a range of needs (e.g., mental health, health, housing, employment) is becoming more common within holistic defense programs. To reduce re-traumatization and assure that mental health needs are identified and addressed, correctional staff—including frontline officers—should be trained on issues of mental health, trauma, screening, confidentiality, and crisis intervention. Specialty courts should undergo rigorous evaluation to determine efficacy of these in reducing re-offending, meeting treatment needs, and preventing individuals from penetrating further into the criminal legal system. Trauma-informed practices and treatment programs for incarcerated women and girls can assist in addressing underlying criminogenic issues such as past victimization and substance abuse. Facilities might also implement family-friendly policies for visitation and communications. Finally, we need to examine restorative and transformative approaches that move away from incarceration and build community resources, including those for prevention and intervention.

DISCUSSION QUESTIONS

1. How can screening practices influence women's and girls' experiences during pre-trial detention and incarceration?
2. You read that the American Bar Association, which is an organization of attorneys, approved a resolution that governments should favor release without money bonds in several instances. How do you understand the arguments about assessing an individual's ability to pay bond fees or bail? What are your thoughts about a broader implementation of policies that eliminate fees for individuals if their

crimes are less severe or based in part on their ability to pay? How might these changes impact our system?

3. This chapter describes multiple types of specialty courts such as mental health courts, drug courts, and courts for veterans or girls. Have you been exposed to specialty courts? Are there some in your area? What are the pros and cons of these types of courts from your perspective? What types of jurisdictions do you think can offer these types of courts and programs?

SECTION III

REENTRY INTO COMMUNITIES

It is clear that women and girls experience many challenges during the reentry process. In a recent review of women's recidivism over several years, the Bureau of Justice Statistics (Alper, Dursose, & Markman, 2018) reported 35% of women were rearrested within the first year after their release. Similarly, the federal Office for Juvenile Justice and Delinquency Prevention (2017) estimates about 55% of youth are rearrested within one year of release. The first chapter in this section provides an overview of the nature of the challenges that women and girls face and common barriers to successful reentry, such as difficulties with transportation, returning to school, or finding employment, as well as continued substance dependence. We also recognize that stable housing, employment, and positive social support are associated with better outcomes. We note that ongoing substance use represents one of the strongest risks for recidivism and that women of color who use substances are at increased risk of recidivism. Black and Latinx women are also more likely to have difficulty obtaining fulltime employment. We end this chapter by asking you to consider the ways in which current policies—such as those regulating occupational licensing, child custody, access to governmental support programs, and services—impact women, girls, and their communities.

The second chapter discusses recent research on best practices and policies to support women's and girls' reenty. In this final chapter, we again draw on the the sequential intercept model to identify points of intervention and recommend evidence-based intervention strategies, including reentry transition planning, service coordination, and the use of specialized probation and parole officers. We dicuss the Assessing, Planning, Identifying, and Coordinating (APIC) model (SAMHSA, 2017), that outlines four steps to enhance reentry success: (1) assess needs and risks, (2) plan for treatment, (3) identify where/how services can be accessed, and (4) coordinate transition to ensure timely access. This model and other best practices we describe in this chapter emphasize coordination of care to decrease gaps in services and barriers to women's and girls' success. In addition, the models and programs described in this chapter utilize collaborative, culturally competent, and trauma-informed approaches. Across both of these chapters, we illustrate how women and girls are affected by their interactions with family members and supervision officers, as well as how structural barriers affect reentry via social policies and regulations enacted at the level of a city, county, or state.

CHAPTER NINE

Challenges of Reentry Into Communities

Introduction

This chapter addresses challenges of reentry, including reengagement with families and communities, negotiating supervision/treatment requirements amid siloed services (e.g., childcare, substance abuse treatment), and securing housing, education, and employment. Particular attention is devoted to how these competing demands exacerbate the collateral consequences of criminal conviction and how these challenges may be further intensified by ongoing traumatization and marginalized status.

Recidivism Rates

In 2018, the Bureau of Justice Statistics released a report examining recidivism rates over 9 years for individuals released from prisons in 30 states (Alper et al., 2018). Recidivism was measured by an arrest, conviction or return to prison after release from prison (see Figure 9.1). The BJS reported that 83% or five of every six individuals released in 2005 were re-arrested by 2014. Almost half (44%) were re-arrested within the first year post-release. On average, these persons were arrested about five times between 2005 and 2014. For women specifically, 77% were re-arrested within the 9-year period with more than one-third (35%) re-arrested in the first year post-release. Similarly, although national recidivism rates for juvenile offenders are not available, summaries across studies suggest 55% of youth are rearrested within one year (OJJDP, 2017). In sum, most persons were not successful in their attempts to reintegrate back into the community.

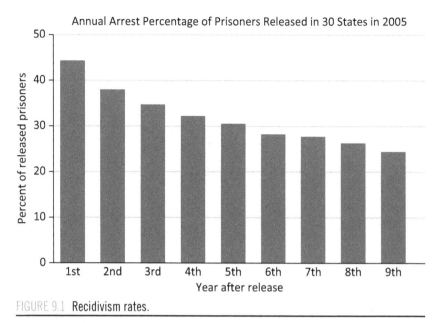

FIGURE 9.1 Recidivism rates.

Note: The denominator for annual percent is 401,288 (total state prisoners released in 30 states in 2005). See table 5 for estimates and appendix table 7 standard errors.

Source: Bureau of Justice Statistics, Recidivism of State Prisoners Released in 2005 data collection, 2005–2014.

Research with larger samples of incarcerated women have identified some protective factors that increase the likelihood of successful reentry. For example, in a study with 506 women by Huebner and colleagues (2010), women who completed high school and who had stable mental health were less likely to recidivate. In addition, women who were mothers of dependent children were less likely to return to prison. Makarios et al. (2010) examined predictors of recidivism among men and women and found that stable employment was similarly associated with greater reentry success, while lack of stable housing, unemployment, and less than high school education were associated with recidivism for both men and women. There is a growing body of research that illustrates the availability of resources and services in one's community, nature of one's support system, and extent of economic disadvantage are strong predictors of recidivism.

Risks for Recidivism

Women face many of the same challenges post-release from incarceration that they struggled with prior to incarceration. They frequently encounter barriers finding employment and housing, obtaining transportation, accessing physical and mental health care and substance use treatment, and locating affordable childcare (Guastafero & Lutgen, 2018).

GETTING REAL 9.1

Because of my DUI, I got a suspended driver's license for 3 years starting the day I got out of prison. ... I can't even get a permit to get back and forth to places—to work, to classes, to grocery shopping, to doctor's appointments— and so I'm relying on other people.

Tammy is an American Indian, aged 27. She got her GED, was working full time prior to her arrest, and living with her three children. Tammy explains she went to prison because she became an alcoholic. She started to drink because everyone around her was drinking; it was the cool thing to do, but then it became a necessity for her. She has been to prison three times but this last time she really got sober, and she doesn't want that life anymore. We interviewed Tammy when she was back in the community and asked about what services she needs to be successful. Because she had three DUIs in a short period, her license was suspended. Tammy has to ask for help to go anywhere, and she thinks some type of transportation services to help her get to appointments would really help. She lives in a snowy, rural place where it is hard to ride her bike to get around, and she is pregnant. Her friends and family do help her out, but she always has to ask. She thinks her aftercare group for substance use is boring and not so helpful, but she is going to try out a new church soon. Tammy feels like she has learned how to see the signs of a violent partner and is better about ending things now; she doesn't put up with that crap. She doesn't like her baby's daddy's lifestyle, but she is letting him stay in her life for the baby. Tammy also acknowledged she doesn't tell people about stressful events now or in her past. She just walls it up, and she should probably go to talk to a counselor. She feels really cold and turned off since her mom died. She can't cry. She is worried about relapsing.

It is critical to understand that a barrier in one area, such as transportation, often leads to difficulties in other areas, such as keeping a job or accessing healthcare. For example, car ownership is a better predictor of obtaining or keeping work than education or previous work experience among low-income women (Bohmert, 2018). Next, physical and mental health problems often make accomplishing tasks like securing housing and employment more difficult. Visher and Bakken (2014) note that women offenders with mental health problems tend to have more difficulty finding employment and housing than those without health problems. In addition, scholars have focused on how neighborhood context, specifically neighborhoods with concentrated disadvantage, increases the difficulties associated with reentry. For example, impoverished neighborhoods typically offer fewer and lower quality services and job opportunities (Huebner et al., 2010).

We can see further evidence of how one barrier (e.g., problems with transportation) can cascade into multiple other difficulties in a study focused on women offenders' access to dependable transportation. Morash and colleagues (2017) followed 366 women offenders living in the Midwest over 3 years. They noted numerous transportation problems, including cost of travel, length of time to travel to work, lack of safety while traveling (e.g. walking to/from public transportation), and legal barriers such as not having valid driver's licenses or driving uninsured vehicles. Women in this study described difficulties with transportation leading to negative outcomes such as missing supervision appointments, job interviews, and medical appointments, and depicted constant stress around the decision to accept the risk of re-arrest when they drove to work, transported their children, or attended required appointments without a valid license or car insurance.

Richie's (2001) study with 42 women who had been arrested and released a minimum of three times provides additional insight into how challenges of reentry intersect with women's histories of mental health and victimization to increase risk of recidivism. The women Richie interviewed frequently highlighted their struggles to manage multiple needs simultaneously. Women described stress and worry about the temporary nature of their housing arrangements, loss of custody of children during reintegration, coping with previous experiences of family violence, and using substances to lessen the impact of traumatic memories, chronic mental health problems, lack of access to medical care, and in some cases, current partner violence. Their narratives illustrate the competing demands faced by the women to obtain work, comply with supervision requirements, work to regain custody of their children, and find housing. Further, many women were taking on these tasks while coping with ongoing or prior violence, as well as current mental health and substance use problems.

A quantitative study by Benda (2005) offers further evidence how women's victimization experiences, mental health, and parenting status influence recidivism. Benda compared 300 men and 300 women on a number of factors including victimization history, mental health, and partner relationships, as well as more commonly assessed measures of criminal history, aggression, employment, education, marital and parenting status, and so on. It is important to note Benda's sample consisted of individuals who opted to complete a military style "boot camp" to decrease their prison sentences. All of the participants were first-time offenders without psychological problems or drug addictions that would prohibit participation in the boot camp. The focus on first-time offenders offers some important insight into factors most affecting individuals who have recently entered the criminal legal system but also excludes the majority of the offender population. In Benda's study, the stronger predictors of recidivism for the women were physical abuse and sexual violence in the past 2 years, problems with their partner, partner engagement in criminal activity, mental health problems, childhood sexual abuse, and selling drugs. In contrast, number of children and positive partner relations were associated with decreased recidivism for these first-time women offenders. Ethnicity and years of education were not associated with recidivism. In another study of women's recidivism, Scott and colleagues (2016) followed 477 women for up to 3 months and noted victimization or trauma in the past year increased likelihood of recidivism by 30%. These authors noted that recent victimization was also associated with substance use, emotional difficulties, and financial problems, again highlighting the likelihood women are coping with multiple challenges simultaneously. In addition, they found living with their children reduced women's recidivism. It is important to note that other studies with large samples of incarcerated women have not found effects of prior victimization histories or parent status on recidivism (e.g., Olson et al., 2016). It is unclear why there are mixed findings and to what extent these differences are due to variations in methods, such as whether interviewers are corrections staff or individuals outside the corrections system, or the different types of assessments tools that were used.

Research with youth suggests similar vulnerability and risk of recidivism associated with victimization and mental health in the trajectories of girls in the criminal legal system. In a study with 402 youth (162 female) aged 11 to 17, prior sexual abuse increased the odds of re-arrest five times for girls whereas it was not associated with boys' recidivism (Conrad et al., 2014). Similarly, number of ACEs or adverse childhood events shortened the time to re-offending for both male and female youth across ethnic groups in a study with over 27,000 total youth (Wolff et al., 2017). Finally, researchers who conducted a study with 587 youth (170 female) found that intersections of gender, ethnicity, and mental health were associated with recidivism such that African American girls with a history of PTSD were at a greater risk of reoffending compared with White or Latinx males or females (Becker et al., 2012).

There a number of studies that have highlighted women's substance use post-release and lack of access to drug treatment services as potent risks for recidivism. For example, in a study of 506 women followed over 8 years, women who were dependent on drugs were three times more likely to fail at reintegration. This effect was heightened for women of color, who were six times more likely to return to prison if they were dependent on drugs (Huebner et al., 2010). Scott and her colleagues (2014) followed 624 women released from jail in the greater Chicago area. They found severity of substance use was one of the strongest predictors of women's recidivism over a 3-year period. They note that this effect was strongest in the first year and emphasize the importance of early access to substance use treatment during reentry. In another large-scale study with about 3,000 women, participating in drug treatment while incarcerated reduced the odds of re-arrest by 23% (Olson et al., 2016). How can we use this information to decrease recidivism rates? What are your thoughts about allocating resources for drug treatment programs and services for formerly incarcerated individuals?

One particularly vulnerable group of system-involved women may be sex workers. Scott and her colleagues (2014) followed a large sample of 624 women released from jail. The authors noted that for this sample, a history of sex work was a significant predictor of recidivism risk. They also reported that women who engaged in sex work frequently had less family support, more housing difficulties, and higher risk of victimization. These combined challenges likely increase women's struggles to reintegrate successfully. In a study focused specifically on women who identified as sex workers (N = 414), women with histories of childhood abuse, prior charges of prostitution, and current drug or alcohol problems were more likely to be re-arrested. In particular, survivors of child abuse were twice as likely to be re-arrested, and using substances also made re-arrest twice as likely (Roe-Sepowitz et al., 2011). Neither ethnicity nor education was associated with re-arrest for prostitution in this sample. Importantly, women who completed a diversion program decreased their risk of being re-arrested by 68%. The program consisted of three components. First, participants attended 36 hours of classes focused on relationships (e.g., boundaries, domestic violence, healthy relationships, STDs). Next, participants completed programs for substance use and prostitution based on the 12-step model, and the third component focused on job skills and training. Thus, we can see heightened risk of recidivism for women with more extensive victimization and substance use histories.

Employment

Offenders' unemployment rate is about five times the national average at 27% (see Figure 9.2) (Couloute & Kopf, 2018). Formerly incarcerated Black and Latinx women face the highest rates of unemployment (40% and 39% respectively) as well as greater difficulty securing full-time work. Formerly incarcerated women are often underemployed, with fewer hours, lower hourly wages, and in temporary positions. Women's difficulties accessing work is particularly important given stable employment is a strong predictor of reentry success. For example, employment reduced risk of recidivism by 83% in a study that included 340 women offenders (Uggen & Kruttschnitt, 1998). Other studies suggest it is not just employment, but specifically earning higher wages that is an important factor for women's re-arrest. Freudenberg and colleagues (2005) followed women released from jail in the New York area during their reentry process and found that employment was associated with lower rates of re-arrest. Furthermore, each $100 increase in salary per week, for up to $500 in additional salary, was associated with 24% reduction in the likelihood of recidivism. In addition to individual women's struggles to obtain work, it is critical that we discuss extensive systemic impediments to post-release employment.

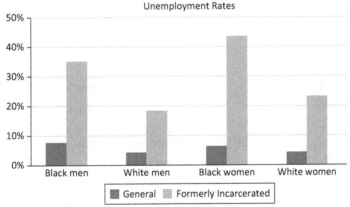

FIGURE 9.2 Unemployment rates (based on unemployment rates provided in Coulette and Kopf (2018)).

There are over 20,000 policies and statutes that limit the employability of individuals with criminal histories. In a report examining how licensure rules affect employment of formerly incarcerated individuals, Rodriguez and Avery (2016) document several key barriers. For example, many states prohibit individuals from obtaining professional or occupational licenses if they have a criminal history of a felony (12,000 license bans) or misdemeanor (6,000 bans). The National Institute of Corrections (Flower, 2010) estimates that these bans result in prohibiting individuals with criminal histories from entering approximately 350 occupations. These include a wide range of professions from medical to construction to personal service (e.g., hair stylists) careers. In addition, many licensing statues include the phrase "good moral character" as criteria for a license, a phrase many argue has been used to deny licensure to individuals with a criminal history. Individuals generally apply to a state board made up of volunteers from a specific profession to obtain a license. How do you think licensure board members judge moral character? Do you think so many professions should prohibit individuals with criminal histories from obtaining occupational licenses?

Reengagement With Family and Social Support Networks

Positive social support and connections with family have been linked to decreased recidivism in women. Cobbina (2010) conducted extensive qualitative interviews with 24 women who were successful in their reintegration efforts during a 2- to 3-year parole period and 26 women who returned to prison while on parole. Women in this study emphasized the role of family support for their successful reintegration, including financial and emotional support, housing, and help with childcare. Women also attributed their success to having supportive probation officers who would listen to and encourage them rather than take a "tough" approach (Cobbina, 2010). The successful women often described their parole officers as mentors who offered pride in their accomplishments and helped them in very concrete ways to access services or find jobs.

In contrast, women who returned to prison noted their support systems did not offer them needed assistance and, in many cases, expected them to engage in criminal activity. They explained that while they could disconnect from friends and community members who were actively using drugs or engaged in criminal activities, it was difficult to sever ties with family members involved in criminal activities. Women in the Cobbina (2010) study also described the problem of returning to live with violent partners who offered housing and support when others did not. However, if the women subsequently tried to escape the violence, they left their place of residence, and subsequently violated terms of their community supervision. The women who returned to prison also described more negative relationships with their parole officers. They noted the parole officers had large caseloads and the women had difficulty communicating with officers.

They described limited interactions, mandates to attend appointments to demonstrate compliance, and very little assistance with reintegration itself.

The women who were successful at reintegrating in Cobbina's (2010) study also described their ability to access a variety of services in their community. They noted receiving assistance with housing, employment, clothing, and other key services. Some of these services were specific to women with a focus on parenting classes and childcare. In contrast, women who were not successful reported struggles finding employment, as well as high stress due to the competing demands of gaining financial independence and still meeting all of the requirements of being on parole. In particular, these women struggled with obtaining the services and care they needed while simultaneously resuming their parenting responsibilities.

GETTING REAL 9.2

Sometimes I feel like I should have just stayed in prison because I come out here and there's nothing here for me; nothing's changed; everything's the same, you know, and it's depressing. I don't have a job, can't even go to school yet, or anything, and things are hard, you know. ... And I've been locked up for a long time, and my mind is kind of still, you know, not ... it's hard.

Christy is a White, 46-year-old woman who served a 4-year sentence for assault. She has been incarcerated seven times. We interviewed her within 6 months of her most recent release. Christy indicated she was not doing well. She was drinking again. She thinks she needs family counseling and anger management to help her deal with the anger and hate she has from being incarcerated. Christy explained she was in the house when her husband murdered somebody. She tried to tell people—a crisis counselor listened—but she still got blamed, too, for the person being murdered. Now she doesn't have her kids; they're gone, and she doesn't have a job, and she can't go to school. She wants to get her GED. She was locked up for a long time, and it has affected her mind. She still has flashbacks and nightmares. People don't understand how hard it is when you get out. There's a lot of stuff she still needs to deal with. Her mom died from alcohol. Christy feels like people around her tell her she's no good, not a good mom. She has to stay quiet and just listen to insults from her uncle when she goes to see her daughter. She wants her kids back, but she doesn't have her own place yet.

Several studies suggest both the importance and the challenges of the parent role for women involved in the legal system. Approximately 80% of these women are primary caregivers for dependent children (Scroggins & Malley, 2010). Over half of incarcerated women (55%) were living with their children prior to their incarceration (Glaze & Maruschak, 2008). When their mothers are incarcerated, children live with a grandparent (45%), father (37%), other relative (23%) or in foster care (11%). Having children in foster care represents serious risk of loss of parental rights for incarcerated women given federal time limits of 15 months of care within a 22-month period specified in the Adoption and Safe Families Act of 1997. In the study by Scott and colleagues (2014) with 624 women released from jail, loss of child custody, particularly within the first 90 days of release, was one of the strongest predictors of women's recidivism. In contrast, retaining custody was strongly associated with reintegration success. However, even when women are strongly motivated to regain custody of their children, keep in mind they must simultaneously secure housing and work and keep their community supervision appointments. McGrath (2012) noted that mothers in the reentry process experienced frequent parole violations for missed supervision appointments, positive drug tests, and inability to meet housing, work, education or treatment requirements.

A qualitative study with 28 mothers in the reentry process highlights women's experiences of competing demands and struggles (Arditti & Few, 2006). These women were incarcerated for an average of 14 months (minimum of 2 months) and on probation at the time of the interview. About 40% of the women met criteria for depression, and half reported current partner violence as well as prior experiences of family violence. Thirteen of the women had current substance dependence and nine were participating in current substance treatment. Only 7 of the 28 women had custody of their dependent children. Most women reported their families helped them during reentry by providing transportation, shelter, financial help, childcare and/or emotional support, but six women reported they received no help from their families. About one-third had obtained full-time work. The average income reported by the women in the sample was under $400 per week, whereas they reported owing an average of over $4,000 in court-related fines. Although this is a small, rural sample, it is clear that women benefitted from family support when it was available, struggled to regain custody of their children, and frequently were coping with mental health or substance use problems, partner violence, difficulties finding work, and serious financial strain.

Supervision Experiences

A consistent concern for women in the reentry process is meeting the requirements of community supervision. Supervision includes women sentenced to probation instead of incarceration and released early or paroled. According to the Bureau of Justice Statistics, women make up 13% of the parole population and 25% of the probation population (Kaeble, 2018). Women under community supervision typically face many requirements such as regular appointments with supervision officers, drug tests and treatment, paying legal fines, securing housing and employment, avoiding contact with known felons, and participating in programs (e.g., education, job preparation). When women fail to meet these requirements, supervision officers issue violations that can include fines, additional requirements or treatment, or sanctions including incarceration.

The use of sanctions is based on the deterrence theory and operant learning. Mowen and colleagues (2018) describe deterrence theory as the idea that individuals' behavior is guided by rational choices that increase pleasure or positive outcomes and decrease pain. In this case, sanctions are intended to decrease the negative outcomes associated with criminal behavior. In contrast, a long history of research on operant learning suggests that positive reinforcement is the most effective way to increase behavior while punishment is less effective at stopping behavior. In a test of these theories, Mowen and colleagues (2018) examined the extent to which supervision officers' use of sanctions or punitive measures versus incentives were associated with offender outcomes. They found that supervision officers' use of praise was associated with lower rates of offending and substance use while sanctions and reprimands were predictive of higher rates of offending and substance use. However, while this research is informative, as it was conducted with a large sample of over 1,500 offenders across 14 states, women were excluded from the sample. While the finding that support or praise is more effective than punishment has critical implications for how supervision officers engage with those under supervision, it is also important to consider the fact that operant theories of learning target the individual's decision making and do not address systemic or social factors that influence engagement in criminal behavior.

Morash and her colleagues have conducted a series of studies on supervision and recidivism among women. In a study published in 2017, they examined whether corrections agents responded to violations with punitive (jail time, drug testing, incarceration) or treatment-oriented (required or increased substance abuse services) responses and subsequent recidivism in a sample of 385 racially diverse women. Women at high risk (more months on parole, more prior arrests) for recidivism were less likely to recidivate when corrections agents utilized treatment responses rather than punitive responses to offenses. Morash and colleagues (2016) found further evidence of this when they noted that intensity of supervision (contacts with supervisor), supportiveness of supervisors' style of interacting with women, and supervisor discussing needs the women perceived as concerns were all associated with reduced risk of recidivism. In particular, they found that corrections agents' style of interacting was indirectly associated with actual number of arrests over 2 years such that women who described corrections officers as supportive experienced less anxiety and distress and subsequently had fewer arrests. In sum, the nature of women's relationships within their informal social support networks as well as the quality of relationships with representatives of the criminal legal system appear to influence women's reentry process.

In another recent study of women on probation and parole, Roddy and colleagues (2018) examined the messages women received from probation and parole officers about employment. They noted that about 40% of the women in a Midwestern sample of women offenders indicated finding employment was a problem. They further explored the nature of assistance offered by supervision officers. Roddy and associates reported that women received relatively limited tangible or direct assistance in obtaining work from supervision officers, but many reported positive messages in the forms of information and encouragement. Women described officers encouraging them to pursue education and skills training as well as offering suggestions about services that would assist them to work on a resume or providing advice about how to present themselves to potential employers (e.g., be honest about your criminal history). In this sample, the most common support offered was information. In addition, the researchers noted that officers often reflected their awareness of the multiple demands facing women (e.g., need for further education, mental health and substance use treatment, parenting concerns) and encouraged them to prioritize efforts to work on these issues and lessened requirements related to employment. In contrast, women reported negative or mixed experiences when agents communicated messages about employment that did not recognize the women's competing needs. How might we use this information to inform training of probation officers? Do you think the skills and responses described as most helpful have a common component of training for probation officers?

Access to Services and Aid

As you read this review, it should be clear that women experience a number of challenges in the reentry process and that these challenges are interdependent, such that difficulty in one arena often is linked to struggles in another area. While the stigma of a criminal history has repeatedly been demonstrated to make it more challenging to obtain employment or housing (Sentencing Project, 2017), it is less well known that women can be denied state or federal assistance due to their criminal history. For example, women who committed felony drug offenses may be denied assistance from the Temporary Assistance to Needy Families (TANF) program. TANF is set up to provide cash to assist families to obtain food stamps, federally subsidized housing, and/or higher education benefits. These funds come from the federal government but are distributed within each state by state agencies. Federal policy prohibits providing TANF aid to felony drug offenders for their lifetimes. Offenders often experience similar difficulties accessing federally subsidized housing and food assistance programs due to crime- and drug-related restrictions in the policies of these programs. For all three of these programs, states have some discretion in who they deem eligible, but, given limited funds, may elect to deny offenders in favor of other applicants (McCarty et al., 2016). Currently, 34 states and Washington DC retain policies denying eligibility on the basis of felony drug offenses (The Sentencing Project, 2017). Similarly, in some states, individuals incarcerated for 12 months or longer are not eligible for Medicaid (Anderson & Javdani, 2018), thus decreasing women's access to health care services.

There have been some efforts to address these gaps in services for formerly incarcerated individuals. The 2008 Second Chance Act provided federal funds to government and nonprofit agencies to assist returning citizens with housing, access to substance use treatment, and employment. As of 2018, the 2008 act had resulted in 800 awards across 49 states to service providers. However, most services are concentrated in urban areas and along the coasts, with many rural states offering one to three programs across the entire state.

A recent study followed 345 drug-involved women under community supervision to examine their needs (e.g., financial, food, housing), access to assistance, and risk of recidivism (Morash et al., 2017). The majority of the women (85%) reported an annual income of under $10,000. Approximately half (55%) were unemployed, and 20% had lived in three or more places during the 6 months they were in the study. By the second interview, women had generally secured assistance for food, but over one-third (36%)

still had unmet housing needs, and one in five (22%) had unmet financial needs. Women with the most unmet needs had the greatest economic risk for recidivism. Further, the women with persistent unmet needs were also more likely to have mental health problems and use substances. Finally, women with unmet housing needs were most likely to also indicate experiences of victimization as adults. While these findings are not surprising, it is important to pause and consider this strong empirical evidence that economic disadvantage is linked with mental health, substance use, and experiences of violence, and that these co-occurring experiences increase the risk of recidivism.

We know that there are often specific barriers that limit individuals' use of services in the general community. There are a few studies that have specifically examined barriers to services for returning citizens. Begun and his colleagues (2016) followed about 300 offenders released from jail, prison, or other community-based correctional facilities to learn about their access to substance use and mental health services and potential barriers to service utilization. They noted consistent difficulty accessing services for both men and women. For example, while 45% of their sample indicated they made efforts to decrease substance use problems during their reentry, only 21% were able to access professional substance abuse treatment services. Similarly, about half (48%) reported they needed mental health services but only 21% entered mental health treatment. Inability to pay for services was the most common barrier. Further, individuals released from jail reported the greatest number of barriers. Because jail is a short-term placement, individuals are often released from jail with minimal post-release planning. Other barriers included balancing competing demands of caring for children, characteristics of the treatment facilities (e.g., staff attitudes toward offenders, long wait periods), lack of knowledge about where to go for treatment, transportation difficulties, shame, and not being ready to change.

In sum, there is clear evidence that women returning to communities need services and supports that target access to housing and transportation; education, employment, and job services; health care, mental health, and substance use treatment; and childcare and parenting skills (Scroggins & Malley, 2010). However, Scroggins and Malley's review of reentry services in 10 large metropolitan areas found there were not sufficient services even in these highly populated areas to meet the needs of women during their reintegration process. First, although the majority of these women have dependent children, childcare was the least provided service. Next, mental health services were provided by only about half of the reentry programs. Medical services were even more limited and often had low capacity with long waiting periods. Interestingly, treatment programs for substance use were among the most commonly offered services. However, we know from other research that women utilize or access substance treatment about half as often as men (Mahmood et al., 2013). Richie's (2001) interviews with formerly incarcerated women offer possible explanations for the apparent contradiction. In her study, women described lack of childcare and experiences of sexual harassment in substance abuse treatment groups as obstacles to obtaining this service. Taken together, this research suggests women would likely benefit most from integrated services, for example a site that combines childcare and treatment services specifically for women.

Housing and transportation assistance were available in fewer than 20% of the programs. Most housing programs were low capacity and included restrictions on length of time that limited their utility for women. Education and job training services were more common across the 10 cities. However, education services were primarily for women who had not completed high school. Given that one-third of women offenders have typically completed high school or their GED, there is a lack of vocational training or college-level courses that would support their ability to gain more skill-based employment. Women did appear to have access to job training and referral sources. Finally, Sroggins and Malley note that these programs tended to provide isolated services in separate locations, requiring women to travel to multiple locations to access these different forms of aid.

SUMMARY

In this chapter, we have reviewed recent and key literature on women's reentry process. At this point, it should be evident that the majority of women (and men) recidivate, often within the first year. Women face multiple demands to secure housing, education, job training, and employment, and to regain custody of their children. Many women take on these charges while coping with ongoing mental health, substance use, physical health problems, and victimization. In addition, women often experience new victimization. The research reviewed illustrates ways in which these stressors co-occur and combine to contribute to women's reentry struggles. Stable housing, employment, and mental health are associated with greater reintegration success. Further, women who have strong, positive support systems are more likely to be successful. This includes families and partners as well as supportive supervision officers. In contrast, ongoing substance use represents one of the strongest risks for recidivism. Although ethnicity itself was generally not associated with women's recidivism, women of color who use substances are at increased risk of recidivism. Black and Latinx women are also more likely to have difficulty obtaining full-time work, further increasing risk of recidivism. Throughout the research, we see women's struggles exacerbated by financial insecurity, disadvantaged neighborhood communities, and lack of positive support systems. We also see additional structural barriers. Current state and federal policies for obtaining assistance (e.g., food, housing, education, health insurance), as well as occupational licensure policies, represent significant barriers for women's ability to find work, particularly secure, skilled work. In addition, lack of needed services (e.g., childcare), difficulty accessing services, and lack of integration and coordination among services are further challenges to the reentry process.

DISCUSSION QUESTIONS

1. What are some of the identified protective factors against recidivism for women?
2. How do different challenges such as transportation, housing, and employment struggles interact to influence recidivism?
3. What are some current barriers to employment for formerly incarcerated individuals?
4. What does research on probation officers' interactions with women suggest are the most effective ways for probation officers to work with women?

CHAPTER TEN

Practice and Policy Implications at Reentry and Community Corrections

Introduction

This chapter includes a brief summary of reentry challenges followed by a discussion of reentry best practices via the APIC model (to be described) and broad recommendations for reentry programs and policies. The sequential intercept model provides a framework for recommended intervention strategies, including reentry transition planning and specialized probation and parole caseloads. A common theme across reentry programs is the importance of coordination of services (e.g., mental and behavioral health, housing, education, transportation) and multisystem planning with attention to the intersectionality of participant identities and cultural competence. We end with a discussion of efforts to change social and legal policies that affect reentry, such as housing-first programs, record expungement, and ban-the-box in employment applications.

Reentry Challenges

As we noted in the previous chapter, most individuals in the reentry period—adults and youth—re-offend. Women who are released from jail or prison contend with multiple demands: to secure housing, employment, job training and/or education; to have transportation; to obtain and participate in needed mental health and substance use services; and, often, to reunite with their children with the aim of assuming a primary caregiving role. In many instances, women are balancing basic needs with efforts to cope with past and/or current victimization, substance use, and mental health problems. Women are less likely to succeed if they are actively using substances, cannot access treatment services, have poorer support systems, are unemployed or underemployed, and are engaged with community supervisors with punitive interactional styles. Economic and neighborhood disadvantage, racial disparities in access to health care and employment or education, and state/federal policies that limit returning citizens' employment opportunities and access to support services are additional structural barriers that negatively impact reentry. Finally, there are mixed results on the effectiveness of reentry programs and services, and in many cases, returning citizens cannot access the services they report needing (Gill & Wilson, 2016).

GETTING REAL 10.1

There's not a lot of stuff out there when you walk out the door to keep you from coming back. They need to get you some kind of intervention when you get out, before you get back into criminal activity—not just $100 and a bus fare. Before you step out that door, you need someone that's going to take the time to help you through the rough spots.

Cindy is a White woman, aged 38, who is in prison for forgery, bank fraud, fraudulent checks, and possession of crack (a probation violation). She thinks she started using drugs because of depression, and the drug use escalated over the years. She grew up sort of a latchkey kid. It was a middle-class household, and her parents didn't beat her or get drunk. She says it was a normal life but unhappy. She'd fly into rages as a child. Her brother sexually abused her from the time she was 10 until he moved out to go into the Army when she was 13 or 14. Even when she got older, he'd say sexual things to her. That makes Cindy worry about her own daughter and about his kids. When she was in ninth grade, she and a friend were brutally raped by some boys from school, and the whole school found out. She was teased and bullied. Cindy smoked pot from age 14 and had to quit school at 15 when she got in trouble for bringing some of her grandmom's pills to school. She started running away a lot, and her parents sent her to a psychiatric school in the mountains, but she ran away from there. When she got home, they tried her in AA and NA and with shrinks. Cindy wasn't serious about any of the programs and used to get drunk or high. She moved in with a guy when she was 17, and he was selling coke. It got worse. By her 18th birthday, she was arrested for occupying a "bawdy house" and was selling her body to get coke.

Sequential Intercept Model at Reentry

As noted in earlier chapters, the sequential intercept model (Munetz & Griffin, 2006) identifies points of intervention to increase access to treatment and decrease the likelihood of reoffending. This model was specifically developed to decrease the rate of incarceration of individuals with serious mental illness. It provides a framework for professionals from multiple systems (e.g., criminal justice, health and human services, housing) to work together to assist formerly incarcerated individuals and decrease recidivism. As a reminder, this model is intended to limit criminalization of mental health by connecting individuals to treatment and support services at "points of interception." Here, reentry can be considered a point of interception—that is, the period of transition between incarceration and return to the community. We have already established that incarcerated women and girls experience mental health and substance use disorders at high rates and that these problems represent a risk for recidivism. However, this model offers an important framework even in the absence of serious mental illness given the frequently complex needs of post-release women and girls via its emphasis on coordination of services. At the point of reentry, this model emphasizes continuity of care. In other words, there is a clear expectation for communication among systems, including sharing key information, and reentering persons should have plans in place to access needed services (e.g., medication, substance use treatment). One example of a best-practice model developed for the reentry intercept (intercept 4) is the APIC model (Osher et al., 2003).

The APIC Model and Reentry Programs

Assessing, planning, identifying, and coordinating (APIC) is a best-practice approach that targets individuals being released from jail (SAMHSA, 2017).

THE APIC MODEL

ASSESS	Assess the individual's needs and potential safety risks.
PLAN	Plan to meet the identified needs with specific treatment programs and services.
IDENTIFY	Identify the agencies that provide the services.
COORDINATE	Coordinate between corrections and community service providers.

These steps seem quite straight forward: (1) Assess needs and risks, (2) plan for treatment, (3) identify where/how services can be accessed, and (4) coordinate transition to ensure timely access. Given that this is a program for individuals in jails, who often have very short durations of incarceration, the goal is to assess post-release risk (low, medium, or high) and needs within 48 hours of entry into the system. There are several measures developed to assess criminogenic needs or problems identified as increasing risk of future criminal behavior. The "big four" criminogenic risk factors assessed by many measures are criminal history, antisocial personality, attitudes, and cognitions. In addition, employment, education, family, and substance use are considered part of the "central eight" factors that should be assessed. The risk-need-responsivity model is a widely used model that emphasizes identifying offenders who are higher risk based on these eight factors and providing responsive services that target the specific, dynamic, or changeable needs of these persons (e.g., you cannot change criminal history, but you can change education level; Andrews & Bonta, 2010). Even as we recognize the widespread application of this model, it is important to note that there are ongoing debates and varied research findings regarding the validity and reliability of risk measures for adults and youth across gender and racial groups (Campbell et al., 2018; Threadcraft-Walker et al., 2018).

In the APIC model, assessment is specifically meant to be client centered. In other words, assessments must reflect the individual's unique needs and awareness of potential barriers (e.g., safety of neighborhood, availability of services, transportation) as well as the strengths of the individual. A recent study examined about 1,000 returning citizens (mostly men) who received reentry services designed to fit their specific service needs compared to those who obtained traditional reentry services. The study found lower recidivism among those whose services "fit" their specific needs (Gill & Wilson, 2016).

Assessments should also be culturally sensitive. This includes awareness of and respect for key cultural values (e.g., emphasis on family or spirituality) and historical experiences of diverse groups of individuals (e.g., past U.S. policies of forced removal of Indigenous children from their families). Pause and consider for a moment why this would matter. If the aim is to assess an individual's needs, barriers to accessing services, and strengths, it is important to consider what might be most motivating and what might represent a barrier to accessing services (e.g., central values) and to what extent the individual may hesitate to share key personal information with a government employee (e.g., current and/or historical experiences that create distrust). A goal across all four steps is to approach the development and implementation of a plan with cultural competence where "cultural competency is the acceptance and respect for difference, a continuous self-assessment regarding culture, an attention to the dynamics of difference, the ongoing development of cultural knowledge, and the resources and flexibility within service models to meet the needs of minority populations" (Cross et al., 1989, p. 17). In other words, corrections staff and reentry service providers are charged to learn, integrate, and utilize information about diverse individuals and groups to best meet the needs of these persons and provide quality services and programs to improve outcomes (Perlin & McClain, 2009). How do you think we can increase cultural competence broadly across the different components of the corrections system? Are students who are pursuing corrections and service careers obtaining this type of training?

A key principle of APIC is the emphasis on taking a systems or community-wide approach to planning for reentry as well as an individualized approach. In the APIC model, the plan for transition is facilitated by a team, including partners from key community agencies offering treatment and support services. For this team to be successful, they will have to take several planned steps. First, they must identify a target population and eligibility requirements for participants. For example, a program may target high-risk or repeat offenders. Next, the roles and responsibilities of staff team members have to be defined. Who has the necessary skills and expertise to conduct an assessment of a person's needs? Which existing community partners can be recruited and informed about the needs of participants? Next, to increase ease of transitions, teams often develop protocols or memoranda of understanding (MOUs) that lay out the expectations and funding mechanisms of services. In addition, teams develop policies for information sharing that uphold privacy rules for personal health information, but which also facilitate provision of services. This might include training staff across sites on how to share and manage confidential information as well as on how to develop universal release forms that can be used across agencies. Finally, each team may implement guidelines to support the individual's transition and connection to service. As you can see, these steps create responsibility for transition at all levels and across systems rather than expecting recently released individuals to navigate these complex service systems on their own. This can help in identifying, accessing, and obtaining the most appropriate services based on specific needs. Implementing programs like this takes time—often years. It may require changes in policies and practices across systems and often necessitates a culture shift so that rehabilitation is a central aim of the system.

While APIC provides a model of best practices for reentry programs, there are also other reentry programs that have been rated as promising based on research. One such program applicable to the reentry intercept involves forensic assertive community treatment (FACT) teams. This model brings together a team of treatment providers and case managers who work with individuals with serious mental illness released from jail or prison to connect these persons to health services, housing, and other support services (SAMHSA, 2019b). This model is an adaptation of the assertive community treatment (ACT) approach, which has a strong evidence base for effectiveness with individuals who have serious mental illness and are involved in the criminal legal system. Similarly, assisted outpatient treatment (AOT) is court-supervised treatment provided in the community. It has been implemented in several states. Outcomes associated with participation in this program include reduced hospitalizations, arrests, incarceration, homelessness, victimization, suicide, and violence against others (SAMHSA, 2019b; Treatment Advocacy Center (TAC), 2016). A common theme across these programs is the identification of the individual's needs and coordination of care by multiple systems.

Community Corrections and Community Support Services

The final intercept in the sequential intercept model is at the point of community corrections and community support services (intercept 5). This intercept focuses on individuals under community supervision, such as those persons on probation or parole. You will recall that over four million adults, 25% of whom were women, were under community supervision in the United States in 2016 (Kaeble, 2018). The majority of these individuals assigned to community supervision are on probation. One strategy that addresses the intercept specific to supervising persons with mental illness is the specialized caseload approach. This intervention strategy focuses on agencies that employ supervision officers who have training in mental health. Ideally, these supervision officers work exclusively with participants who have mental illness, they carry smaller caseloads (e.g., 45 probationers compared to 120), participate in regular training relevant to working with individuals with mental illness (20–40 hours per year), actively coordinate services for probationers as a member of a team, and use positive compliance strategies rather than sanctions (Skeem & Lougren, 2006; Skeem et al., 2018). There is limited research on the effectiveness of specialty supervision, but the few existing studies suggest that participants are more likely to access services and less likely to violate parole or probation. In a 2018 study, Skeem and colleagues compared specialty and traditional supervision of 359 individuals with mental health problems and found that specialty supervision was less costly than traditional supervision when costs associated with crises and recidivism were taken into account. Specifically, persons assigned under specialty supervision were less likely to rely on emergency care and inpatient services. Further, probationers assigned to traditional supervision were 2.68 times more likely to be re-arrested within 2 years (Skeem et al., 2017).

Recommendations for Effective Reentry Programs and Community Supervision

In 2017, the Bureau of Justice Assistance (BJA) published a report with recommendations for reentry programs and supervision based on interviews with site coordinators for 22 adult offender reentry demonstration projects (Lindquist et al., 2015). As you review these recommendations, you will see some overlap with the APIC model. Yet, there is also some new information regarding how to meet the aims of assessment. The report also offers concrete tips regarding team planning and coordination of services as well as on how to increase access to services. First, these site coordinators indicated the importance of taking sufficient time to plan and identify what policies and processes must change to successfully implement these types of reentry programs. For example, they noted that the program must have buy-in or support from all partners. This may require a shift in culture or thinking on the part of corrections officers, starting with staff in leadership roles. Community corrections staff are tasked with maintaining public safety, often via restricting or monitoring supervisee behaviors. Shifting the professional focus to the supervisee's rehabilitation, health, and needs can take time and training. In addition, site coordinators encouraged efforts to obtain support from leaders in the community to gain positive visibility of the program. They argued these types of support increase the likelihood of program success, enhance community partner participation, and sustain funding. Further, community partners such as health care providers must be educated about the corrections process and supervisee's needs to be effective partners. Site coordinators recommended regular meetings to identify needs and potential barriers, plan reentry transitions, and educate and build trust among team members. This also allows team members to consider funding and reimbursement processes, to plan the best use of available resources (e.g., coordinating transportation to health care and supervision appointments), and to share information.

The ways information is protected are often different in corrections compared to health care settings. Site coordinators recommended training on how and what information to share, including developing a universal release form that could be used across sites and/or a shared, central database. As you may infer, these types of activities, intended to enhance system coordination, can take extensive planning and collaboration among systems. In addition, some sites suggested including a formerly incarcerated individual as a team member to assist in planning. Another common recommendation is to identify needs and then allow service providers' access to persons while still incarcerated. This can assist with post-release planning and can establish a health care provider-client relationship prior to release. Site coordinators also note the need for better assessment tools for corrections officers to identify trauma and mental health concerns and related needs.

Next, site coordinators for these reentry programs indicated the importance of identifying a target population for the reentry program. These coordinators note that it is important to have flexibility in the eligibility criteria for participants of reentry programs. Specifically, it is sometimes difficult to address unmet needs for the highest need groups when programs are full, yet stricter eligibility criteria may deny services to women and girls who would indeed benefit from them; this requires some balance. Next, effective supervision or case management staff should be trained, skilled in building relationships and working with populations with mental health concerns, assigned reasonable caseloads, and trained to be respectful in their interaction with returning citizens. Effective case management includes in-depth knowledge of area services, state and federal eligibility requirements, and knowledge of how to navigate bureaucracies of differing aid agencies. Further, corrections staff, supervision officers, and community partners can be most effective when they are representative of or similar to the populations they are working with, including being formerly incarcerated themselves, culturally competent, and located in individuals' communities. The site coordinators provided the perspective that supervision was more effective when supervising officers incorporated recognition of success and incentives for participation as well as tangible help (e.g., transportation) or flexibility (e.g., allow lower risk persons to call in for supervision appointments). Similar to recommendations from Richie in 2001 and Scroggins et al. in 2010, these coordinators also recommended developing "hub services," such that services were located closely together to increase access.

Youth and Reentry

Finally, there are some recommendations specific to youth and reentry. The Office of Juvenile Justice and Delinquency Prevention noted key barriers for youth returning to communities include stigma for seeking treatment, difficulty reengaging in school, and navigating multiple systems (Development Services Group, 2017). At this time, results of studies of existing reentry programs for youth are mixed. The Office of Juvenile Justice and Delinquency Prevention (OJJDP) recognize the need for innovative programs and case management to assist youth in the reentry process.

Gender-Responsive Approaches

This series of recommendations from the adult offender reentry demonstration projects is not specific to women and girls, but is clearly relevant to their success. A study of recidivism risks among 477 women over 3 years reminds us to consider gender-specific as well as gender-neutral risks for women's recidivism (Scott et al., 2016). For example, living with one's children was a protective factor in reducing recidivism for women in this study. Thus, women who are actively caregiving or reuniting with their families may need family housing, parenting education, and support services (e.g., childcare) as a component of their reentry plan. In contrast, experiences of victimization post-release were associated with increased recidivism. In this study, almost half of the women reported new experiences of violence, and these experiences increased risk of recidivism by 30%. Studies of recidivism in girls also highlight the role of trauma and victimization as predictors of reoffending (Conrad et al., 2014; Wolff et al., 2017). These findings support integration of trauma-informed approaches in reentry planning for women and girls post-release.

The National Resource Center on Justice Involved Women published gender-responsive practice guidelines specific to women's reentry (Ramiriz, 2016) that overlap some in content with the recommendations previously described but place a greater emphasis on quality of relationships and trauma-informed approaches. Borrowing from Benedict (2008), these guidelines identify five key characteristics of gender-responsive practice: (a) relational: establishing mutually respectful and empathic relationships with women; (b) strength based: identifying and utilizing women's strengths in reentry planning; (c) trauma informed: assess and recognize that historical and current trauma exposure can impact women's participation in services; (d) holistic: provide comprehensive case management that is situated to respond to complex and multiple needs; and (e) culturally competent: staff and services that recognize and value women's diversity.

Morash (2010) explores the effectiveness of gender-responsive supervision by probation and parole officers in her book *Women on Probation and Parole*. Morash recognizes existing criticisms of this form of supervision, noting that it can lead to more intense checking on women and control over women by officers, resulting in a higher risk of women violating their probation or parole and reincarceration. To address concerns about whether gender-resposive supervision is effective in helping women be more successful in their reentry process, Morash compares a gender-responsive supervision approach utilized in one county to a traditional supervision approach used in a similar county. Using a primarily qualitative case study approach, Morash conducts an in-depth exploration of women's experiences of supervision and notes that women receiving gender-responsive supervision in her study did report more intense and frequent contacts with supervision officers, resulting in more identification of women violating their supervision, but also leading to more referrals for treatment and other services and greater access to work-related resources.

Policy Concerns and Recommendations

We know women and girls who were formerly incarcerated face many disadvantages as they struggle to reintegrate into their communities. In the chapter on reentry, we briefly discussed policies that prevent returning citizens from accessing employment and various forms of assistance or aid for housing, food, education, and so on. Here, we revisit these policies with the aim of increasing the visibility of the collateral consequences of these social and legal policies and the ways in which they increase economic marginalization of returning citizens. Then we present some current recommendations and policy change efforts.

Depending on the crimes an individual committed, ex-offenders may lose benefits, including federal student loans and participation in the Temporary Aid to Needy Families program, the Supplemental Nutrition Assistance program, and Supplemental Security Income for the elderly and disabled (Bannon et al., 2010; Hall et al., 2016). As we noted before, states have some discretion determining eligibility for these types of assistance programs (McCarty et al., 2016). Yet, as of 2016, 34 states and Washington DC had policies denying eligibility on the basis of felony drug offenses (Sentencing Project, 2017). Even in states where eligibility has been increased, such as Massachusetts, women are not eligible for 12 months after release unless they are pregnant, the primary caretaker of a child under 2 or with a disability, or they are a documented victim of domestic violence (Hall et al., 2016). Similarly, in some states, individuals incarcerated for 12 months or longer are not eligible for Medicaid (Anderson & Javdani, 2018). These instances of reduced or eliminated eligibility for assistance are examples of collateral consequences of criminal convictions and can have long-lasting impact on individuals' reintegration into their communities. There are tools available to states and corrections agencies to work on eligibility requirements and assist individuals to access these services. SOAR or SSI/SSDI Outreach, Access and Recovery is a program offered via the Substance Abuse and Mental Health Services Administration to train case workers to help ex-offenders regain these benefits if they are eligible. Similar trainings are available to assist corrections professionals to support returning citizens' applications for Medicare and Medicaid services.

We know risk of recidivism is greatest in the first year post-release. It is important that we question the rationale for denying these forms of assistance to individuals with felony records and ask why lengthy waiting periods for eligibility or revocation of services are used to deny service during this critical juncture—particularly for those services essential to health and well-being, such as aid to needy families and Medicare. These programs can be a lifeline to persons struggling to reintegrate into families and communities while trying to address mental and physical health issues, remain drug free, and seek employment.

Many occupations require licenses. States again have the ability to determine eligibility for occupational licenses and many prohibit a range of occupations on the basis of any felony conviction. As we noted before, the National Institute of Corrections (Flower, 2010) estimates that these policies prohibit former offenders from entering approximately 350 occupations. Criteria for exclusion vary from state to state and include occupations as diverse as dance-hall operators, contractors, dieticians, and barbers. Other examples of post-incarceration policies that increase barriers for returning citizens are state laws for revocation of driver's licenses and eligibility for public housing assistance. Individuals with drug- or sex-related convictions can be denied public housing, and in many states, driver's licenses are revoked after any criminal conviction (Hall et al., 2016). Applying for a new license once released is expensive and takes time. Consider again the finding from Morash and colleagues (2017) that women reported that problems in transportation led to missing supervision appointments, job interviews, and medical appointments, contributing to high stress and risk of re-arrest when driving. Here, we see the link between policies revoking driver's license and increased risk of recidivism when women do not attend supervision appointments or secure employment.

Changing these policies by increasing eligibility of formerly incarcerated persons would reduce notable barriers for employment, housing, education, disability income, health care, and food assistance in this population. Significant revision or elimination of these existing policies could substantially reduce disproportionate economic marginalization of returning citizens.

There is some evidence of legislative support for increasing returning citizens' access to assistance. For example, the 2008 Second Chance Act provides federal funds to government and nonprofit agencies to assist returning citizens with housing, access to substance use treatment, and employment. However, the number of programs per state varies tremendously. For example, more rural states like Idaho, Utah, Wyoming, South Carolina, Mississippi, and West Virginia have 10 to 20 programs across the state whereas more densely populated states like California, New York, and Ohio have 100 or more funded programs.

Another legislative effort, primarily at the state level, includes recent expansion of the opportunity for individuals with minor or misdemeanor crimes who do not reoffend to apply for record expungement (Prescott & Starr, 2019). Prescott and Starr recently obtained de-identified statewide data to examine the effectiveness of record expungement in Michigan. First, they noted very few, about 6%, of those eligible for record expungement applied. In Michigan, individuals may only apply for expungement if they have a single conviction after a period of 5 years. Individuals who were incarcerated for their crimes were less likely to apply. Applications require several steps, including mailing copies of the application to multiple offices. Women, particularly Black women convicted of minor felony crimes, were most likely to apply and be granted record expungement. Individuals who did obtain record expungement had low rates of re-arrest or new convictions within 5 years, and typically obtained better paying jobs within 1 year of the record expungement. Pennsylvania created automatic record expungement for certain convictions after 10 years in 2018, and similar bills for automatic record expungement passed in California and Utah in 2019. Based on their findings, these authors recommend decreasing the hurdles or steps involved in the application process for record expungement and broadening automatic expungement within 5 years to support reentry success for first-time offenders, particularly in regard to employment.

There has also been notable action to change employment barriers via the "ban-the-box" movement. The ban-the-box movement began in 2004 as a result of efforts by formerly incarcerated individuals and their families. The aim of this movement was to remove a question about conviction history from employment application forms and place a greater emphasis on applicants' qualifications for the position. Ban the box has been adopted by 35 states and 150 cities, and in 12 states, ban-the-box policies have been extended to include private employers (Avery, 2019). In addition, the Equal Employment Opportunities Commission (EEOC) has issued guidelines for businesses, encouraging them to consider time since the conviction, the extent to which the specific conviction is associated with the employment opportunity, and mitigating circumstances. Some states have also enacted legislation, including fair chance licensing reforms, to limit consideration of convictions related to the occupation or to convictions in the past 2 to 5 years in applications for occupational licenses (Ensellem et al., 2018). It is important to note that there is some controversy about the effectiveness of the ban-the-box policy, with some research suggesting that if employers do not have specific information about criminal record, they are more likely to rely on stereotypes about demographic information such as race (e.g., that a Black man is more likely to have a criminal record; Doleac, 2016) to evaluate a job applicant.

Organizations have also demonstrated how to engage in policy reform to advocate on behalf of system-involved populations. The Corporation for Supportive Housing (see csh.org), started by Julie Sandorf and co-funded by three major charities, partners with local communities to develop low-cost housing that is integrated with health care and other services. The main pathways for their efforts include lending funds, consulting, advocating for policy reform, and working to change existing government systems. This organization began by developing stable housing for homeless populations but has expanded to include a focus on system-involved individuals (the FUSE initiative). This group specifically works to collect and use data to address social and racial inequity in accessible housing and to decrease reliance on crisis care (e.g., emergency rooms, jails, and shelters). Another policy initiative that has been piloted in some states is the "housing-first" approach (Roman, 2009). This approach works to transition formerly incarcerated persons with mental illness into housing with associated support services directly from jail or prison. In many cases, this housing is not permanent. A study of formerly homeless participants in a housing-first program indicated individuals who were in unstable housing spent more time in prison compared to those assigned stable housing (Kerman et al., 2018). There is little data specific to women offenders and this program.

SUMMARY

There have been clear advances in policy efforts to improve the reentry process, but it is also clear that a number of social and legislative barriers remain for individuals in the reentry process. Further, results of the effectiveness of reentry programs are mixed. But we are seeing a greater emphasis on evaluating program effectiveness and evidence-based practices and programs. A consistent message across the sequential intercept model, the APIC approach, research studies with returning citizens, and reentry program staff is the importance of systems coordinating with one another and providing comprehensive services. An additional key component that is compatible with these models is the incorporation of a trauma-informed approach. As you may recall, a trauma-informed approach is based on guiding principles of (a) safety; (b) transparency and trustworthiness; (c) peer support; (d) collaboration and mutuality; (e) empowerment, voice, and choice; and (f) cultural, historical, and gender issues (SAMHSA, 2014). There is clear overlap in the trauma-informed and gender-responsive approaches. Both emphasize the importance of considering women's and girls' experiences of victimization as services are planned and provided. Both approaches also emphasize the importance of building trusting relationships with individuals who are reentering communities. This again overlaps with research findings and recommendations we have reviewed in this chapter, noting that the quality of relationships between returning citizens, corrections and supervision staff, and providers influences outcomes, and that communication and collaboration among all parties is key. Taken together, these approaches emphasize the importance of buy-in or support across agencies, among leadership, and in the community. Changing climates and shifting away from a punitive to a rehabilitative approach in reentry planning and supervision will take time. However, readers such as yourselves who take interest in women's pathways to incarceration, experiences during incarceration, and experiences post-release are taking critical first steps in changing and impacting the corrections system.

DISCUSSION QUESTIONS

1. What are some of the key steps recommended for successful reentry programs?
2. What are "wraparound services" and why are they recommended to support successful rentry? What services might be particularly helpful for women?

3. This chapter references the importance of sharing information across providers and services. Why might this be important and how can this be facilitated?

4. What are ways that we can change systemic barriers to access to aid or employment? What efforts are currently under way to make these changes?

Conclusion

In this text, we have drawn on existing theories and research to illustrate the variety of ways women's and girls' life experiences, social identities, and the laws and policies in their communities influence their risk of entering the criminal legal system, their experiences in the system, and the reentry process. We have highlighted the high rates of adversity and exposure to interpersonal violence as well as mental and physical health problems experienced by system-involved women and girls, and noted how women's and girls' social identities (e.g., their ethnicity, sexual identity, gender identity, and access to resources) intersect and are associated with their risk of incarceration. We, as authors of this book, also have asked you to consider how behaviors come to be defined as criminal. For example, we have pointed out that many behaviors labeled as criminal, such as running away, drug use, or sex work can also be described as survival strategies used by women and girls with limited resources in the face of multiple adversities and exposures to violence.

As we described women's and girls' entry into the system, involvement with the system, and efforts to leave the system, we also provided examples of potential ways to change the system from within. We drew on the sequential intercept model and trauma-informed approaches to identify points of interception where workers in the system could change policies and decision-making processes. For example, we discussed examining and changing policies and procedures to be responsive to trauma survivors rather than retraumatizing women and girls. We also noted many points of discretion in decision making by key personnel in the legal system (e.g., law enforcement officers, juvenile intake officers, defendants, prosecutors, judges, correctional officers, probation/parole officers) and the possibility of changing jurisdiction-specific and institution-specific protocols that affect how individuals' behaviors are labeled, the pathways through the system, and the possibility of utilizing alternative methods of addressing criminal behaviors, depending on the nature and severity of the crime. We noted that individuals of different backgrounds and intersecting identities are at varied risk for more punitive responses and that access to resources plays a significant role in individuals' risk of detention. We also emphasized and encouraged the use of standardized screening and assessment tools to assess women's and girls' needs and the importance of connecting individuals to needed services to decrease time spent in the criminal legal system, deter criminogenic behavior, and decrease risk of reoffending.

Important next steps for effective reform from within the criminal legal system require advances in evidence-based practice and policy and multi-system administrative data integration. First, while we describe some efforts at evidence-based practice and policy in this text, there is clear need for partnerships among researchers and system-involved practitioners to identify the most effective screening tools and programs to address the treatment needs of system-involved women and girls. Further, while there are ongoing policy efforts to address some of the issues identified by scholars and advocates for reform, additional work is necessary to disseminate policy recommendations at all levels. For example, federal institutions such as the Substance Abuse and Mental health Administration (SAMHSA) have issued guidelines for adopting trauma-informed approaches, but it is not clear that this information is reaching and being effectively implemented in many county and state institutions. Similarly, although there is growing recognition that data integration across systems would likely improve access to services and service coordination, many barriers to effective multisystem administrative data integration remain.

Many of our recommendations for best practices focus on changing behaviors and decision-making processes of system-involved personnel and processes within the criminal legal system. We have also advocated that changing the system must include a commitment from leaders within the criminal legal system to examine our laws, policies, and operations. Throughout this text, we have emphasized the need for corrections to work with other institutions and systems to address social inequities such as access to health care, safe communities, affordable housing, and quality education.

However, to decrease the collateral damage incurred by our current carceral methods, many activists, theorists, researchers, and formerly incarcerated individuals have argued the need for broader, systemic change. Many have suggested a key avenue for change is to shift our focus away from the criminal legal system and concentrate resources and efforts of reform outside of the established corrections institutions. For example, we discuss efforts to prevent entry into the criminal legal system at early points of interception (e.g., working with crisis workers and behavioral health service providers) as well as efforts to change policies regarding licensure and employment for individuals with criminal records.

The work of author and civil rights attorney Alec Karakatsanis, in his 2019 book *Usual Cruelty*, offers criticism of continuing to try to reform the current criminal legal system from within and provides suggestions of reform efforts located external to the current legal system. Karakatsanis argues the current system cannot be fixed internally due to the extensive, existing inequities in our broader society. Some of his suggestions are similar to recommendations offered within this text, such as examining and changing how we label and respond to criminogenic behaviors. But Karakatsanis goes on to argue that to engage in effective change, the power to make reforms should shift from key personnel within the criminal legal system (e.g., police, attorneys, judges, supervision officers) to individuals, communities, and institutions outside of the legal system. Karakatsanis draws on the concept of restorative justice, which emphasizes repairing the harm caused by a criminal behavior rather than our current focus on punishment for the behavior. He offers suggestions of allocating or reinvesting resources currently used by the criminal legal system to communities to address social inequities such as housing quality and affordability and access to quality health care, stable financial institutions, and funding schools. Karakatsanis goes further and asserts that the extensive damage caused by our current system and processes should be addressed via a system of reparations to those who have suffered collateral damage due to lack of resources—for example, the individuals who have been held in jail for the lack of ability to pay fines. Reflect on what we have discussed throughout this book. Do you think that reforms from within the system are making needed progress to reduce impacts of crime and incarceration? What strategies outside of the system hold the most promise for transforming the way we address crime?

It will take efforts from within and external to the current criminal legal system to make significant impacts on the rate of incarceration of women and girls in our country. We hope that reading this text has provided you with information and tools to assist you as you interact with or work in this system.

References

Aaron, L., & Dallaire, D. (2010). Parental incarceration and multiple risk experiences. *Journal of Youth and Adolescence, 39*(12), 1471–1484.

Abin-Lackey, C. (2014, February 5). *Profiting from probation: America's 'offender-funded' probation industry.* Human Rights Watch. https://www.hrw.org/report/2014/02/05/profiting-probation/americas-offender-funded-probation-industry

Abram, K. M., Teplin, L. A., King, D. C., Longworth, S. L., Emanuel, K. M., Romero, E. G., & Olson, N. (2013). *PTSD, trauma, and comorbid psychiatric disorders in detained youth* (NCJ 239603). U.S. Department of Justice, Office of Justice Programs, Office of Juvenile Justice and Delinquency Prevention. https://ojjdp.ojp.gov/sites/g/files/xyckuh176/files/pubs/239603.pdf

Abreu, D., Parker, T., Noether, C., Steadman, H., & Case, B. (2017). Revising the paradigm for jail diversion for people with mental and substance use disorders: Intercept 0. *Behavioral Science Law, 35*(5–6), 380–395.

Administration for Children and Families (ACF). (2013). *Human trafficking briefing series: Emerging practices within child welfare responses.* Author.

Alexander, M. (2012). *The New Jim Crow.* New Press.

Alexander, M. (2018, November 8). The newest Jim Crow: Recent criminal justice reforms contain the seeds of a frightening system of "e-carceration." *New York Times.* https://www.nytimes.com/2018/11/08/opinion/sunday/criminal-justice-reforms-race-technology.html

Alper, M., Durose, M. R., & Markman, J. (2018). *2018 update on prisoner recidivism: A 9-year follow-up period (2005–2014)* (NCJ #250975). Bureau of Justice. https://www.bjs.gov/content/pub/pdf/18upr9yfup0514.pdf

American Psychiatric Association. (2013). *Diagnostic and statistical manual of mental disorders* (5th ed.) Author.

American Psychological Association. (2017). *End the Use of Restraints on Incarcerated Women and Adolescents during Pregnancy, Labor, Childbirth, and Recovery.* https://www.apa.org/advocacy/criminal-justice/shackling-incarcerated-women.pdf

Anderson, E., Beemsterboer, N., Beninacasa, R., & Van Werkom, B. (2014, May 19). *As court fees rise, the poor are paying the price.* NPR. http://www.npr.org/2014/05/19/312158516/increasing-court-fees-punish-the-poor

Anderson, V., & Javdani, S. (2018). Physical health needs and treatment for female offenders returning to society. In L. Carter and C. Marcum (Eds.), *Female offenders and reentry: Pathways and barriers to returning to society* (pp. 28–44). Routledge.

Andrews, D. A., & Bonta, J. (1994). *The psychology of criminal conduct.* Anderson.

Andrews, D. A., & Bonta, J. (2010). Rehabilitating criminal justice policy and practice. *Psychology, Public Policy, and Law, 16*(1), 39–55. https://doi.org/10.1037/a0018362

Appelbaum, K., Hickey, J., & Packer, I. (2001). The role of correctional officers in multi-disciplinary mental health care in prison. *Psychiatric Services, 52*(10), 1343–1347.

Arditti, J. A., & Few, A. L. (2006). Mothers' reentry into family life following incarceration. *Criminal Justice Policy Review, 17*(1), 103–123. https://doi.org/10.1177/0887403405282450

Arnold, R. (1992). Women of color: Processes of victimization and criminalization of Black women. *Social Justice, 17*(3), 153–166.

Atkins, C. (2019, May 29). New law ends use of restraints on pregnant inmates as advocates push for more to be done. *NBC News.* https://www.nbcnews.com/politics/donald-trump/new-law-ends-use-restraints-pregnant-inmates-advocates-push-more-n1007526

Avery, B. (2019, July 1). *Ban the box: US cities, counties and states adopt fair hiring policies.* National Employment Law Project. https://nelp.org/publication/ban-the-box-fair-chance-hiring-state-and-local-guide/

Balko, R. (2018, September 18). There's overwhelming evidence that the criminal-justice system is racist. Here's the proof. *Washington Post.* https://www.washingtonpost.com/news/opinions/wp/2018/09/18/theres-overwhelming-evidence-that-the-criminal-justice-system-is-racist-heres-the-proof/?noredirect=on

Bannon, A., Nagrecha, M., & Diller, R. (2010). *Criminal justice debt: A barrier to reentry.* Brennan Center for Justice.

Barnert, E. S., Dudovitz, R., Nelson, B. B., Coker, T. R., Biely, C., Li, N., & Chung, P. J. (2017). How does incarcerating young people affect their adult health outcomes? *Pediatrics, 139*(2), e20162624.

Beck, A. J. (2014). *Sexual victimization in prisons and jails reported by inmates, 2011–12: Supplemental tables: Prevalence of sexual victimization among transgender adult inmates.* Bureau of Justice Statistics. https://www.bjs.gov/content/pub/pdf/svpjri1112_st.pdf

Beck, A. (2015). *Use of restrictive housing in U.S. prisons and jails, 2011–12* (NCJ #249209). Bureau of Justice Statistics. https://www.bjs.gov/content/pub/pdf/urhuspj1112.pdf

Becker, S. P., Kerig, P. K., Lim, J. Y., & Ezechukwu, R. N. (2012). Predictors of recidivism among delinquent youth: Interrelations among ethnicity, gender, age, mental health problems, and posttraumatic stress. *Journal of Child & Adolescent Trauma, 5*(2), 145–160.

Beckett, K., Nyrop, K., Pfingst, L. (2006). Race, drugs, and policing: Understanding disparities in drug delivery arrests. *Criminology, 44*(1), 105–137. https://doi.org/10.1080/19361521.2012.671798

Begun, A. L., Early, T. J., & Hodge, A. (2016). Mental health and substance abuse service engagement by men and women during community reentry following incarceration. *Administration and Policy in Mental Health, 43*(2), 207–218. https://doi.org/10.1007/s10488-015-0632-2

Belknap, J. (2004). Meda Chesney-Lind. *Women & Criminal Justice, 15*(2), 1–23.

Belknap, J. (2014). *The invisible woman: Gender, crime, and justice.* Cengage.

Belknap, J., & Holsinger, K. (2006). The gendered nature of risk factors for delinquency. *Feminist Criminology, 1*(1), 48–71.

Belknap, J., & Whalley, E. (2013). The health crisis among incarcerated women and girls. In E. Waltermaurer & T. Akers (Eds.), *Epidemiological criminology: Theory to practice* (pp. 95–106). Routledge.

Benda, B. B. (2005). Gender differences in life-course theory of recidivism: A survival analysis. *International Journal of Offender Therapy and Comparative Criminology, 49*(3), 325–342. https://doi.org/10.1177/0306624X04271194

Benedict, A. (2008). The five CORE practice areas of gender-responsiveness. CORE Associates, LLC.

Benedict, A. (2014). *Using trauma-informed practices to enhance safety and security in women's correctional facilities.* Bureau of Justice Assistance. https://bja.ojp.gov/sites/g/files/xyckuh186/files/Publications/NRCJIW-UsingTraumaInformedPractices.pdf

Bersani, B., & Piquero, A. (2016). Examining systematic prevalence, trends, and divergence in self-reported and official reported arrests. *Journal of Quantitative Criminology, 33*(4), 835–857.

Binswanger, I. A., Merrill, J. O., Krueger, P. M., White, M. C., Booth, R. E., & Elmore, J. G. (2010). Gender differences in chronic medical, psychiatric, and substance-dependence disorders among jail inmates. *American Journal of Public Health, 100*(3), 476–482. https://ajph.aphapublications.org/doi/abs/10.2105/AJPH.2008.149591

Blackmon, D. (2008). *Slavery by another name: The re-enslavement of Black Americans from the Civil War to world*. Doubleday.

Blakinger, K. [@keribla]. (2019, December 18). *Thread: And it's not just the journey* [Tweet]. https://twitter.com/keribla/status/1207328104697470977

Blevins, K., & Soderstrom, I. (2015). The mental health crisis grows on: A descriptive analysis of DOC systems in America. *Journal of Offender Rehabilitation, 54*(2), 142–160. https://doi.org/10.1080/10509674.2015.1009965

Bocanegra, K. (2017). Community and decarceration: Developing localized solutions. In M. Epperson & C. Pettus-Davis (Eds.), *Smart decarceration: Achieving criminal justice transformation in the 21st century* (pp. 115–133). Oxford University Press.

Bohmert, M.N. (2018) Transportation Issues. In L. Carter and C. Marcum (Eds.), *Female offenders and reentry: Pathways and barriers to returning to society* (pp. 5–27). Routledge

Bottiani, J., Bradshaw, C., & Mendelson, T. (2016). A multilevel examination of racial disparities in high school discipline: Black and White adolescents' perceived equity, school belonging, and adjustment problems. *Journal of Educational Psychology, 109*(4), 532–545.

Brand, J., & Pishko, J. (June 14, 2018). Bail reform: Explained. *The Appeal*. https://theappeal.org/bail-reform-explained-4abb73dd2e8a/

Brandt, A. L. S. (2012). Treatment of persons with mental illness in the criminal justice system: A literature review. *Journal of Offender Rehabilitation, 51*(8), 541–558. https://doi.org/10.1080/10509674.2012.693902

Bravo, K., Espinosa, E., & Friel, C. (2018, October 23). Anaheim father facing deportation after testifying against daughter's molester, family says. *KTLA*. https://ktla.com/2018/10/22/anaheim-father-facing-deportation-after-testifying-against-daughters-molester-family-says/?utm_source=The+Appeal&utm_campaign=7675d2f1a8-EMAIL_CAMPAIGN_2018_08_09_04_14_COPY_01&utm_medium=email&utm_term=0_72df992d84-7675d2f1a8-58396775

Brennan, T., Breitenbach, M., Dieterich, W., Salisbury, E. J., & van Voorhis, P. (2012). Women's pathways to serious and habitual crime: A person-centered analysis incorporating gender responsive factors. *Criminal Justice and Behavior, 39*(11), 1481–1508. https://doi.org/10.1177/0093854812456777

Bronson J., & Berzofsky, M. (2017, June). *Indicators of mental health problems reported by prisoners and jail inmates, 2011–12* (NCJ 250612). Bureau of Justice Statistics. https://www.bjs.gov/content/pub/pdf/imhprpji1112.pdf

Bronson, J., & Carson, E. A. (2019). *Prisoners in 2017* (NCJ 252156). Bureau of Justice Statistics. https://www.bjs.gov/content/pub/pdf/p17.pdf

Brower, J. (2013). *Correctional officer wellness and safety literature review*. National Institute of Corrections. http://nicic.gov/library/028104

Brown, J. (2018, October 15). Changing the narrative on opioids: BU Center for Humanities forum examines crisis through history, culture, literature. *The Brink*. http://www.bu.edu/articles/2018/changing-the-narrative-on-opioids/

Browne, A. (1987). *When battered women kill*. Free Press.

Browne, A., Miller, B., & Maguin, E. (1999). Prevalence and severity of lifetime physical and sexual victimization among incarceration women. International *Journal of Law and Psychiatry, 22*(3–4), 301–322.

Campbell, C., Papp, J., Barnes, A., Onifade, E., & Anderson, V. (2018). Risk assessment and juvenile justice. *Criminology & Public Policy, 17*(3), 525–545. https://doi.org/10.1111/1745-9133.12377

Carson, E. A., & Sabol, W. J. (2016). *Aging of the state prison population, 1993–2013* (NCJ #248766). Bureau of Justice Statistics. https://www.bjs.gov/content/pub/pdf/aspp9313.pdf

Center for American Progress and Movement Advancement Project (CAPMAP). (2016). *Unjust: How the broken criminal justice system fails transgender people*. http://www.lgbtmap.org/criminal-justice-trans

Centers for Disease Control and Prevention (no date). *Traumatic brain injury in prisons and jails: An unrecognized problem*. https://www.cdc.gov/traumaticbraininjury/pdf/Prisoner_TBI_Prof-a.pdf

Centers for Disease Control and Prevention (CDC). (2011). Health disparities and inequalities report—United States, 2011. *Morbidity and Mortality Weekly Report, 60*, 1–116. https://www.cdc.gov/mmwr/pdf/other/su6001.pdf

Centers for Disease Control and Prevention (CDC). (2013). Health disparities and inequalities report—United States, 2013. *Morbidity and Mortality Weekly Report, 62*(3), 1–189. https://www.cdc.gov/mmwr/pdf/other/su6203.pdf

Cepeda, E. (2016, September 19). Cepeda: The myth of immigrants and crime. *Roanoke Times*. https://www.roanoke.com/opinion/columns_and_blogs/cepeda-the-myth-of-immigrants-and-crime/article_23e2b232-47d4-5bc5-9327-99bba742e346.html

Chesney-Lind, M. (1989). Girls' crime and woman's place: Toward a feminist model of female delinquency. *Crime & Delinquency, 35*(1), 5–29.

Clear, T. (2009). Incarceration and communities. *Criminal Justice Matters, 75*, 26–27.

Clear, T., Rose, D., & Ryder, J. (2001). Incarceration and the community: The problem of removing and returning offenders. *Crime & Delinquency, 47*(3), 335–351.

Clear, T., Rose, D., Waring, E., & Scully, K. (2003). Coercive mobility and crime: A preliminary examination of concentrated incarceration and social disorganization. *Justice Quarterly, 20*(1), 33–64.

Coates, T. (2015). *Between the world and me*. Spiegel & Grau.

Cobbina, J. E. (2010). Reintegration success and failure: Factors impacting reintegration among incarcerated and formerly incarcerated women. *Journal of Offender Rehabilitation, 49*(3), 210–232. https://doi.org/10.1080/10509671003666602

Conrad, S. M., Tolou-Shams, M., Rizzo, C. J., Placella, N., & Brown, L. K. (2014). Gender differences in recidivism rates for juvenile justice youth: the impact of sexual abuse. *Law and Human Behavior, 38*(4), 305–314. https://doi.org/10.1037/lhb0000062

Couloute, L., & Kopf (2018). *Out of prison and out of work: Unemployment among formerly incarcerated people*. Prison Policy Initiative. https://www.prisonpolicy.org/reports/outofwork.html

Cramer, L., Goff, M., Peterson, B., & Sandstrom, H. (2017). *Parent-child visiting practices in prisons and jails: A synthesis of research and practice*. Urban Institute.

Crenshaw, K. (2013). From private violence to mass incarceration: Thinking intersectionally about women, race, and social control. *UCLA Law Review, 59*, 1418–1472.

Crenshaw, K., Ocen, P., & Nanda, J. (2015). *Black girls matter: Pushed out, overpoliced, and underprotected*. Center for Intersectionality and Social Policy Studies.

Cross, T. L., Bazron, B. J., Dennis, K. W., & Isaacs, M. R. (1989). *Towards a culturally competent system of care: Vol. I*. National Technical Assistance Center for Children's Mental Health, Georgetown University Child Development Center.

Daly, K. (1992). Women's pathway to felony court: Feminist theories of lawbreaking and problems of representation. *Review of Law and Women's Studies, 2*(1), 11–52.

Davidson, J., Pasko, L., & Chesney-Lind, M. (2011). "She's way too good to lose": An evaluation of Honolulu's girls court. *Women & Criminal Justice, 21*(4), 308–327.

Davis, E., Whyde, A., & Langton, L. (2018). *Contacts between police and the public, 2015* (NCJ 251145). Bureau of Justice Statistics: Special Report. https://www.bjs.gov/content/pub/pdf/cpp15.pdf

DeCou, C., Lynch, S. M. & Cole, T. (2016). Physical and sexual victimization predicts suicidality among women in prison: Understanding ethnic and trauma-specific domains of risk. *Current Psychology, 36*, 774–780. https://doi.org/10.1007/s12144-016-9465-8

DeHart, D. D. (2008). Pathways to prison: Impact of victimization in the lives of incarcerated women. *Violence Against Women, 14*(12), 1362–1381. https://doi.org/10.1177/1077801208327018

DeHart, D. (2009). *Poly-victimization among girls in the juvenile justice system: Manifestations and associations to delinquency* (NCJRS #228620). U.S. Department of Justice.

DeHart, D. (2018). Women's pathways to crime: A heuristic typology of offenders. *Criminal Justice & Behavior, 45*(10), 1461–1482. https://doi.org/10.1177/0093854818782568

DeHart, D., & Iachini, A. (2019). Mental health and trauma among incarcerated persons: Development of a training curriculum for correctional officers. *American Journal of Criminal Justice, 44*(3), 457–473.

DeHart, D., Lize, S., Priester, M. A., & Bell, B. (2017). Improving the efficacy of administrative data for evaluation of holistic defense. *Journal of Social Service Research, 43*(2), 169–180.

DeHart, D. D., & Lynch, S. M. (2012). Gendered pathways to crime: The relationship between victimization and offending. In C. Renzetti, S. Miller & A. Gover (Eds.), *Routledge International Handbook of Gender and Crime Studies*. Routledge.

DeHart, D., Lynch, S., Belknap, J., Dass-Brailsford, P., & Green, B. (2014). Life-history models of female offending: The role of serious mental illness and trauma in women's pathways to jail. *Psychology of Women Quarterly, 38*(1), 138–151. https://doi.org/10.1177/0361684313494357

DeHart, D. D., & Moran, R. (2015). Poly-victimization among girls in the justice system: Trajectories of risk and associations to juvenile offending. *Violence Against Women, 21*(3), 291–312.

DeHart, D., Shapiro, C., & Clone, S. (2018). "The pill line is longer than the chow line": The impact of incarceration on prisoners and their families. *The Prison Journal, 98*(2), 188–212.

DeHart, D. D., Smith, H. P., & Kaminski, R. H. (2009). Institutional response to self-injury among inmates. *Journal of Correctional Health Care, 15*(3), 129–141. https://doi.org/10.1177/1078345809331444

Development Services Group, Inc. (2017). *Juvenile reentry*. Office of Juvenile Justice and Delinquency Prevention. https://www.ojjdp.gov/mpg/litreviews/Aftercare.pdf

Dirks, D. (2004). Sexual revictimization and retraumatization of women in prison. *Women's Studies Quarterly, 32*(3/4), 102–115.

Drapkin, M. (2009). *Management and supervision of jail inmates with mental disorders*. Civic Research Institute.

Dolan, K., & Carr, J. (2015). *The poor get prison: The alarming spread of the criminalization of poverty*. Institute for Policy Studies.

Doleac, J. (2016, March 31). *"Ban the box" does more harm than good*. Brookings Institute. https://www.brookings.edu/opinions/ban-the-box-does-more-harm-than-good/

Duley, K. (2007). Un-domesticating violence. *Women & Therapy, 29*(3–4), 75–96.

Eason, J. (2017). *Big house on the prairie: Rise of the rural ghetto and prison proliferation*. University of Chicago Press.

Editorial Board. (2013, August 12) Racial discrimination in stop-and-frisk. *New York Times*. https://www.nytimes.com/2013/08/13/opinion/racial-discrimination-in-stop-and-frisk.html

Ehrmann, S., Hyland, N., & Puzzanchera, C. (2019). *Girls in the juvenile justice system* (NCJ 251486). National Report Series Bulletin. https://ojjdp.ojp.gov/sites/g/files/xyckuh176/files/pubs/251486.pdf

Eliason, M., Taylor, J., & Williams, R. (2004). Physical health of women in prison. *Journal of Correctional Health, 10*(2), 175–203. https://doi.org/10.1177/107834580301000204

Ellis, K. (2018). Contested vulnerability: A case study of girls in secure care. *Children and Youth Services Review, 88*, 156–163. https://doi.org/10.1016/j.childyouth.2018.02.047

Encyclopædia Britannica (2018). *Slave code.* https://www.britannica.com/topic/slave-code

Enns, P., Yi, Y., Comfort, M., Goldman, A., Lee, H., Muller, C., Wakefield, S., Wang, E., & Wildeman, C. (2019). What percentage of Americans have ever had a family member incarcerated? Evidence from the Family History of Incarceration Survey (FamHIS). *Socius: Sociological Research for a Dynamic World, 5,* 1–45.

Ensellem, M., Avery, B., & Hernandez, P. (2018, May 15). *Fair chance licensing reform takes hold in the states.* National Employment Law Project. https://www.nelp.org/publication/fair-chance-licensing-reform-takes-hold-states/

Ewing, W., Martinez, D., & Rumbaut, R. (2015, July 13). *The criminalization of immigration in the United States.* American Immigration Council. https://www.americanimmigra-tioncouncil.org/research/criminalization-immigration-united-states

Fabelo, T., Thompson, M. D., Plotkin, M., Carmichael, D., Marchbanks, M. P., III, & Booth, E. A. (2011). *Breaking schools' rules: A statewide study of how school discipline relates to students' success and juvenile justice involvement.* Council of State Governments Justice Center, Public Policy Research Institute of Texas, & A&M University.

Feld, B. (2009). Violent girls or relabeled status offenders? An alternative interpretation of the data. *Crime & Delinquency, 55*(2), 241–265.

Felitti, V., Anda, R., Nordenberg, D., Williamson, D., Spitz, A., Edwards, V., Koss, M., & Marks, J. (1998). Relationship of childhood abuse and household dysfunction to many of the leading causes of death in adults: The Adverse Childhood Experiences (ACE) study. *American Journal of Preventive Medicine, 14*(4), 245–258.

Fellner, J. (2006). A corrections quandary: Mental illness and prison rules. *Harvard Civil Rights-Civil Liberties Law Review, 41,* 391–412.

Ferszt, G., & Clarke, J. (2012). Health care of pregnant women in U.S. state prisons. *Journal of Health Care for the Poor and Underserved, 23*(2), 557–569.

Finkelhor, D., Turner, H., Hamby, S., & Ormrod, R. (2011). Polyvictimization: Children's exposure to multiple types of violence, crime, and abuse. *Juvenile Justice Bulletin.* https://www.ncjrs.gov/pdffiles1/ojjdp/235504.pdf

Fitzgerald, E., Elspeth, S., Hickey, D., & Biko, C. (2015). *Meaningful work: Transgender experiences in the sex trade.* National Center for Transgender Equality.

Florida Legislature Office of Program Policy Analysis and Government Accountability (FLOPPAGA). (2016). *Placement challenges persist for child victims of commercial sexual exploitation; questions regarding effective interventions and outcomes remain.* Author.

Flower, S. M. (2010). *Employment and female offenders: An update of the empirical research* (NIC #024662). U.S. Department of Justice. https://s3.amazonaws.com/static.nicic.gov/Library/024662.pdf

Ford, J., & Trestman, R. (2005). *Evidence-based enhancement of the detection, prevention, and treatment of mental illness in correctional systems: Final report.* U.S. Department of Justice. https://www.ncjrs.gov/pdffiles1/nij/grants/210829.pdf

Ford, J., Trestman, R., Osher, F., Scott, J., Steadman, H., & Robbins, P. (2007). *Mental health screens for corrections. Research for Practice Brief.* U.S. Department of Justice. https://www.ncjrs.gov/pdffiles1/nij/216152.pdf

Freudenberg, N., Daniels, J., Crum, M., Perkins, T., & Richie, B. E. (2005). Coming home from jail: The social and health consequences of community reentry for women, male adolescents, and their families and communities. *American Journal of Public Health, 95*(10), 1725–1736. https://doi.org/10.2105/AJPH.2004.056325

Ghandnoosh, N. (2017). Minimizing the maximum: The case for shortening all prison sentences. In M. Epperson & C. Pettus-Davis (Eds.), *Smart decarceration: Achieving criminal justice transformation in the 21st century* (pp. 115–133). Oxford University Press.

Ghandnoosh, N., Rovner, J., & Yoo, J. (2017). *Immigration and public safety.* Washington, DC: The Sentencing Project.

Gehring, K., & Van Voorhis, P. (2014). Needs and pretrial failure: Additional risk factors for female and male pretrial defendants. *Criminal Justice and Behavior, 41*(8), 943–970.

General Assembly of the Commonwealth of Pennsylvania. (2011). *The effects of parental incarceration on children: Needs and responsive services* [Report of the Advisory Committee Pursuant to House Resolution 203 and Senate Resolution 52 of 2009]. Author.

Gersten, A. (2019, September 24). *Prisons disproportionately ban books on race and civil rights, PEN America report finds.* PasteMagazine.com https://www.pastemagazine.com/books/banned-books/prisons-disproportionately-ban-books-on-race-and-c/

GetLegal.com (2016). *The criminal justice system.* https://www.getlegal.com/legal-info-center/criminal-law/criminal-justice-system/Gilfus, M. (1992). From victims to survivors to offenders: Women's routes of entry and immersion into street crime. *Women & Criminal Justice, 4*(1), 63–89.

Gill, C., & Wilson, D. B. (2016). Improving the success of reentry programs: Identifying the impact of service-need fit on recidivism. *Criminal Justice and Behavior, 44*(3), 336–359. https://doi.org/10.1177/0093854816682048

Giovani, T. (2012). *Community-oriented defense: Start now.* Brennan Center for Justice.

Glaze, L. E., & Maruschak, M. L. (2010, March 30). *Parents in prison and their minor children* (NCJ #222984). Bureau of Justice Statistics: A Special Report. https://www.bjs.gov/content/pub/pdf/pptmc.pdf

Glazer, E., Sassaman, H. J., & Wool, J. (2017, October 25). *Debating risk-assessment tools: Experts weigh in on whether algorithms have a place in our criminal justice system.* The Marshall Project. https://www.themarshallproject.org/2017/10/25/debating-risk-assessment-tools

Godfrey, B., & Soper, S. (2018, May 22). *Prison records from 1800s Georgia show mass incarceration's racially charged beginnings.* The Conversation. http://theconversation.com/prison-records-from-1800s-georgia-show-mass-incarcerations-racially-charged-beginnings-96612

Godsoe, C. (2015). Punishment as protection. Harvard Law Review, *52*(5), 1313–1384.

Goldstein, J. (2013, August 12). Judge rejects New York's stop-and-frisk policy. *New York Times.* https://www.nytimes.com/2013/08/13/nyregion/stop-and-frisk-practice-violated-rights-judge-rules.html

Golzari, M., Hunt, S. J., & Anoshiravani, A. (2006). The health status of youth in juvenile detention facilities. *Journal of Adolescent Health, 38*(6), 776–782. https://doi.org/10.1016/j.jadohealth.2005.06.008

Graham, K. (2013). Overcharging. *Santa Clara Law Digital Commons.* https://digitalcommons.law.scu.edu/facpubs/608/

Grant, J., Mottet, L., & Tanis, J. (2011). *Injustice at every turn: A report of the National Transgender Discrimination Survey.* https://www.transequality.org/sites/default/files/docs/resources/NTDS_Report.pdf

Green, B., Dass-Brailsford, P., de Mendoza, A., Mete, M. Lynch, S., DeHart, D., & Belknap, J. (2016). Trauma experiences and mental health among incarcerated women. *Psychological Trauma: Theory, Research, Practice, & Policy, 8*(4), 455–463.

Green, K., Ensminger, M., Robertson, J., & Juon, H. (2006). Impact of adult sons' incarceration on African American mothers' psychological distress. *Journal of Marriage and Family, 68*(2), 430–441.

Guastafero, W. & Lutgen, L. (2018). Women with substance use disorders reentering the community. In L. Carter and C. Marcum (Eds.), *Female offenders and reentry: Pathways and barriers to returning to society* (pp. 76–107). Routledge.

Gueta, K. (2017). The experience of prisoners' parents: A meta-synthesis of qualitative studies. *Family Process, 57*(3), 767–782.

Hall, T. L., Wooten, N. R., & Lundgren, L. M. (2016). Postincarceration policies and prisoner reentry: Implications for policies and programs aimed at reducing recidivism and poverty. *Journal of Poverty, 20*(1), 56–72. https://doi.org/10.1080/10875549.2015.1094761

Hanser, R. (2018). *Essentials of community corrections*. SAGE.

Harris, A. (2016). *A pound of flesh: Monetary sanctions as punishment for the poor*. Russell Sage Foundation.

Hattery, A., & Smith, E. (2018). *Policing Black bodies: How Black lives are surveilled and how to work for change*. Rowman & Littlefield.

Hatzenbuehler, M., Keyes, K., Hamilton, A., Uddin, M., & Galea, S. (2015). The collateral damage of mass incarceration: Risk of psychiatric morbidity among nonincarcerated residents of high-incarceration neighborhoods. *American Journal of Public Health, 105*(1), 138–143.

Hayes, C. (2017). *A colony in a nation*. Norton.

Hinton, E., Henderson, L., & Reed, C. (2018). *An unjust burden: The disparate treatment of Black Americans in the criminal justice system*. New York, NY: Vera Institute of Justice.

Hoffman, H., Byrd, A., & Kightlinger, A. (2010). Prison programs and services for incarcerated parents and their underaged children: Results of a national survey of correctional facilities. *Prison Journal, 90*(4), 397–416.

Huebner, B. M., DeJong, C., & Cobbina, J. (2010). Women coming home: Long-term patterns of recidivism. *Justice Quarterly, 27*(2), 225–254. https://doi.org/10.1080/07418820902870486

Human Rights Watch (HRW). (2014). *Profiting from probation: America's "offender-funded" probation industry*. https://www.prisonlegalnews.org/media/publications/Human%20Rights%20Watch%20-%20Private%20Probation%20Report%2C%202014.pdf

Human Rights Watch (HRW). (2015, May 12). *Callous and cruel: Use of force against inmates with mental disabilities in US jails and prisons*. https://www.hrw.org/report/2015/05/12/callous-and-cruel/use-force-against-inmates-mental-disabilities-us-jails-and#233cc9

Ingoldsby, E., & Shaw, D. (2002). Neighborhood contextual factors and early-starting antisocial pathways. *Clinical Child and Family Psychology Review, 5*(1), 21–55.

Ireland, J. (2002). *Bullying among prisoners: Evidence, Research, and Intervention Strategies*. Brunner-Routledge.

James, A. (2019). Ending the incarceration of women and girls. *Yale Law Journal Forum, 128*, 772–790.

Jones, A. (2019, May). *Does our county really need a bigger jail: A guide for avoiding unnecessary jail expansion*. Prison Policy Initiative. https://www.prisonpolicy.org/reports/jailexpansion.html

Jones, R. (2016, August 14). How Trump remixed the republican "Southern Strategy." *The Atlantic*. https://www.theatlantic.com/politics/archive/2016/08/how-trump-remixed-the-republican-southern-strategy/495719/

Kaeble, D. (2018). *Probation and parole in the United States, 2016* (NCJ 251148). Bureau of Justice Statistics. https://www.bjs.gov/content/pub/pdf/ppus16.pdf

Kaeble, D., & Cowhig, M. (2018) *Correctional populations in the United States* (NCJ 251211). Bureau of Justice Statistics. https://www.bjs.gov/content/pub/pdf/cpus16.pdf

Kajstura, A. (2019). *Women's mass incarceration: The whole pie 2019*. Prison Policy Initiative. https://www.prisonpolicy.org/reports/pie2019women.html

Kakade, M., Duarte, C., Liu, X., Fuller, C., Drucker, E., Hoven, C., Fan, B., & Wu, P. (2012). Adolescent substance use and other illegal behaviors and racial disparities in criminal justice system involvement: Findings from a US national survey. *American Journal of Public Health, 102*(7), 1307–1310.

Karakatsanis, A. (2020). *Usual cruelty: The complicity of lawyers in the criminal injustice system*. The New Press.

Khaleeli, H. (2016, May 30). #SayHerName: Why Kimberlé Crenshaw is fighting for forgotten women. The Guardian. https://www.theguardian.com/lifeandstyle/2016/may/30/sayhername-why-kimberle-crenshaw-is-fighting-for-forgotten-women

Kelly, A. (2017, February 1). Survey: Arizona voters support alternatives to bail. *AZPM News*. https://news.azpm.org/p/news-topical-politics/2017/2/1/105609-survey-arizona-voters-support-alternatives-to-bail/

Kendi, I. (2016). *Stamped from the beginning: The definitive history of racist ideas in America*. Nation Books.

Kennedy, D. (2012). "The good mother": Mothering, feminism, and incarceration. *William & Mary Journal of Women & the Law, 18*, 161–200.

Kennedy, R. (2011). *Race, crime, and the law*. Vintage.

Kerman, N., Sylvestre, J., Aubry, T., & Distasio, J. (2018). The effects of housing stability on service use among homeless adults with mental illness in a randomized controlled trial of housing first. *BMC Health Services Research, 18*(1), 190. https://doi.org/10.1186/s12913-018-3028-7

Kessler, R. C., Berglund, P. A., Demler, O., Jin, R., Merikangas, K. R., & Walters, E. E. (2005). Lifetime prevalence and age-of-onset distributions of DSM-IV disorders in the National Comorbidity Survey Replication (NCS-R). *Archives of General Psychiatry, 62*(6), 593–602.

Kifer, M., Hemmens, C., & Stohr, M. (2003). Goals of corrections: Perspectives from the line. *Criminal Justice Review, 28*(1), 47–69.

Kochel, T., Wilson, D., Mastrofski, S. (2011). Effect of suspect race on officers' arrest decisions. *Criminology, 49*(2), 473–512.

Kosciw, J., Graytak, E., Palmer, N., & Boesen, M. (2014). *The 2013 National School Climate Survey: The experiences of lesbian, gay, bisexual and transgender youth in our nation's schools*. GLSEN.

Korn, J., Kraemer, W., & Coggins, E. (2015). *Massachusetts Correctional Institute Framingham Peer Support program*. http://apps1.seiservices.com/SAMHSA/CMHS_webinars2015/Resources%5C2_Massachusetts%20Presentation.pdf

Lang, J. (2011). *What is a community court? How the model is being adapted across the United States*. Bureau of Justice Assistance. https://www.courtinnovation.org/sites/default/files/documents/What%20is%20a%20Community%20Court.pdf

Langton, L., & Durose, M. (2016. October 27). *Police behavior during traffic and street stops, 2011* (NCJ 242937). Bureau of Justice Statistics: Special Report. https://www.bjs.gov/content/pub/pdf/pbtss11.pdf

Lau, K. S., Rosenman, M. B., Wiehe, S. E., Tu, W., & Aalsma, M. C. (2018). Race/ethnicity, and behavioral health status: First arrest and outcomes in a large sample of juvenile offenders. *Journal of Behavioral Health Services & Research, 45*(2), 237–251.

LeFlouria, T. (2015). *Chained in silence: Black women and convict labor in the New South*. University of Chapel Hill.

Lindquist, C., Willison, J. B., Rossman, S., & Hardison, J. (2015). *Second chance act adult offender reentry demonstration programs: Implementation challenges and lessons learned*. Urban Institute.

LoBianco, T. (2016, March 24). *Report: Aide says Nixon's war on drugs targeted Blacks, hippies*. CNN. https://www.cnn.com/2016/03/23/politics/john-ehrlichman-richard-nixon-drug-war-blacks-hippie/index.html

Lustbader, S. (2020, January 7). Problem-solving courts promise a kinder, gentler system. Are they impeding progress? *The Appeal*. https://mailchi.mp/theappeal/daily-appeal-347551?e=dd538c1ae4

Lynch, S., DeHart, D., Belknap, J., & Green, B. (2012). *Women's pathways to jail: The roles and intersections of serious mental illness & trauma* (NCJ 240558). Bureau of Justice Assistance. https://www.bja.gov/Publications/Women_Pathways_to_Jail.pdf

Lynch, S., DeHart, D., Belknap, J., Green, B., Dass-Brailsford, P., Johnson, K., & Whalley, E. (2014). A multi-site study of the prevalence of serious mental illness, PTSD, and substance use disorders in women in jail. *Psychiatric Services, 65*(5), 670–674. https://doi.org/10.1176/appi.ps.201300172

Lynch, S., DeHart, D., Belknap, J., Green, B., Dass-Brailsford, P., Johnson, K., & Wong, M. (2017). An examination of the associations among victimization, mental health, and offending in women. *Criminal Justice & Behavior*, (44)6, 796–814. https://doi.org/10.1177/0093854817704452

Lynch, S. M., Heath, N. M., Matthews, K. C., & Cepeda, G. J. (2012). *Seeking Safety*: An intervention for trauma exposed incarcerated women? *Journal of Trauma & Dissociation*, *13*(1), 1–14. https://doi.org/10.1080/15299732.2011.608780

Mahmood, S. T., Vaughn, M. G., Mancini, M., & Fu, Q. J. (2013). Gender disparity in utilization rates of substance abuse services among female ex-offenders: A population-based analysis. *American Journal of Drug & Alcohol Abuse, 39*(5), 332–339.

Makarios, M., Steiner, B., & Travis, L. F. III. (2010). Examining the predictors of recidivism among men and women released from prison in Ohio. *Criminal Justice and Behavior, 37*(12), 1377–1391.

Martin, E. (2017, May). Hidden consequences: The impact of incarceration on dependent children. *NIJ Journal, 278*, 1–7.

Martin, M., Colman, I., Simpson, A., & McKenzie, K. (2013). Mental health screening tools in correctional institutions: A systematic review. *BMC Psychiatry, 13*, 275–285.

Maruschak, L., Berzofsky, M. & Unangst, J. (2015). *Medical problems of state and federal prisoners and jail inmates, 2011–12* (NCJ 248491). Bureau of Justice Statistics. https://www.bjs.gov/content/pub/pdf/mpsfpji1112.pdf

McCarter, S. (2017). The school-to-prison pipeline: A primer for social workers. *Social Work, 62*(1), 53–61.

McCarty, M., Falk, G., Aussenberg, R. A., & Carpenter, D. (2016, November 28). *Drug testing and crime-related restrictions in TANF, SNAP, and housing assistance.* Congressional Research Service. https://fas.org/sgp/crs/misc/R42394.pdf

McCorkel, J. (2013). *Breaking women: Gender, race, and the new politics of imprisonment.* New York University Press.

McCullumsmith, C. B., Clark, C. B., Perkins, A., Fife, J., & Cropsey, K. L. (2013). Gender and racial differences for suicide attempters and ideators in a high-risk community corrections population. *Crisis, 34,* 50–62. https://doi.org/10.1027/0227-5910/a000160

McGrath E. (2012). Reentry courts: Providing a second chance for incarcerated mothers and their children. *Family Court Review, 50*(1), 113–127.

McGrew, K. (2016). The dangers of pipeline thinking: How the school-to-prison pipeline metaphor squeezes out complexity. *Educational Theory, 66*(3), 341–367.

McKillop, M., & Boucher, A. (2018, February 20). *Aging prison populations drive up costs.* PEW Charitable Trusts. https://www.pewtrusts.org/en/research-and-analysis/articles/2018/02/20/aging-prison-populations-drive-up-costs

Messina, N., & Grella, C. (2006). Childhood trauma and women's health outcomes in a California prison population. *American Journal of Public Health, 96*(10), 1842–1848. https://doi.org/10.2105/AJPH.2005.082016

Meyer, I., Flores, A., Stemple, L., Romero, A., Wilson, B., & Herman, J. (2017). Incarceration rates and traits of sexual minorities in the United States: National Inmate Survey, 2011–2012. *American Journal of Public Health, 107*(2), 267–273.

Miller, J. (2008). *Getting played: African American girls, urban inequality, and gendered violence.* New York University Press.

Morash, M. (2010). *Women on probation and parole: A feminist critique of community programs and services.* UPNE.

Morash, M., Kashy, D. A., Bohmert, M. N., Cobbina, J. E., & Smith, S. W. (2017). Women at the nexus of correctional and social policies: Implications for recidivism risk. *British Journal of Criminology, 57*(2), 441–462. https://doi.org/10.1093/bjc/azv124

Morash, M., Kashy, D. A., Smith, S. W., & Cobbina, J. E. (2016). The connection of probation/parole officer actions to women offenders' recidivism. *Criminal Justice and Behavior, 43*(4), 506–524. https://doi.org/10.1177/0093854815626490

Morris, E., & Perry, B. (2017). Girls behaving badly? Race, gender, and subjective evaluation in the discipline of African American girls. *Sociology of Education, 90*(2), 127–148.

Motivans, M. (2019) *Federal justice statistics, 2015–16* (NCJ 251770). *Bulletin.* https://www.bjs.gov/content/pub/pdf/fjs1516.pdf

Mowen, T. J., Wodahl, E., Brent, J. J., & Garland, B. (2018). The role of sanctions and incentives in promoting successful reentry: Evidence from the SVORI data. *Criminal Justice and Behavior, 45*(8), 1288–1307. https://doi.org/10.1177/0093854818770695

MST Services. (2018, September 18). *How can we stop the school-to-prison pipeline?* http://info.mstservices.com/blog/can-we-stop-the-school-to-prison-pipeline

Mumola, C. (2000). *Incarcerated parents and their children* (Special Report). Bureau of Justice Statistics.

Munetz, M. R., & Griffin, P. A. (2006). Use of the sequential intercept model as an approach to decriminalization of people with serious mental illness. *Psychiatric Services, 57*(4), 544–549. https://doi.org/10.1176/ps.2006.57.4.544

Murray, J., & Farrington, D. (2005). Parental imprisonment: Effects on boys' antisocial behaviour and delinquency through the life-course. *Journal of Child Psychology and Psychiatry, 46*(12), 1269–1278.

Murray, J., Farrington, D., & Sekol, I. (2012). Children's antisocial behavior, mental health, drug use, and educational performance after parental incarceration: A systematic review and meta-analysis. *Psychological Bulletin, 138*(2), 175–210.

Najavits, L., & Hien, D. (2013). Helping vulnerable populations: A comprehensive review of the treatment outcome literature on substance use disorders and PTSD. *Journal of Clinical Psychology, 69*(5), 433–479.

Nanda, J. (2012). Blind discretion: Girls of color and delinquency in the juvenile justice system. *UCLA Law Review, 59*, 1502–1539.

National Center for Transgender Equality (NCTE). (2018). *LGBTQ people behind bars: A guide to understanding the issues facing transgender prisoners and their legal rights.* https://transequality.org/transpeoplebehindbars

National Institute on Mental Health (2020). *Mental illness.* https://www.nimh.nih.gov/health/statistics/mental-illness.shtml

National Legal Aid Defenders Association (NLADA). (2008). *Making our case: Utilizing performance measurement to promote holistic advocacy and community-oriented defense.* Open Society Institute.

National Partnership for Pre-Trial Justice. (2020). *Advancing pre-trial justice: Training, implementation, and research for fair, just, effective pre-trial practices.* https://www.psapre-trial.org/

National PREA Resource Center (2019). *Prison Rape Elimination Act.* https://www.prearesourcecenter.org/about/prison-rape-elimination-act-prea

National Public Radio (NPR). (2019, October 2). Political prisoners? [Podcast]. https://www.npr.org/transcripts/764809210

National Resource Center on Justice Involved Women. (no date). *The use of restraints on pregnant women in jails and prisons.* http://cjinvolvedwomen.org/the-use-of-restraints-on-pregnant-women-in-jails-and-prisons/

National Task Force on the Use of Restraints with Pregnant Women under Correctional Custody. (2012) *Best Practices in the Use of Restraints with Pregnant Women Under Correctional Custody.* U.S. Department of Health and Human Services. Department of Justice Grant No. 2010-DJ-BX-K080.

Nellis, A. (2016, June 14). *The color of justice: Racial and ethnic disparity in state prisons.* The Sentencing Project. https://www.sentencingproject.org/publications/color-of-justice-racial-and-ethnic-disparity-in-state-prisons/

Newell, W. (2013). The legacy of Nixon, Reagan, and Horton: How the tough on crime movement enabled a new regime of race-influenced employment discrimination. *Berkeley Journal of African-American Law & Policy, 15*(1), 3–36.

Norwood, C. (2019, February 13). *Anti-drug smuggling policies are increasingly isolating prisoners*. https://www.governing.com/topics/public-justice-safety/gov-prison-jails-drugs-restrictions-inmates.html

Novisky, M., & Peralta, R. (2020). Gladiator school: Returning citizens' experiences with secondary violence exposure in prison. *Victims & Offenders*. http://doi.org/10.1080/15564886.2020.1721387

Office of Juvenile Justice and Delinquency Prevention (OJJDP). (2017). *Juvenile Reentry. Model Programs Guide*. https://www.ojjdp.gov/mpg/litreviews/Aftercare.pdf

O'Keefe, M. L., & Schnell, M. J. (2007). Offenders with mental illness in the correctional system. *Journal of Offender Rehabilitation, 45*(1–2), 81–104. https://doi.org/10.1300/J076v45n01_08

Ocen, P. (2012). The new racially restrictive covenant: Race, welfare, and the policing of Black women in subsidized housing. *UCLA Law Review, 59*, 1541–1582. http://www.uclalawreview.org/pdf/59-6-4.pdf

Office of the Inspector General (OIG). (2018). *Review of the Federal Bureau of Prisons' management of its female inmate population*. U.S. Department of Justice.

Olson, D. E., Stalans, L. J., & Escobar, G. (2016). Comparing male and female prison releasees across risk factors and postprison recidivism. *Women & Criminal Justice, 26*(2), 122–144. https://doi.org/10.1080/08974454.2015.1083930

Oluo, I. (2018). *So you want to talk about race*. Seal.

Osher, F., Steadman, H. J., & Barr, H. (2003). A best practice approach to community reentry from jails for inmates with co-occurring disorders: The APIC model. *Crime & Delinquency, 49*(1), 79–96.

Owen, B. (2017). Security is not safety: Gendered harms in women's prisons. *Penal Reform International*. https://www.penalreform.org/blog/security-is-not-safety-gendered-harms-in-womens/

Pasko, L. (2017). Beyond confinement: The regulation of girl offenders' bodies, sexual choices, and behavior. *Women & Criminal Justice, 27*(1), 4–20.

Patrick, K. (2017). National snapshot: Poverty among women and families, 2016. Washington, DC: National Women's Law Center.

Perlin, M. L., & McClain, V. (2009). "Where souls are forgotten": Cultural competencies, forensic evaluations, and international human rights. *Psychology, Public Policy, and Law, 15*(4), 257–277.

Petrosino, A., Turpin-Petrosino, C., & Guckenburg, S. (2010). *Formal system processing of juveniles: Effects on delinquency*. Campbell Systematic Reviews, 6(1), 1–88. https://doi.org/10.4073/csr.2010.1

Policy Research Associates (PRA). (2012). *Promising practices guide: Supporting the recovery of justice-involved consumers*. NAMI. https://static1.squarespace.com/static/599ee1094c0dbff62a07fc13/t/59af1347dbe3974ceaa105cd/1376071503025/PromisingPractices.pdf

Policy Research Associates (PRA). (2017). *The sequential intercept model: Advancing community-based solutions for justice-involved people with mental and substance use disorders*. https://www.prainc.com/wp-content/uploads/2018/06/PRA-SIM-Letter-Paper-2018.pdf

Poteat, V. P., & Scheer, J. (2016). Sexual orientation-based disparities in school and juvenile justice discipline: A multiple group comparison of contributing factors. *Journal of Educational Psychology, 108*(2), 229–241.

Potter, G. (2013). *The history of policing in the United States, Part 1*. Eastern Kentucky University. https://plsonline.eku.edu/insidelook/history-policing-united-states-part-1

Potter, H. (2015). *Intersectionality and criminality: Disrupting and revolutionizing studies of crime*. Routledge.

Prescott, J. J., & Starr, S. B. (2019, March 16). Expungement of criminal convictions: An empirical study. http://dx.doi.org/10.2139/ssrn.3353620

Priester, M. A., Cole, T., Lynch, S. M., & DeHart, D. D. (2016) Consequences and sequelae of violence and victimization. In Carlos Cuevas (Ed.), *Wiley-Blackwell handbook on the psychology of violence* (pp. 100–120). Wiley-Blackwell.

Primeau, A., Bowers, T. G., Harrison M. A., & Xu. (2013). Deinstitutionalization of the mentally ill: Evidence for transinstitutionalization from psychiatric hospitals to penal institutions. *Comprehensive Psychology, 2,* 2.

Prison Policy Initiative (PPI). (2013). *Jail postcard-only mail policies.* https://www.prison-policy.org/factsheets/postcardsfactsheet.pdf

Rabuy, B., & Kopf, D. (2015). *Separation by bars and miles: Visitation in state prisons.* https://www.prisonpolicy.org/reports/prisonvisits.html

Rabuy, B., & Kopf, D. (2016). *Detaining the poor: How money bail perpetuates an endless cycle of poverty and jail time.* https://www.prisonpolicy.org/reports/incomejails.html

Rabuy, B., & Wagner, P. (2015). *Screening out family time: The for-profit video visitation industry in prisons and jails.* https://www.prisonpolicy.org/visitation/report.html

Radatz, D., & Wright, E. (2017). Does polyvictimization affect incarcerated and non-incarcerated adult women differently? An exploration into internalizing problems. *Journal of Interpersonal Violence, 32*(9), 1379–1400.

Ramirez, R. (2016). *Reentry considerations for justice involved women.* National Resource Center on Justice Involved Women. https://cjinvolvedwomen.org/wp-content/uploads/2016/07/Reentry-Considerations-for-Justice-Involved-Women-FINAL.pdf

Ramirez-Barrett, J., Ruhland, E., Whitham, H., Sanford, D., Johnson, T., & Dailey, R. (2006). *The collateral effects of incarceration on fathers, families, and communities.* Council on Crime and Justice.

Ray, N. (2006). *Lesbian, gay, bisexual and transgender youth: An epidemic of homelessness.* National Gay and Lesbian Task Force Policy Institute and the National Coalition for the Homeless.

Reaves, B. (2013). *Felony defendants in large urban counties, 2009.* Bureau of Justice Statistics.

RED. (n.d.). *The school to prison pipeline: The issue, the solution, and guiding principles to consider.* https://stoprecidivism.org/the-school-to-prison-pipeline/?gclid=EAIaIQob-ChMIkf7okIj85wIVD5SzCh1-iQ66EAAYASAAEgLbJ_D_BwE

Richie, B. (1995). Compelled to crime: *The gender entrapment of battered Black women.* Routledge.

Richie, B. E. (2001). Challenges incarcerated women face as they return to their communities: Findings from life history interviews. *Crime & Delinquency, 47*(3), 368–389.

Robbins, T. (2013, November 19). *Little-known immigration mandate keeps detention beds full.* National Public Radio. https://www.npr.org/2013/11/19/245968601/little-known-immigration-mandate-keeps-detention-beds-full

Robertson, O. (2007). *The impact of parental imprisonment on children.* Quaker United Nations Office.

Roddy, A. L., Morash, M., Adams, E. A., Holmstrom, A. J., Smith, S. W., & Cobbina, J. E. (2018). The nature and effects of messages that women receive from probation and parole agents in conversations about employment. *Criminal Justice and Behavior, 46*(4), 550–567. https://doi.org/10.1177/0093854818811385

Rodriguez, M., & Avery, B. (2016). *Unlicensed and untapped: Removing barriers to state occupational licenses for people with records.* National Employment Law Project. https://s27147.pcdn.co/wp-content/uploads/Unlicensed-Untapped-Removing-Barriers-State-Occupational-Licenses.pdf

Roe-Sepowitz, D. E., Hickle, K. E., Loubert, M. P., & Egan, T. (2011). Adult prostitution recidivism: Risk factors and impact of a diversion program. *Journal of Offender Rehabilitation, 50*(5), 272–285.

Roman, C. (2009, May). *Moving toward evidence-based housing programs for persons with mental illness in contact with the justice system.* CMHS National GAINS Center. https://pdfs.semanticscholar.org/3e45/254f5705d46ffaa81763ad5f7103d190fb63.pdf

Roos, L., Afifi, T., Martin, C., Pietrazak, R. Tsai, J., & Sareen, J. (2016). Linking typologies of childhood adversity to adult incarceration: Findings from a nationally representative sample. *American Journal of Orthopsychiatry, 86*(5), 584–593.

Rubin, H. T. (2014). Courts for girls: An emerging specialty. *Juvenile Justice Update, 20*(4), 1–12.

Salisbury, E., & Van Voorhis, P. (2009). Gendered pathways: A quantitative investigation of women probationers' paths to incarceration. *Criminal Justice and Behavior, 36*(6), 541–566.

San Francisco Partnership for Incarcerated Parents. (2003). *Children of incarcerated parents: A bill of rights.* http://www.parentinginsideout.org/the-children-of-incarcerated-parents-bill-of-rights/

Schaffner, L. (2006). *Girls in trouble with the law.* Rutgers University Press.

Scholars Strategy Network. (2016, April 11). *The achievements of specialty courts in the United States.* https://scholars.org/contribution/achievements-specialty-courts-united-states

Schnittker, J., Massoglia, M., & Uggen, C. (2012). Out and down: Incarceration and psychiatric disorders. *Journal of Health and Social Behavior, 53*(4), 448–464. https://doi.org/10.1177/0022146512453928

Schoenly, L. (2010). *He's faking it: How to spot inmates' invented illnesses.* Corrections One. https://www.correctionsone.com/correctional-healthcare/articles/2008884-Hes-faking-it-How-to-spot-inmates-invented-illnesses/

Schouten, R. (2012). The insanity defense: An intersection of morality, public policy and science. *Psychology Today.* https://www.psychologytoday.com/us/blog/almost-psychopath/201208/the-insanity-defense

Scott, C. (2010). *Handbook of correctional mental health.* American Psychiatric Association.

Scott, C. K., Grella, C. E., Dennis, M. L., & Funk, R. R. (2014). Predictors of recidivism over 3 years among substance-using women released from jail. *Criminal Justice and Behavior, 41*(11), 1257–1289. https://doi.org/10.1177/0093854814546894

Scott, C. K., Grella, C. E., Dennis, M. L., & Funk, R. R. (2016). A time-varying model of risk for predicting recidivism among women offenders over 3 years following their release from jail. *Criminal Justice and Behavior, 43*(9), 1137–1158. https://doi.org/10.1177/0093854816632551

Scroggins, J. R., & Malley, S. (2010). Reentry and the (unmet) needs of women. *Journal of Offender Rehabilitation, 49*(2), 146–163. https://doi.org/10.1080/10509670903546864

Sentencing Project. (2017). *State advocacy update: Efforts to address federal drug felony ban on public benefits.* https://www.sentencingproject.org/news/state-advocacy-update-ban-ban-efforts-address-federal-drug-felony-ban-public-benefits/

Sentencing Project. (2019). *Factsheet: Incarcerated women and girls: 1980–2017.* https://www.sentencingproject.org/publications/incarcerated-women-and-girls/

Sered, D., & Johnson, A. (2019, November 21). Imagining a post-incarceration world. *The Appeal Podcast.* https://theappeal.org/topics/podcasts/

Sexton, L., Jenness, V., & Sumner, J. M. (2010). Where the margins meet: A demographic assessment of transgender inmates in men's prisons. *Justice Quarterly, 27*(6), 835–866.

Sharp, S. (2014). *Mean lives, mean laws: Oklahoma women prisoners.* Rutgers.

Sharp, S., Peck, M., & Hartsfield, J. (2012). Childhood adversity and substance use of women prisoners: A general strain theory approach. *Journal of Criminal Justice, 40,* 202–211.

Skeem, J. L., & Louden, J. E. (2006). Toward evidence-based practice for probationers and parolees mandated to mental health treatment. *Psychiatric Services, 57*(3), 333–342.

Skeem, J. L., Manchak, S., & Montoya, L. (2017). Comparing public safety outcomes for traditional probation vs specialty mental health probation. *JAMA Psychiatry, 74*(9), 942–948. https://doi.org/10.1001/jamapsychiatry.2017.1384

Skeem, J. L., Montoya, L., & Manchak, S. M. (2018). Comparing costs of traditional and specialty probation for people with serious mental illness. *Psychiatric Services, 69*(8), 896–902. https://doi.org/10.1176/appi.ps.201700498

Southern Poverty Law Center (SPLC). (2016). *Shadow prisons: Immigrant detention in the South.* Author.

Stahl, A. (2018, October 24). *Advocates say Brooklyn D.A.'s office is prosecuting transgender people in self-defense cases.* The Appeal. https://theappeal.org/advocates-say-brooklyn-da-is-prosecuting-transgender-people-in-self-defense-cases/

Steffensmeier, D., Painter-Davis, N., & Ulmer, J. (2017). Intersectionality of race, ethnicity, gender, and age on criminal punishment. *Sociological Perspectives, 60*(4), 810–833. https://doi.org/10.1177/0731121416679371

Stoneleigh Foundation & Maternity Care Coalition. (2019). *Executive summary: A rising tide—Understanding incarceration's multigenerational impact on women, girls, and communities.* https://maternitycarecoalition.org/wp-content/uploads/2019/04/Executive-Summary-A-Rising-Tide.pdf

Stumpf, J. (2006). The crimmigration crisis: Immigrants, crime, and sovereign power. *American University Law Review, 56*(2), 367–419.

Substance Abuse and Mental Health Services Administration (SAMHSA). (2012). *Identifying mental health and substance use problems of children and adolescents: A guide for child-serving organizations.* U.S. Department of Health and Human Services.

Substance Abuse and Mental Health Services Administration (SAMHSA). (2013). *Creating a trauma-informed criminal justice system for women: Why and how.* Author.

Substance Abuse and Mental Health Services Administration (SAMHSA). (2014). *SAMHSA's concept of trauma and guidance for a trauma-informed approach* (HHS Publication No. (SMA) 14–4884). Author.

Substance Abuse and Mental Health Services Administration (SAMHSA). (2017). *Guidelines for successful transition of people with mental or substance use disorders from jail and prison: Implementation guide* (SMA16-4998). Author.

Substance Abuse and Mental Health Services Administration (SAMHSA). (2019a). *Law enforcement and behavioral health partnerships for early diversion.* https://www.samhsa.gov/gains-center/grants-grantees/early-diversion

Substance Abuse and Mental Health Services Administration (SAMHSA). (2019b). *Principles of community-based behavioral health services for justice-involved individuals: A research-based guide.* Office of Policy, Planning, and Innovation.

Sullivan, L. (2009). *The SAGE glossary of the social and behavioral sciences.* SAGE.

Swavola, E., Riley, K., & Subramanian, R. (2016). *Overlooked: Women and Jails in an Era of Reform.* Vera Institute of Justice.

Takei, C. (2018). *President Trump, stop and frisk is both unconstitutional and ineffective.* ACLU. https://www.aclu.org/blog/criminal-law-reform/reforming-police-practices/president-trump-stop-and-frisk-both

Tasca, M., & Turanovic, J. (2018). *Examining race and gender disparities in restrictive housing placements* (Document #252062). National Criminal Justice Reference Service.

Teplin, L. A., Abram, K. M., & McClelland, G. M. (1996). Prevalence of psychiatric disorders among incarcerated women. *Archives of General Psychiatry, 53*(6), 505–512. https://doi.org/10.1001/archpsyc.1996.01830060047007

Thatcher, D. (2004). Order maintenance reconsidered: Moving beyond strong causal reasoning. *Journal of Criminal Law & Criminology, 94*(2), 381–414.

Threadcraft-Walker, W., Threadcraft, M. M., Henderson, H., & Rembert, D. (2018). Gender, race/ethnicity and prediction: Risk in behavioral assessment. *Journal of Criminal Justice, 54*, 12–19. https://doi.org/10.1016/j.jcrimjus.2017.11.001

Treatment Advocacy Center (TAC). (2016). *Promoting assisted outpatient treatment.* http://www.treatmentadvocacycenter.org/fixing-the-system/promoting-assisted-outpatient-treatment

Treatment Innovations. (2019). *Seeking Safety.* https://www.treatment-innovations.org/

Trestman, R. L., Ford, J., Zhang, W., & Wiesbrock, V. (2007). Current and lifetime psychiatric illness among inmates not identified as acutely mentally ill at intake in Connecticut's jails. *Journal of the American Academy of Psychiatry and the Law, 35*(4), 490–500.

Tripodi, S., & Pettus-Davis, C. (2013). Histories of childhood victimization and subsequent mental health problems, substance use, and sexual victimization for a sample of incarcerated women in the U.S. *International Journal of Law and Psychiatry, 36*(1), 30–40.

Torrey, E., Kennard, A., Eslinger, D., Lamb, R., & Pavle, J. (2010). *More mentally ill persons are in jails and prisons than hospitals: A survey of the states.* Treatment Advocacy Center.

Uggen, C., & Kruttschnitt, C. (1998). Crime in the breaking: Gender differences in desistance. *Law and Society Review, 32*(2), 339–366.

U.S. Census (n.d.). *Quick facts.* https://www.census.gov/quickfacts/fact/table/US/PST045217

U.S. Department of Justice. (2015). *Investigation of the Ferguson Police Department.* Author.

U.S. Department of Justice. (2016). *Report and recommendations concerning the use of restrictive housing.* Author.

U.S. Sentencing Commission. (2018). Demographic differences in sentencing: An update to the 2012 Booker report. *Federal Sentencing Reporter, 30*(3), 212–229.

VERA Institute of Justice. (2018). *Unlocking the black box of prosecution* (Webtool). Author.

Visher, C. A., & Bakken, N. W. (2014). Reentry challenges facing women with mental health problems. *Women & Health, 54*(8), 768–780.

Von Hoffmann, E. (2015, March 6). How incarceration infects a community: Disease-based models help researchers understand how prison-admission rates are linked to the health of a neighborhood. *The Atlantic.* https://www.theatlantic.com/health/archive/2015/03/how-incarceration-infects-a-community/385967/

Wagner, P., & Jones, A. (2019). *State of phone justice: Local jails, state prisons, and private phone providers* [Press release]. https://www.prisonpolicy.org/phones/state_of_phone_justice.html

Wagner, P., & Rabuy, B. (2017). *Following the money of mass incarceration.* Prison Policy Initiative.

Washington Post. (1971, July 29). President signs D.C. crime bill. https://www.washingtonpost.com/politics/president-signs-dc-crime-bill/2012/06/07/gJQA4JyALV_story.html?utm_term=.eb2b69859633

Wattanporn, K., Holtfreter, K. (2014). The impact of feminist pathways research on gender-responsive policy and practice. *Feminist Criminology, 9,* 191–207.

Widom, C. (January, 2000). Childhood victimization: Early adversity, later psychopathology. *National Institute of Justice Journal, 1–9.*

Widom, C., & Maxfield, M. (2001). *An update on the "Cycle of Violence"* (NCJ #184894). U.S. Department of Justice.

Wilson, J., & Kelling, G. (1982, March). Broken windows: The police and neighborhood safety. *Atlantic Monthly,* 29–38.

Wodahl, E. (2006). The challenges of prisoner reentry from a rural perspective. *Western Criminology Review, 7*(2), 32–47.

Wolff, K. T., Baglivio, M. T., & Piquero, A. R. (2017). The relationship between adverse childhood experiences and recidivism in a sample of juvenile offenders in community-based treatment. *International Journal of Offender Therapy and Comparative Criminology, 61*(11), 1210–1242. https://doi.org/10.1177/0306624X15613992

Wolff, N., Shi, J., & Siegel, J. (2009). Patterns of victimization among male and female inmates: Evidence of an enduring legacy. *Violence & Victims, 24*(4), 469–484.

YWCA. (2017). *End racial profiling and the criminalization of communities of color.* https://www.ywca.org/what-we-do/advocacy/policy-priorities/racial-justice-and-civil-rights/

Zahn, M., Agnew, R., Fishbein, D., Miller, S., Winn, D. Dakoff, G., Kruttschnitt, C., Giordano, P., Gottfredson, D., Payne, A., Feld, B., & Chesney-Lind, M. (2010). *Girls Study Group: Understanding and responding to girls' delinquency.* U.S. Department of Justice.

Index

CPSIA information can be obtained
at www.ICGtesting.com
Printed in the USA
LVHW101919060721
692016LV00004B/16